Globalization and Governance

Globalization and Governance

Essays on the Challenges for Small States

EDITED BY ANN MARIE BISSESSAR

McFarland & Company, Inc., Publishers
Jefferson, North Carolina, and London

The editor wishes to
acknowledge the assistance
of Ms. Simone Francis.

LIBRARY OF CONGRESS CATALOGUING-IN-PUBLICATION DATA

Globalization and governance : essays on the challenges for
small states / edited by Ann Marie Bissessar.
    p.   cm.
Includes bibliographical references and index.

    ISBN 0-7864-1965-2 (softcover : 50# alkaline paper)

    1. Globalization.   2. States, Small.   I. Bissessar, Ann Marie.
JZ1318.G57863   2004
303.48'2 — dc22   2004020168

British Library cataloguing data are available

Cover image © 2004 Artville, LLC

Manufactured in the United States of America

McFarland & Company, Inc., Publishers
  Box 611, Jefferson, North Carolina 28640
   www.mcfarlandpub.com

Contents

Part Two: The Economics of Globalization

Part Three: Cultural and Social Integration

Preface

Ann Marie Bissessar

Globalization, following Albrow, might be defined as all those processes in which the peoples of the world are incorporated into a single, global society; and while it is true that the idea of "global society" is open to quibble, there can be no doubt the pace and intensity of global interactions have increased almost exponentially over the last few decades. Nothing on this scale has been witnessed before. Understandably, there have been several attempts to conceptualize and interpret what is undoubtedly a revolutionary phase in history; and understandable, too, is that this has given rise to much debate and intensity on political platforms as well as the academic podium.

These debates, however, can safely be described as following three major tendencies: political, economic and cultural. Critics who focus on the political inevitably point to the status of the state and conclude either that it is in retreat (Strange 1996; Camilleri and Falk 1992) or that the state has reconstituted itself to confront the challenges posed by globalization, thereby transforming itself into a "competition state" (Cerny 1977; Mann 1997). The debates among the economics-minded are even fiercer. These critics hold that globalization is nothing new (Dunning 1993; Hurst and Thompson 1996; Hoogevelt 1993), that international transactions are in the logic of capitalism and that the trade along the silk route goes back centuries. A major contention of these critics is that the economic benefits of globalization are unevenly spread, prompting Rodrick to inquire whether globalization has not gone too far. The multi-national corporations (MNCs), in particular, are viewed as the villains of the period.

Much anxiety and resentment also derives from what is perceived as the cultural consequence of globalization. Some protest that globalization is taking us headlong into "homogenization of the world" (Sachs 1992); others warn of new fault lines that would lead to "a clash of civilizations"

1

and international conflict along those lines (Huntington 1993). Others lament that cultural globalization will end with the Americanization of the world (Hall 1991). The changing role of the state and the new styles of governance, the economic consequences of globalization and the cultural shifts that these entail are the issues that are now energizing the debate on globalization, whether perceived in objective or subjective terms. The essays are offered as a contribution from the point of view of small states to the ongoing debates.

The first part of this book, "Globalization and Governance," commences with "Globalization and the Caribbean" by Vaughan A. Lewis. Lewis suggests that integration of the Caribbean into the global economy was slowed by British efforts to join the European Common Market and Community. However, the concept of integration was always foremost on the agenda of Caribbean governments and was pushed by economic pressures during the 1970s and 1980s, and more recently by organizations such as the World Trade Organization, the dynamic of North American, and the Free Trade Areas of the Americas. Lewis laments that the new process of internationalization — referred to as globalization — leaves no room for small countries in the Caribbean.

Justin Daniel, in his piece entitled "The Cotonou Agreement and the ACP-EU Partnership: Towards a Reevaluation of Politics?" agrees with Lewis to a large extent in his evaluation of the Cotonou Agreement and the ACP. He suggests that any agreement must operate within an institutional framework but questions the basis of the agreement, which is built on standards defined by other financial backers and institutions, and whether these standards could be attained in developing countries.

Philip D. Osei's "Tripartite Social Partnerships in Small States: Barbados and Jamaica in Comparative Perspective" is a comparative assessment of Barbados and Jamaica's corporatist experiment with a new tripartite social partnership as a strategy for national development. He notes that the benefits to be derived from the partnership included anticipated economic growth, protection of jobs, safeguarding the existing parity of the rate of exchange of the local currency to the U.S. dollar, and less inflation. He notes, though, that while Barbados has made significant strides, the same has not been true of Jamaica. He proposes that one factor that may have been responsible for the difference is the social capital of the respective countries.

In "Globalization, Diversity and Civil Society in the Caribbean: Integration by Design or Default?" Jack Menke argues that an important precondition for regional integration in the Caribbean is the existence of a strong democracy in the individual states with civil society as the backbone. His article assesses the problems and the possible role of the civil society in strengthening institutional capacities at the national and regional level. He recommends that what may be needed is a new approach, which he refers to as "integration by design."

Gale Rigobert offers a refreshing view of a very new challenge in the Caribbean in her article "The Digital Divide: A New Imperialism?" She argues that contrary to the claim that information communication technology presents an historic opportunity for developing countries to develop their own productive and creative capacities, the old developmental problems, the North-South socioeconomic distinctions and associated problems persist.

The editor, in "Governance in a Small State," argues that the practice of "good governance," which originated in the Nordic countries and which relied mainly on market mechanisms, is faced with challenges in a small developing country. She contends that the reform of structures, tools and processes of governance has to conform to the political systems and cultures of a particular society in order for it to attain its objectives.

Ronald Marshall's article, "Globalization, Governance and Integration: The Case of Health Care Service as a Predictor of Social Stability," is more specific. He contends that globalization must be harnessed to health care delivery systems in order to bring about requisite changes to alleviate suffering and death. In research carried out in various institutions involved in the delivery of health care in Trinidad and Tobago, he found that firms and line ministries were not aware of the benefits to be derived from harnessing the potential of globalization.

Sadia Niyakan-Safy's contribution, "Rethinking Globalization's Discontent," builds on the argument that while globalization has aggravated the socioeconomic, political and cultural problems of the poorer countries of the world, the process itself is by no means responsible for these problems. Indeed, she argues that the problem is primarily that policy responses have been inadequate to deal with the challenges of the globalization.

The second part of this book, "The Economics of Globalization," is, as the title suggests, an economic enquiry into the process and impact of globalization. It is quite appropriate to begin this section with an article by a professor of economics; Ramesh Ramsaran gives us "Inequality and the Division of Gains at the Global Level: Some Reflections." He contends, like Roderick, that the globalization process is benefiting some countries but that a large number are left behind. This disparity raises serious questions about how well the international community is addressing the concerns of poor nations, who have little influence on the decisions affecting them.

Roger Hosein's "Small Regional Trade Agreements (RTAs) and Export Performance of Member Countries: Trinidad and Tobago's Experience Within CARICOM" explores the impact of membership in the regional body, CARICOM, on Trinidad and Tobago's export patterns. He notes that during the period 1973–1998, the exports of Trinidad and Tobago to CARICOM reflect a bias in favor of the protected regional market.

The final piece in Part Two, Bhoendranatt Tewarie and Roger Hosein's "Open Regionalism: The FTAA and Implications for CARICOM Development," notes that as with all arrangements, membership in the Free Trade Area of the Americas has both benefits and costs. The benefits, they suggest, include the potential creation of trade and expansion in the preferential market base of CARICOM states. The costs, however, include the exposure of fragile infant industries to more competitive extra-regional firms. They argue that the FTAA should be viewed as both an opportunity and challenge for CARICOM countries and that CARICOM members should use the occasion to reposition themselves globally.

The final part of this book, in a lighter vein, concerns "Cultural and Social Integration." John La Guerre starts off this part by looking at cultural policy in a plural society. In "Cultural Policy, Globalization and the Governance of Plural Societies" he argues that there has never been a carefully conceived policy for Trinidad and Tobago and that the forces of globalization have seriously complicated the task of constructing such a policy.

Ann-Marie Pouchet's piece, "Caudillismo: A Framework of Resistance," explores the tradition from which Hugo Chavez, the president of Venezuela, emerged. His, she notes, is the tradition of the "strongman," the *caudillo*. She proposes two hypotheses: one, that this type of leader is a product of the environment; the other, that the national and international rejection of the strongman is part of the dynamic that keeps him in power.

References

Albrow, Martin. 1989. *Bureaucracy*. London: Pall Mall Press Ltd.

Cerny, Philip. 1997. "Paradoxes of the Competition State: The Dynamics of Political Globalization." *Government and Opposition*. Vol. 32, No. 2, Spring 1997.

Dunning, John. 1993. *The Globalization of Business*. London: Routledge.

Hirst, Paul, and Grahame Thompson. 1996. *Globalization in Question: The International Economy and Possibilities of Governance*. Cambridge: Polity Press.

Hoogvelt, H. Ankie. 1997. *Globalization and the Post-Colonial World. The New Political Economy of Development*. Baltimore: The John Hopkins University Press.

Mann, Michael. 1997. "Has Globalization Ended the Rise and Rise of the Nation-State?" *Review of International Political Economy* 4.3 Autumn: 472–496.

PART ONE.

Globalization and Governance

Globalization and the Caribbean

Vaughan A. Lewis

We can fairly say that the regimes that took the Caribbean states into independence after 1962 expected the systems of protected integration into the global economy to continue indefinitely. This protected integration took the form of the Commonwealth Preference system, which ensured a market, generally but not always, for Caribbean agricultural exports. These exports were themselves mostly produced and marketed by firms carrying metropolitan (British, Dutch, French) nationality, implanted within the particular colony or territory. The same institutional arrangement characterized the production and export of oil from Trinidad and Tobago. The analysis of the "plantation economy" school has aptly described the arrangements for the Caribbean, demonstrating the extent of their integration into the global economy as dominated by one or other metropolitan node.

A similar mode of organization, too, came to characterize the new postwar export of bauxite from Jamaica, Guyana and Suriname, though the locus (home base) of the relevant firms changed from the United Kingdom to North America. The process of "industrialization by invitation" further increased the North American presence through the establishment of branch plants for mainly light manufacturing industries in the region. These branch plants were guaranteed a protected market, not by the metropole, but by the colonial territories, which were gaining increasing discretion as to development policy and were soon to be independent.

This paper was prepared for a panel discussion at a conference called "Globalization, Governance and Integration," sponsored by the Department of Behavioural Sciences, Faculty of Social Science, University of the West Indies, St. Augustine, Trinidad and Tobago, West Indies, 26–27 September 2002.

Finally, the systems of finance and telecommunications followed the mercantilist or neomercantilist patterns of productive investment, being extensions of the various metropoles (in the case of banking and insurance, now including Canada).

For the Anglophone Caribbean this form of integration into the global economy, particularly as it concerned the agricultural commodities, first came under systemic challenge when the British government announced at the beginning of the 1960s that it intended to seek accession to the European Common Market and Community, after its initial rejection of the option of joining in the formation of what was stated to be an "ever closer union." Caribbean governments immediately saw the implications of this for the region's protected agricultural trade, as evidenced particularly in statements at the time by Dr. Eric Williams of Trinidad and Tobago and the Jamaican trade minister, Robert Lightbourne.

Williams, leading a country now anticipating a greater dependence on petroleum than on sugar or citrus, and pursuing industrialization for foreign exchange and national income, was somewhat sanguine about this development, not expecting much from any arrangement to protect West Indian commodities. As he observed in early 1967: "The United Kingdom is about, public reports indicate, to give up this system of Commonwealth Preferential arrangements, by going into the European Common Market. It is unthinkable that the preferences for citrus and sugar will survive British entry into the European Common Market, and the whole mood in the world today is against preferences" (Williams 1967).

Yet, he averred in 1968: "All the evidence available so far points to an extremely long delay before Britain can gain entry into the Community. Thus what will otherwise have been an imperative necessity might well be transmuted into an opportunity for us to reduce our dependence on Britain either by lowering our cost of production or by judicious forms of economic diversification" (Williams 1968).

On the other hand, the Jamaican minister took the lead in stressing the need for Caribbean countries to obtain what he called "bankable assurances" from the British Government that such protection could be achieved and maintained. We shall return to this.

It will be recalled that stress on the other aspects of the neomercantilist arrangements in financial services and the mineral industries came nearly a decade later, as domestic nationalist pressure exerted against the government of Trinidad and Tobago led that government to seek a so-called Third Way between the existing arrangements and the socialist/communist arrangements of Cuba. This strategy relied on a version of the old British Fabian socialist doctrine of taking over the "commanding heights" of the economy, even if, in some cases, permitting minority equity to foreign investors. This led to a substantial reorganization of ownership of the Trinidad oil industry — though it should be observed that this was occurring at a time when the industry was thought to be in a declining production (or maturing) phase; to the placing of the ownership of banks and insurance in private Trinidadian hands through purchase of equity (localization); and the government's complete control of the sugar lands and the production of sugar.

By the first half of the 1970s, though under less overt pressure and partly responding, more than its Trinidad counterpart, to wider ideological and policy trends in the Third World, the government of Jamaica came to pursue a similar strategy. Though it could already be perceived that foreign investment in the bauxite industry was winding down, there was, among the Jamaican political, technocratic and (in some measure) business elites, the perception that the prospects for continuing strong demand for bauxite-alumina exports were good; that they could continue to work effectively and to mutual satisfaction with the multinationals in the production process; and that therefore the international channels for the marketing of bauxite would remain intact.

Guyana, at this time, went a step further than Jamaica in full-scale nationalization of the bauxite producing system, though largely for ideological reasons having to do with domestic political competition between government and opposition, both asserting the ideology of Marxism-Leninism. This was accompanied by state purchase and ownership of agricultural (sugar) activities and financial institutions, and substantial state regulation of others (rice).

The partial or whole delinking of what might be called the "national economic appendages" from the multinational economic systems in which they were embedded, undertaken too at a time of intense American preoccupation with the alleged penetration of communist influences in the Caribbean, did not, and indeed could not, have anticipated the dramatic recession that developed in the Western Hemisphere, deeply affecting large states of South America as well as small ones in the Caribbean Basin. This brought in its train a sharp decline after 1975/6 in the prices for sugar and bauxite, and a declining demand for aluminum, in conjunction with the fact that the multinationals had, simultaneously, begun to explore new locations for exploitation of bauxite in Australia and Brazil. And while, for Trinidad and Tobago, the price of oil exploded after the events in the Middle East, this exerted intense pressure on other Caribbean economies leading to extensive debt.

With respect to the agricultural and mineral commodities, governments' attempts at partial delinking and self-directed management of the countries' development was not successful, partially due to the unfavorable environment of the time. The economic recession, partly a function of the American attempt to correct its burst of deficit financing during and after the Vietnam War, brought in its train a new ideology of economic development. This emphasized privatization (following Thatcher), economic stabilization, and deregulation of state-dominated economic activities. These policies were promoted as paths to the *relinking* of the failed economies in the Hemisphere, isolated from investment. And importantly, with such failure the regimes found themselves facing the disintegration — particularly in the Caribbean — of the incipient welfare and mass-supporting social policy systems that formed, as an inheritance from British Labour ideology, the basis of the implicit understanding between nationalist-labor governments and their populations, for their assuming and maintaining power after the advent of universal suffrage.

The return to a so-called market economy, emphasizing the importance of attracting foreign investment to develop the old plantation industries and attracting investment from new spheres of multinational production, is typified by the return of Michael Manley to government in Jamaica in 1989, conceding that the international environment was not favorable to the policies that he had espoused in the 1970s. These new initiatives were fully pursued too by governments of Trinidad and Tobago after 1986, in response to the recession that gripped that country with the fall of oil prices in the early '80s. Their objective was, in part, to break the metropolitan protectionist logjam that had inhibited the growth of their new industries working with petroleum products and derivatives. The prospect of extensive resources of natural gas further induced the governments' new orientation, given the dearth of national financial resources for the kind of self-directed industrial programs pursued after the first oil price boom. Guyana, by the beginning of the 1990s, was also seeking to reinvite the bauxite multinationals and the English sugar company, Bookers, back to their local mineral and agricultural locations.

At the CARICOM level, these initiatives, and the new orientation they implied, of relinking to the North Atlantic economy, were reflected in agreement by heads of government to the Nassau Understanding on Structural Adjustment of 1984. It can also be said that this was a collective response to the strategic initiative of the United States in legislating the Caribbean Basin Initiative of 1981, which would facilitate multinational investment in the region. It also seemed to be an admission that global economic conditions were forcing renewed forms of multilateral integration on the basis of common rules and regulations. These left no space for a Third World–directed international economic order.

These new orientations in the Caribbean, historically the most internationally integrated countries of the Western Hemisphere, we can see as small scale reflections of a phenomenon that has come to be recognized at the wider hemispheric level. We can, in retrospect, see that the United States' determination towards post-Vietnam war recovery, in the context of its increasing awareness of the effects of European economic integration on that region's economic growth, forced a further determination on the United States' part towards meeting the competition developing within the North Atlantic economy. The hemispheric effects of this were seen, from a Caribbean perspective, in traditionally statist and protectionist Mexico's decision to join GATT (the General Agreement on Tariffs and Trade), and then negotiate NAFTA (the North American Free Trade Agreement) with the United States and Canada.

This institutional linking of Mexico to the North Atlantic economy — Mexico being a super-large economy compared with those of the Caribbean Basin states— is, in effect a form of magnet drawing all Western Hemispheric countries in the same direction. And this phenomenon has gained even greater force with the revolution in the technology of communications and electronics which, in inducing what has been called "a compression of time and space," has given mobility to capital flows in the world economy that can, as events in Mexico have shown, be both constructive and destructive, and not easily susceptible to the unilateral control of even the most substantial developing countries' governments.

The globalization that is partially the result of what we have described above, combined with determined American efforts at regulating its processes (through the World Trade Organization [WTO] and a certain control over flows of concessionary finance), has, naturally, had an important effect on regional efforts at integration initiated from *within* developing regions in the Western Hemisphere, as in other regions. It is obvious that the South American attempt at integration — in, for example, MERCOSUR — has been powerfully affected by Argentina's swift deregulation and adjustment to the liberalizing North Atlantic economy, and by that country's determination (now failed) to find an anchor in the United States financial system (note Menem's desire to take this to its logical conclusion of "dollarization"). We can also see that the integration effort has been affected by the partially domestically-induced financial weakness of Brazil, which even in the midst of its struggle for more equitable access to the United States market for its agricultural commodities, finds itself dependent on US mediation in its search for the temporary financial resources needed by its economy.

In that context, the small Caribbean economies and their intended collective Single Market and Economy could hardly be exempt from such forces. We prefer, in fact, to say that they are almost exemplary of the effects of those forces. The movement of the European Community (EC), agreed in 1986, to the Single Economic Market of 1992, signaled the reconstruction of the historic and comfortable protectionist and preferential system which had, with Britain's access to the EC, now left its Commonwealth moorings and settled into the Lomé cum Cotonou Conventions of the EU/ACP states.

But it can be posited that the movement from Commonwealth to Lomé/Cotonou, and the United States–forced subordination of the regime's future arrangements to WTO compatibility, marks the end of the influence of old, and more modernized, mercantilist economy for the Caribbean, certainly as far as its agricultural commodities are concerned. The WTO's ruling on the US–Latin American–EU–Caribbean dispute, when taken in conjunction with the unequal size and capabilities of the parties involved, seems to justify this conclusion; a conclusion that also seems applicable to the Caribbean sugar industries as Europe seeks, in the context of the North Atlantic struggle, to extend the "Everything but Arms" proposal to all least developed countries.

As the prime minister of Barbados has ruefully observed: "The problems in the sugar industry will arise because the market for sugar is going to be very difficult to hold. Europe has decided that countries that hitherto could supply it, but can supply tens of millions of tons of sugar will after the year 2007 be able to sell sugar on the European market on the same terms as we can" ("Bleak Future").

As the governments of the banana-producing countries of the Caribbean have found out, the accepted dominance of the rules-based WTO leaves little space for subordinate-system institutional protection. The very process of European Union liberalization to which these countries' export-agriculture regimes were subordinated, and which offered *interim* institutional protective devices, has been itself subordinated to the WTO system in such a manner, and at such speed, that any arrangements made have seemed to have a permanent instability built into them. (I have argued elsewhere that to the extent that the United States has played a substantial part in inducing this state, and to the extent that this state is likely to be reproduced in the regime that comes into being with the Free Trade Area of the Americas (FTAA), this latter agreement should have, like the European integration system, compensatory mechanisms for member-states of lesser weighting — such mechanisms to be separate from any "special and differential provisions" as to treaty implementation that might be agreed for the Caribbean states as a consequence of their small size.)

The tenor of this paper, then is, that precisely because of the manner of their incorporation, and the extreme and one-sided integration into both components of the North Atlantic economy, the Caribbean economies are the objects of a dual set of pressures, simultaneously exerted. The arrangements that have been made for them in the past are being globalized into obsolescence. The arrangements that they made for themselves before the advanced liberalization that now characterizes the North Atlantic economy — namely the customs union and common market arrangements, and then the 1992 CARICOM Single Market arrangements — are being overlaid by the requirements of the WTO, and within the Western Hemisphere by the projection of the NAFTA scheme into the FTAA, whose proposed provisions in some cases are more advanced, in terms of liberalization, than those of the WTO. Similarly, CARICOM countries have established arrangements that take advantage of the fact that they can work with highly skilled resources, of a scale appropriate to their population sizes, and have responded to the "compression of time-space phenomenon — namely the provision of off-shore financial services." Yet these activities would appear to fall victim to the competition between the two poles of the North Atlantic economy engaged in trying to ensure a level playing field between themselves.

One possible exception to such a pessimistic scenario would appear to be the situation of Trinidad and Tobago with a new commodity in global demand by the metropolitan economy, though the organizational form of the exploitation of the economy would appear to be of the traditional type. This new initiative must be looked at in scale, as a part of the wider geo-economic arena that encompasses both that country and Venezuela. And it was, no doubt, in anticipation of the competition between herself, Venezuela and Mexico that Trinidad was anxious, soon after the signing of the NAFTA agreement, to pronounce herself ready for admission. (In this she was joined by Jamaica, though from a different production orientation.) This orientation has also implied that, through the 1990s, Trinidad should act with dispatch to ensure what might be referred to as maximum institutional integration with the United States, in the sense of signing all relevant treaties relating to investment, tax information and security — the latter two bearing on the concerns of great significance to the United States of money laundering and narcotics movement.

This orientation of Trinidad and Tobago suggests a differentiation between her interests — or at least the pace of her implementation of her interests — in the Hemisphere, vis-à-vis other CARICOM partners, in much the same way that the character of North American investment in

Costa Rica has induced a certain movement away from her Central American neighbours. However, the fact that (in 1998) 38 percent of Trinidad and Tobago's export trade was with CARICOM partners suggests the need for some continuing institutional connection beneficial to all the partners.

Considerations of geopolitics and geo-economics might also in some measure qualify the validity of the long term effects of current liberalization processes on Guyana, as against those we deem as applying to many other CARICOM countries. In the medium term, our projections can stand, to the extent that the country's mineral system is not seen as a strategic part of any major multinational entity or system's priorities; and Guyana's sugar production, though larger in scale than other Caribbean states, still can be subject to the effects of the Everything But Arms initiative. In addition, the imbalance between population and land area, in the absence of any dynamic towards external investment and/or technological innovation that would reduce this imbalance, does not suggest any substantial process of strategic relinking of the country's economy into the North Atlantic system.

Yet from the perspective of Guyana's location within the sphere of northern South America — dominated by a Brazil/Venezuela nexus and influenced by the continuing legal jurisdiction of France in one of the territories of the area — different possibilities, in the longer term, for its economy might be posited; though it would be an element in different subsystems subject either to the dynamic of North American and FTAA integration processes, or to European initiatives in the Hemisphere (for example, the recent Guyana Plateau Initiative from the European Union).

In general, then, the analysis here has stressed the extent to which historical internationalization of Caribbean economies has meant that those countries' experience of "integral linkage" has been extensive; that the deep or extensive integration of the economies has gone through various phases, though always with a guarantor of the "rules of the game" once local regimes were disposed to observe them.

The new process of internationalization — referred to as globalization — leaves no room for protector or guarantor. Yet, though there is an admission, following the difficulties of the 1980s, that some form of renewed integral relationship is required, the centrality of the Caribbean position in the relevant (North Atlantic) system is diminished, as such assets as those countries possess do not make them a "substantial stake" in the current competition.

It would appear that the new global rules of trade and production as imposed by WTO are determining the status of Caribbean nations and the nature of their relationship within the new structures to which they have sought, or been forced, to adapt. Yet the region's claim for special and differential treatment is not looked at favorably, as WTO technocrats and dominant states take cognizance of the reintegration in the last 20 years into the globalized economy of "small" countries like Singapore and New Zealand, without such "Special and Different" treatment. Finally, the positions of some countries in CARICOM, in their search for new positions of integration or linkage, appear more favorable than others; however, the implications of this for the CARICOM system are not yet clear.

References

Best, L., and K. Levitt. 1975. "Character of Caribbean Economy." In George Beckford (ed.), *Caribbean Economy: Dependence and Backwardness*. Mona, Jamaica: Institute of Social and Economic Research.

"Bleak Future for Sugar", *Barbados Nation*, 3 September 2002.

Lewis, Vaughan A. 2001. "Caribbean Adjustment in the Current Global Readjustment." Mimeograph. Prepared for the conference "Globalization and the Wider Caribbean: Challenges and Opportunities" at the Ibero-American Institute, Berlin, Germany, 14 May 2001.

The Nassau Understanding: The Structural Adjustment and Closer Integration for Accelerated Development in the Caribbean Community. Nassau, Bahamas; CARICOM Secretariat. 7 July 1984.

Williams, Eric. 1967. *Speech to the House of Representatives by Dr the Rt. Hon Eric Williams, Prime Minister of Trinidad and Tobago, on the Entry of Trinidad and Tobago into the Organization of American States, 3rd February 1967*. In Roy Preiswerk (ed.), *Documents on International Relations*. University of Puerto Rico: Institute of Caribbean Studies, 1970.

_____. 1968. *Trinidad and Tobago and the European Economic Community*. Excerpt from a speech by Dr the Rt. Hon Eric Williams, Prime Minister of Trinidad and Tobago, April 1968. In Preiswerk, *op.cit.*

The Cotonou Agreement and the ACP-EU Partnership: Towards a Reevaluation of Politics?

Justin Daniel

Abstract

In a sense, the Cotonou Agreement represented the end of the Lomé system. Falling into line with the principles of the World Trade Organization (WTO), the European Union (EU) by the introduction of the Cotonou Agreement appeared to limit its ambition to accompany the integration of African, Caribbean and Pacific (ACP) states into the globalized economy. However, the alignment of ACP states with the common regime of free trade agreements signed by the EU and their standardization within the device of cooperation, as well as their exposure to the logic of international competition as a modality of integration into the globalized economy, were measures that pointed to a profound change in their thinking.

This paper attempts to probe the potential and the limits of this new partnership. Two major points are raised: on the one hand, the promotion and the extension of the device of political dialogue among states; and on the other hand, the attempt to reevaluate politics through policy dialogue. Finally, the paper will look at the likely impact of the Cotonou Agreement on the functioning of the political and administrative systems of the ACP countries.

The Cotonou Agreement, which was signed on June 23, 2000, by the EU and the ACP states was the result of a long process of negotiation spanning the period between September 1998 and February 2000. The Agreement intended to capitalize on 25 years of experience representing, through the successive Lomé Conventions, a model in North-South relations. From the outset the Agreement was premised on the idea of partnership. Thus, the conventions under this agreement established an institutional dialogue to allow the European Community (EC) as well as the ACP states to present their respective points of view, to make their demands, and to prevent legal disputes. The conventions therefore opened up issues to frank debate that the political neutrality and ideological polarization accompanying the Cold War had formerly made difficult.

Over the years, however, this institutional partnership gradually deteriorated. The dialogues that took place did not address the fundamental objectives of the Agreement and was further hindered by the formalism and unwieldiness of the procedures. At the same time, however, the EU extended its cooperation towards several other regions located either at its immediate periphery or in Latin America or Asia.

It was clear, however, that the joint institutions, funded by the European Development Fund (EDF), resisted this change of policy. It should be recalled that these institutions were responsible for revising the Agreement before 2020. They therefore suggested that a major introduction of the Agreement was to make political dialogue one of its fundamental pillars. This dialogue was also to be a decisive component of the general and sector-based policies that underlay the strategies of commercial and financial cooperation.

This brief presentation will accordingly highlight the institutional framework within which the political dialogue will unfold, before trying to reveal the advantages and the limitations of the new partnership. The exercise is less easy than it appears at first sight. An agreement is the consequence of a series of frequent and subtle compromises, which can be interpreted only through the different points of views as they emerge. In other words, the cold analysis of an agreement or document deserves to be supplemented by the attentive observation of the protagonists' attitudes during the negotiations, and of the behaviour of the actors involved in the enforcement of the agreement, once the latter comes into effect. In this case, however, because of the lack of sufficient data, it seems unrealistic to attempt any evaluation of the first effects of the new agreement.

Given these limitations, a scrutiny of the Agreement's provisions yields two sets of observations:

1. those relating to the introduction and the extension of political dialogue between the various countries and

2. those connected to the attempt at a re-evaluation of political environment of the various states.

Introduction and Deepening of Political Dialogue in the Various Countries

The EU's approach to cooperation and development tended to be premised on conditions that were introduced by financial backers and international institutions such as the OECD's Development Assistance Committee, the institutions of Bretton Woods (the World Bank and the International Monetary Fund) and, of course, the WTO.

The Cotonou Agreement, however, continued to rely on dialogue as a tool since this allowed for the management of the partnership between the states; it offered them an overall and coherent approach to achieve the objectives of cooperation, and enabled them to arrive at policies to overcome common problems such as the struggle against poverty, the progressive integration of ACP countries into the world economy, and sustainable development.[1] These objectives, however, could not be achieved without insisting on political adjustments on the part of the respective partners.

The insistence on a unified political objective was not meaningless, since the institutional framework on which it was premised was the result of over 25 years of cooperation. However, there is no denying that the new agreement left some problems unresolved. One major issue was the lack of experience within the organization regarding the coordination of joint institutions and, more generally, the management of the dramatic changes that would affect the cooperation between the EU and the ACP states involved.

Undeniable Potentialities

The main features of the institutional framework of cooperation were established at the inception of the ACP-EEC Convention on the February 28, 1975. Three bodies combined to decide and to discuss political issues.

The first such institution, the ACP-EU Council of Ministers, was essentially the executive body. As a supreme decision-making institution, it had a wide range of responsibilities including defining the priorities pertaining to ACP-EU cooperation, assessing the performance of the latter and, if necessary, introducing measures to remove the obstacles that might hinder it, without forgetting its essential role in the overall political dialogue.

The next organ, the Committee of Ambassadors, normally attended the Council of Ministers and prepared the sessions. This committee was, theoretically, involved with presenting solutions to problems linked to the implementation of cooperation policies. The Committee meets regularly, follows the terms outlined in the Agreement in working closely with the Council, and is responsible for any matter that is passed on for implementation by the Council of Ministers. Far from being the operational arm as established under the Lomé Convention, however, the present committee seems to have confined itself during the last years to a minor role; namely, participation in planning the agenda of the Council of Ministers on the basis of rather cursory exchanges.

Finally, and in spite of its consultative status, the Joint Parliamentary Assembly plays an important role by giving a political boost to the Cotonou system. It is composed of equal numbers of EU and ACP members of parliaments (or, failing this, representatives designated by the parliament of each state). Its role was to promote the democratic processes through dialogue and consultation; facilitate greater understanding between the peoples of the EU and those of the ACP states; raise public awareness of development issues; discuss issues pertaining to development and the ACP-EU partnership; and put in motion the decision-making mechanisms to achieve the objectives of the Agreement (Article 17). It must be added that the opinions, recommendations or resolutions of the Joint Parliamentary Assembly submitted to the European Council and to the European Commission have had an indisputable influence on the latter and, in a general way, on the ACP-EU process of cooperation. Yet, there have been few structural changes in these three organs since 1975. Thus an evaluation of the Cotonou Agreement would suggest that it hopes to benefit from the previous experience of the Lomé conventions and from the advantages inherent in the partnership approach.

There can be no doubt, however, that the multilateral framework of the partnership presents a number of advantages. For instance, it allows numerous countries of the ACP group to access the European decision-makers while, taken individually, they could hardly have this opportunity, and it nurtures exchanges on subjects to which the peoples are particularly sensitive, while these subjects are not always compatible with a bilateral framework.[2] Two other factors distinguish the institutional device of dialogue between the ACP states and the EU and underline its interest. On the one hand, its permanent (or almost permanent) character ensures the persistence of the exchange while, on the other hand, the joint dimension of institutions allows the maintenance of balance within the partnership.[3]

However, it one thing to maintain an institutional device whose originality and advantages are unmistakable, but it is another to go beyond the limits or the insufficiencies of the aforementioned device and the practices that are associated with it. With respect to this second point, different studies[4] as well as the reflections presented in the *Green Paper* tabled by the European Commission in 1996[5] urged the various actors to evaluate the function and the results of the institutionalised system of dialogue. A major concern was that the ACP group was far from being homogeneous. This sometimes tended to aggravate nationalistic sentiments, and even, in some cases, to strengthen the weight of the European Commission and the EDF Committee during the decision-making process.[6] What actually emerged, then, was a mainly national approach during the stage of implementation of the individual programs.[7] In addition, nongovernmental organizations as well as social and economic organizations, to a large extent, were excluded from the institutions of the previous Lomé Conventions because of the interstate dimension of EU-ACP cooperation.[8] Finally, three factors combined to produce what some termed an "erosion of the institutional partnership."[9] First, a lack of confidence between the parties resulted in a high degree of formalism and reliance on bureaucratic practices. Second, the informality of dialogue pertaining to political questions has led to the lack of any concrete conclusion or commitment. Third, the tendency of political debates between the two parties to focus on a relatively narrow set of issues (primarily linked to political conditionality) and to be organized in a rather rigid manner (for example, in high-level ministerial meeting) left little scope for open and frank discussions.[10] Added to these was the issue of the marginalization within the framework of ACP-EU dialogue in the general policy implemented by the EU. Because much of the debate on cooperation were directed towards other European countries or ACP states, this gave rise to a lack of linkage between the ACP forum and the other European authorities.[11]

One understands, under these conditions, that the Cotonou Agreement seeks to make political dialogue one of the decisive instruments of the partnership. Of course, political dialogue is not new in ACP-EU cooperation. This idea was expressed in the previous conventions and it is inherited from a long tradition going back at least to Yaounde and marked by strong institutionalisation, a sign of mutual recognition from both partners.

Moreover, this idea really began to stand out with the third Convention signed in Lomé in 1984; namely, a convention that already had opted for an intensification of the dialogue conceived as the means to increase the efficiency of cooperation.[12] However, the Cotonou Agreement identified the key feature of the political dialogue by emphasizing its deepening and its widening. Three directions seemed to have been introduced to ensure this objective: namely, the diversification and flexibility of the framework within which this dialogue took place. Consequently, the Agreement stated explicitly that dialogue "shall be formal or informal according to the need, and conducted within and outside the institutional framework, in the appropriate format, and at the appropriate level including regional, sub-regional or national level" (Article 8).

Clearly, the intention of the agreement was to take into account the objection previously raised: that dialogue between the partners was organized in a too rigid and formal manner. It also served to ensure that issues should be addressed at the levels where they arose, in particular at the intra-national levels. The new programming system in financial cooperation, for example, made provisions for the establishment of a single strategy of national cooperation for each ACP state through dialogue with the recipient country. It was thus the national level which was adopted in this particular case, but the choice of other levels could be made in the other domains such as the negotiation of economic partnerships at the regional level, or the defence of ACP interests at the global level in international fora.

In a more general way, it was clear that the purpose of the new approach was to allow more flexibility and the possibility of adapting the system of cooperation to necessarily changeable realities. Finally, it must be added that this dialogue also took place in an operational perspective, through multiple committees and working groups, among which were included the Joint ACP-EC Ministerial Trade Committee (Article 38) and the ACP-EC Development Finance Cooperation Committee (Article 32 of the Annexes to the Agreement).

Generally, the Cotonou Agreement endeavoured to capitalize on the previous experience under the Lomé regime while putting the political dialogue, organized within a framework of equality and partnership, at the center of the system of cooperation. One major objective was to combine dialogue by the various political groups into an essential tool to ensure that policies were broad-based. Unlike the Lomé agreement, the Cotonou Agreement broke the longstanding tradition that conferred an almost exclusive responsibility for the promotion of growth and development on the central governments. Instead, it allowed a wide range of actors to become true partners in the development process within the framework of the ACP-EU cooperation. Thus, non-state actors were associated not only with the application of the projects but also with political dialogue, and the Cotonou Agreement operated within a substantially widened field in order to better design policies for ACP-EU countries. The introduction of this new agreement aimed manifestly at relaunching and consolidating the ACP-EU dialogue, which had faced serious problems under the Lomé regime. However, it left a set of problems unresolved, which some suggested would present challenges for the future.

Policy Challenges

Two sets of challenges are worth mentioning: the first resulted from problems inherent in the adoption of different rules and procedures, while the second concerned the capacity of the Cotonou Agreement to produce, based on political dialogue, the expected effects.

In some respects, the Cotonou Agreement expressed various principles whose implementation proved easier said than done, especially when these principles followed complex and tense debates, reflected fragile compromises or resulted from a rather cursory treatment during the process of negotiation. Thus, the extension to non-state actors of the partnership relation between the ACP states and the EU raised several practical problems[13] including the definition and the selection of the actors destined to participate in the dialogue and to have access to the sources of financing, the criteria of selection, the issue of determining the authorities competent to proceed with this selection, the transparency of the procedure, and the evaluation of the legitimacy and the capacity of the non-state actors.

It was clear, then, that the Agreement provided rather succinct answers, doubtless taking into account the extreme variety of situations met in the different ACP states. Differences between these countries included the organizational capacities as well as expectations. It should be recalled, however, that Article 6 made reference to "Civil Society in all its forms according to national characteristics." It entrusted the parties (ACP governments and the EU), with the task of recognition of non-state actors by identifying three criteria of selection, namely, the extent to which these actors addressed the needs of the population, their specific competencies, and the democratic and transparent dimension of their organization and management.

These provisions were supposed to bring about a relatively level playing field, more concerned with local realities than the former rigid and formal framework, which had served to exclude legitimate nongovernmental organizations. But they could, at the same time, also generate tensions and resistances. Some non-state actors voiced their concern that some of the articles defined under this agreement could open the way to processes of arbitrary selection, particularly in countries confronted with problems of governance or those against the idea of participative development.[14]

It goes without saying, that the support that was provided by the agreement to increase the capacity-building of these actors (Articles 4, 5, 7, 33) was a critical element to its success. Essentially, these Articles could have included measures to allow for exchange of information (the traditional Achilles' heel of ACP-EU cooperation) and support for non-state actors at various levels (national, regional and global) to organize themselves as more effective representative structures and as partners in the dialogue. However, this was a relatively new area in which the ACP-EU cooperation had little experience or competence. They had little knowledge of organizations and networks of non-state actors who might become dependent on a structural financial assistance program especially at a time when governments seemed hesitant to support capacity-building.[15]

Additionally, the modalities of implementation of a dialogue structured on the basis of new public-private partnerships taking place at the national, regional and global levels were rather vague since the agreement confined itself to a pragmatic approach claiming to be respectful of the characteristics of each country. Here, also, the political willingness of the ACP states to involve those actors in the dialogue, and the deliberate mobilization of mechanisms provided by the agreement to build their capacities, may have turned out to be decisive factors.

Finally, the Joint Parliamentary Assembly, which was directly involved in promoting political dialogue and democratic processes, had to face a substantial challenge. The first involved its internal structuring and the reinforcement of its legitimacy. The members of the ACP parliament sit, unlike their European counterparts who belong to structured and organized groups, according to a national representation.[16] This lack of a proper structure was a grave issue especially because of the lack of homogeneity within the ACP states. It was, therefore, no doubt important to favor regional coordination. Besides, under the regime of Lomé, apart from the fact that all the ACP states were not provided with a parliament, those who had it were not always represented by members of parliament. Thus, a new orientation was adopted, aimed at conferring a renewed legitimacy to the Joint Parliamentary Assembly and maximizing the chances of succession to the new partnership. It henceforth consisted of members democratically elected in their respective countries and not appointed by the government and the party in power. This choice was clearly indicative of some measure of progress. However, in order to evaluate progress, it would be necessary to take into account the differentiated evolution of the democratic processes among the different countries[17] in order to make sure of the democratic legitimacy and the independence of the members of parliament.

In addition, the Assembly provided for, according to the spirit of the Cotonou Agreement, another major innovation under the shape of regional Assembly meetings. During regular intervals, representatives of an ACP subregion met with European members of the Assembly. These initiatives coincided with meetings of representatives of civil society and with the economic forces of the region, in order to find answers geared towards specific problems. However, while this was a worthy principle, it presupposed the parameters and goals of the aforesaid regions,[18] along with the culture of the civil society. It was a misconceived supposition, since these factors varied from one political system to the other. It also, in many cases, overestimated the economic forces likely to be mobilized and involved in the partnership.

While these were certainly practical problems that could have been ironed out, a more general problem emerged. This was the capacity of the aforementioned Agreement to produce, on the basis of a strengthened political dialogue, the expected benefits. In other words, the critical issue was the real impact of the Cotonou Agreement on the consecration of democracy and human rights as essential elements. Issues such as the emergence of a new function of "peace-building and conflict prevention and resolution" (Article 9); the growing conditionality (struggle against corruption and suspension of the cooperation in the "grave cases of corruption"); the commitment of the ACP states to the fight against irregular immigration in Europe; evaluation of their performances relating to institutional reforms; and transparency and efficiency in the use of financial assistance were major questions which are still to be resolved.

Were these conditions sufficient to put an end to the erosion of the institutional partnership amply underlined under the previous conventions? Could they favor a proper fit between cooperation, development and the enforcement of democratic principles as well as that of good governance? Certainly, the European approach towards the states under which these principles were enunciated was rather specific.

It emphasized institutional cooperation aimed at facilitating the promotion of a democratic mode of corporation rather than emphasizing sanctions. This approach incorporated a number of measures, which generally ranged from informal pressure towards the states concerned, to the enforcement of a trade embargo for the gravest cases.[19]

As Franck Petiteville pointed out, however, this approach met "fundamental limits which are those of any cooperative diplomacy facing extremely conflicting political processes." For example, authoritarian regimes were reluctant to introduce sanctions (Nigeria, Sudan); were unable to prevent situations of crises, which limited the European strategy of enforcement, *a posteriori*, of humanitarian actions (in war situation) or sanctions (after coups d'état); and were unable to resolve gaps between the means of cooperation and the scale of some conflicts (Rwandan genocide, and civil and border wars in the region of the Great Lakes).[20]

In short, the Cotonou Agreement conferred a decisive role by way of political dialogue. In a more general way, it insisted on definition of the political environment. These two aspects formed part of the major choices adopted by the contracting parties. Their enforcement, and their success, involved a long and exacting process that depended on the introduction of a number of operational devices. However, the main objective of dialogue, notably in the light of the strategy of ACP-EU cooperation and the role accorded to the political environment, suggests that the Agreement was in fact a real attempt at reevaluation of the politics, both in the exchanges between partners and in the domestic functioning of ACP states.

Towards a Reevaluation of Politics: The Policy Dialogue

One of the critical questions political scientists raise when analysing policies is, Does politics matter? Or, What is the role of politics in the definition and the implementation of policies? Trying to answer this question amounts to admitting that political thought is historically crossed by at least two traditions. Constantly reactivated, not in an abstract way or under the shape of a timeless invariant, these two traditions tend to espouse the dominant ideas and ideological context of the moment. They alternately dominate the intellectual scene — without ever succeeding in totally eliminating the opposite option — and contribute to legitimization of the actions of political authorities. The first tradition, the beginnings of which go back to Machiavelli, takes a technical and determinist approach to politics, and was adopted some years ago by the International Monetary Fund (IMF) and the World Bank. The second, the impact of which was noticeable in the seventies, for example, tends to confer a determining role to politics raised sometimes to the status of a deus ex machina.

It is with reference to this dialectic that the distance covered since the first Yaoundé Convention in 1963 can be understood, and that the meaning and the scope of the policy dialogue proposed by the Cotonou Agreement can be interpreted. In this respect, two observations stand out. On one hand, there is an indisputable widening of the political field; on the other hand, we see the ambivalent character of the attempt to reevaluate politics.

The Widening of the Political Field

The content and the field of politics, such as they can be grasped through the exchanges between the ACP states and the EU, evolved considerably in the course of successive agreements. The first three Lomé conventions introduced the concept of neutrality as a political option.[21] In the context of the Cold War, the political aspects of cooperation were not addressed or were replaced by other concerns such as maintaining the dialogue with all the ACP states, independently of their belonging to the sphere of influence of communism, capitalism or to the nonaligned group. The almost blind respect for the principle of sovereignty of its partners led the European Economic Community to avoid any judgement on their ideological, political or economic choices. Such a posture was not, however, exempt from ambiguity, owing to the fact that it corresponded to a highly political choice aimed at preserving dialogue and cooperation with the ACP states. This naturally excluded certain delicate issues, but served at the same time "as a shock absorber while the bilateral relations were tense."[22]

As a result, it was necessary to wait for Lomé III when an attempt (Article 4 of the Convention) was made to address the question of human dignity (although not yet human rights); the emphasis was put on economic, cultural and social rights rather than on civil and political rights. It appeared, then, that during this phase policy did not matter or policy did not determine politics. In other words, the cooperation and trade policies that were at the heart of the ACP-CE dialogue had no power to influence politics. This neutrality gave rise, particularly at the international level, to strong ideological polarization.

The revision and reintroduction of Lomé IV and Lomé IV Agreements marked a turning point. The respect for human rights became a fundamental part of Europe-ACP relations. Implicit in these agreements was the understanding that any violation of human rights, democratic principles, the rule of law, or any of the other essential elements of the Convention, could result in a sanction of partial or total suspension of economic aid.

The objectives outlined for the ACP-EU cooperation were in keeping with a process of EU cooperation directed not only towards its immediate periphery (central and oriental Europe, the Mediterranean Sea, the Commonwealth of Independent States), but also towards the emerging regions of Asia and Latin America.[23] These objectives suggested the end of the Lomé system, with the exception of the sphere of partnership negotiation underlying the joint institutions analysed above. Above all, it clearly echoed not only the liberal representation of the globalized economy and the multilateral doctrine of the WTO, but also the political interventions of institutions such as the IMF and the World Bank in developing countries.[24] Formerly, it will be recalled, these institutions had based their doctrines on the basic principle of separating the economic sphere from the political sphere.[25]

From this point of view, the Cotonou Agreement, by asserting strongly the political dimension of the EU-ACP relationship, intended to take into account a principle which expressed itself at first at the global multilateral level. Espousing this new approach appeared to give priority to politics over economics.

Firstly, the Agreement widened the area of policies linked to the dialogue by introducing the policies of peace consolidation and conflict prevention as well as migratory policies. It created, in addition to respect for democratic principles and for the rule of law, good governance by way of dialogue between governments and civil society. In brief, the aim was twofold. First, it established a framework to allow the ACP states to resolve problems of instability and the difficulties connected with their institutional weaknesses, which hindered the functioning of aid and trade instruments put in place by Lomé. Second, it reaffirmed the link between the Common Foreign and Security Policy (CFSP).

The Agreement also set out clearly the idea of integrated development in order to protect the balance and the interaction between the economic, social, cultural and political dimensions of development. In other words, the conditions of the Agreement proposed a global strategy of development based on a rejection of any separation between economics and politics, and focused on the struggle against poverty. As Françoise Moreau pointed out, "the political dimension of poverty-reduction was now considered to be an integral part of the development processes."[26]

In sum, in order to circumvent the ideological depolarisation brought about by the end of the Cold War, the Cotonou Agreement recognized explicitly the political dimension of the EU-ACP relationship. Far from being reduced to a simple set of technical prescriptions underscored by an ideology strongly supported by the prevailing liberalism, which was not geared to supporting national particularism, politics was elevated as an essential component of development, even if its content nurtured apparently lively exchanges during the negotiations. Such was the significance of the debate which was formed around the idea of good governance.[27] Another concept that was widely accepted was that of the rule of law (Article 9.2).

Simultaneously, emphasis was placed on the necessity of building institutional capacities in order to improve the political framework within which the exchanges and the investments were to develop. In a way, it contributed to the reengineering of the role of the state, even though the latter was no longer considered as the only actor capable of mobilizing the necessary resources for development. However, at least four conditions had to be satisfied in order to achieve the changes expected. These conditions included going beyond the simple statement of general principles, enriching these general principles with new relevant practices, mobilizing adequate means on both sides, and finally, capitalizing on the acquired experience since the signing of the first Lomé Convention.

The Reevaluation of Politics: An Ambivalent Approach

The will to reevaluate politics could be explained by the growing awareness of the difficulties encountered by the partnership proposed by the Lomé Convention. It is at this point relevant to quote this brief passage from the *Green Paper* on the EU-ACP relationship, where the main problems were summed up as follows:

> Indeed, it has proved hard to put initial intentions, based on the principle of equal partners, into practice since the institutional weakness of the recipient countries, their dependence on aid, a growing conditionality, and the Community's tendency like other donors, to take the place of their faltering partners, a tendency prompted by a growing concern for effectiveness, have seriously undermined the principle of partnership.[28]

This appraisal of the institutional partnership and the EC-ACP cooperation led to a need for two clear policy directions. On the one hand, it was felt that a policy should allow for the progressive emergence of an "asymmetric partnership" in the various ACP countries. On the other hand, what became urgent was the need to reconsider the method by which aid was delivered, especially when aid was used as a substitute to a true development policy. It was agreed, though, that these objectives could be achieved by mobilizing new methods such as appropriation by the recipient countries or allocation of resources based on quantitative and qualitative assessment of each country's needs and performances.

This dual policy led to an emphasis on institutional and political strengthening and made it one of the decisive topics of the EU-ACP dialogue. It was understood, though, that the enforcement of the new system of political cooperation had to first overcome one major obstacle, namely, the absence of political cohesion within the EU. The likely resistance in certain ACP states (notably those confronted with internal crises and those facing attempts to promote a political partnership) could become complicated because of the difficulty that the EU confronts when defining a common approach. Hence, there is a risk of persistence in a system of double standards reflecting the predominance of divergent national interests and limiting, at the same time, the scope of the political partnership.

It is needless to return here to the debates governing the determination of the practical modalities of the Agreement and its operational devices by the joint institutions, notably the Committee of Ambassadors. These principles and, more generally, the political conditionality upon which the new partnerships were founded, would have to be fed by political dialogue and would have to feed it in return. The Agreement also presupposed the use of technical cooperation by the EU within the framework of its political interventionism.

Beyond the norm of sound management and political conditionality, it seems difficult to be unaware of the debate concerning the nature and the function of the state in the ACP societies. Obviously, that debate is useful for understanding a number of issues relating to history, to the sociopolitical motives of state action, to culture, and to the multiplicity of actors and factors at work in economic interventionism. From this point of view, it is one thing to establish the principles of cooperation oriented towards a multidimensional development, but it is another to establish understanding and consideration on behalf of institutions entrusted with attaining such an ambition, or to determine the specifics of long-term sociopolitical trajectories.

Indeed, only such an approach, which inevitably is both plural and complex, can allow the understanding and management, through long-term policy, of the opposition and the resistance likely to accompany state reform, and inherent in the process of transformation itself. Such an approach helps to clarify "which actor is the most credible, and must be favoured, in such or such country between the private sector and the public sector, if a budget deficit is the result of the erring ways of the economic policy and a social guarantee for the reforms, if a coup d'état is the nth attempt of monopolizing the national cake, or the first step of a serious political reconstruction in a country where the state lost for a long time any legitimacy."[29]

This problem relates to assessing the influence of the institutional framework — in which the importance of both parties is underscored — on possible innovations in development policies. While some may suggest that this is insignificant, this issue nevertheless becomes critical for the development debate and is borne out by recent policy literature that suggests "the conclusion may be surprising that the influence of the institutional framework, although unmistakable, is very ambiguous."[30] How does one articulate, however, the components of the relationship resulting from the normative conception of governance and more or less assumed by the EU — participation, transparency, accountability — and how does one grasp and analyze the strong preferences among the target populations with which public projects are concerned?

"Governance" stands out in international institutions and relations under a definition which makes it "a paragon of the liberal ideal of an opened economy, where the information circulates freely, where the legislative framework is favourable to the entrepreneurs and where any public deficit must be fought."[31] The concept is described as a "naturalized" synthesis of political democracy and the market economy. This normative bias tends to reduce considerably its scope by transmuting governance into a simple norm, widely deprived of its analytical content, which is nevertheless useful when examining complex political phenomena.[32] Additionally, this transformation is far from producing any insight, more than indispensable, on the practical and precise consequences of state reform.

The approach, in terms of reevaluation of the state, does not escape a certain ambivalence since it goes together with an overestimation of "civil society." Indeed, a double problem arises: the emergence of the constituents of civil society is implicitly connected to a decline in legitimacy of the states, which gradually lost their monopoly over the concerns of the population, while having retained their dialogue with the EU.

Unquestionably, the state and the political system are, in a number of ACP countries, connoted negatively: they are viewed as headquarters of arbitrary power and ineffectiveness; they are frequently presented as the real, or main, reasons behind underdevelopment evils; and their incapacity to face governance problems is constantly highlighted. Symmetrically, the qualities of civil society "make indispensable the appeal to it in four areas of action: development, democracy, governance and humanitarian assistance. The necessity of a strong civil society, acting in 'partnership' with the market forces and with a reduced and purified state, returns as a leitmotiv in the discourses of both the financiers and the progressive activists: what should be done, is 'to strengthen' it, 'to organize it', even 'to reform' and 'to educate it.'"[33]

One critical issue is that of representativeness of various interest groups and their ability to renounce their 'singular' interest and to act as checks and balances on each other.[34] The renunciation of a monastic vision of politics thus involves the change in a number of ACP states from an embryonic form of representative democracy to a much more complex "functional democracy,"[35] providing the arena for representative pluralism. If this concept met resistance from what may be considered solidly established democracies,[36] it is easy to imagine the tensions that could result from it in ACP states. The introduction of such a concept would involve new tools or instruments. Because there are so many units involved, one such tool might be the introduction of a common, unifying objective. Other considerations may be the subordination of individual interests to one singular interest, membership of intermediate bodies selected on the basis of non-universalising criteria,[37] proliferation of private networks, and religious movements and community-based organizations defending specific interests (such as geographic, professional, or economic). Another problem results from the difficulty in grasping the concept of "civil society." This term has not been easy to define theoretically since its meaning varies considerably from one context to another. This obstacle, however, was circumvented by the Joint Declaration relating to the partnership actors. They included a concise definition within the Agreement that noted that "Civil Society in all its forms according to national characteristics" is an actor of cooperation.[38] As Yolette Azor-Charles put it: "…in certain countries, civil society is not yet well-defined, hence the need to agree on a specific definition. In other countries, most non-state actors are not consulted or even informed about this cooperation. There is also a fear that such players would want to take over something of the role of the State."[39]

In other words, the mobilization of civil society has to be accompanied by a strong democratic culture. It follows that, if most of the observers welcome this major innovation — the involvement of the non-state organizations in political dialogue — they assume that this innovation will be a big challenge during the coming years. Whether it will be a challenge or an obstacle only time can tell.

Endnotes

1. See on this matter, Andrea Koulaïmah-Gabriel, "La coopération ACP-UE: un partenariat institutionnel," in L'Union européenne et les pays ACP, edited by Jean-Jacques Gabas (Paris: Karthala, 1999), 77–95.

2. Andrea Koulaïmah-Gabriel, "La coopération ACP-UE: un partenariat institutionnel," 78.

3. Ibid., p. 79.

4. See Jean-Jacques Gabas, L'Union européenne et les pays ACP (Paris: Karthala, 1999); Jean-Jacques Gabas, La convention de Lomé en questions: "Les relations entre les pays (ACP) et l'Union européenne après l'an 2000 (Paris: Karthala, 1998); Franck Petiteville, La coopération économique de l'Union européenne entre globalisation et politisation," Revue française de science politique (2001): 431–458.

5. European Commission, Green Paper on relations between the European Union and the ACP countries on the eve of the 21st century: Challenges and options for a new partnership (Luxembourg: 1997). Office for Official Publications of the European Committees.

6. Roger Blein, "Adapter les institutions aux nouveaux enjeux des relations entre l'Union européenne et les pays ACP,' in Jean-Jacques Gabas, L'Union européenne et les pays ACP, op. cit.: 98–104.

7. Ibid.

8. Ibid.

9. Andrea Koulaïmah-Gabriel, "La coopération ACP-UE: un partenariat institutionnel," op. cit.

10. ECDPM, Cotonou Infokit: Political Dialogue 19 (Maastricht: ECDPM, 2001).

11. Ibid.
12. Michel Waelbroeck et al., *Le Droit de la Communauté Européenne: La Convention de Lomé*, vol. 13, (Brussels: Editions de l'Université de Bruxelles, 1990) 512.
13. See ECDPM, *Infokit Cotonou: Le renforcement des capacités* 11 (Maastricht: ECDPM, 2001).
14. Ibid.
15. See ECDPM, *Infokit Cotonou: Le renforcement des capacités* 11 (Maastricht: ECDPM, 2001).
16. Youssof Ouedraogo, "Le système institutionnel de Lomé," in *L'Union européenne et les pays ACP*, edited by Jean-Jacques Gabas, *op. cit.*, 117.
17. Kenneth Karl, "Assemblée parlementaire paritaire ACP-UE: c'est parti!," *Courrier ACP-UE*, January–February 2001, 7.
18. Ibid.
19. Franck Petiteville, "La coopération économique de l'Union européenne entre globalisation et politisation," *op. cit.*: 446–447. See also on this point Dieter Frisch, "La dimension politique dans les rapports avec les partenaires de Lomé," in *La convention de Lomé en questions: les relations entre les pays (ACP) et l'Union européenne après l'an 2000*, edited by Jean-Jacques Gabas *op. cit.*: 55–64. This author notably writes: " It is necessary to resist the temptation to use too easily this weapon [the sanctions]. First, because cooperation pursues objectives of long-term development — and is not part of the *stop* and *go* of everyday politics. Secondly, the cooperation is supposed to help the man and not regimes which, then, suffer generally a little from sanctions. And, finally, a suspension of cooperation means, according to the experience, the interruption of the dialogue and, thus, a total loss of influence on the evolution of things in the country in question. It is thus a weapon to use carefully " (62).
20. Ibid., 447.
21. Dominique David, "Plus de 40 ans de relations Europe-ACP," *Le Courrier ACP-UE*, September 2000; see also Dieter Frisch, "La dimension politique dans les rapports avec les partenaires de Lomé," *op. cit.*
22. Ibid., 56.
23. Franck Petiteville, "La coopération économique de l'Union européenne entre globalisation et politisation," *op. cit.*, 432.
24. Christian Chavagneux, "Le FMI et la Banque mondiale tentés par la politique," *Esprit*, June 2000, 101–117.
25. Marie-Claude Smouts, "Du bon usage de la gouvernance en relations internationales," *Revue internationale des sciences sociales* 155 (1998).
26. Françoise Moreau, "The Cotonou Agreement — new orientations," *The ACP-EU Courier*, September, 2000, 7.
27. See, for example, Kusha Harakisingh, "On the Front Line: The Lomé Experience Dissected," in *Caribbean Survival and the Gglobal Challenge*, edited by Ramesh Ramsaran (Boulder, Colorado: Lynne Rienner Publishers, 2002), 366–383.
28. *Green Paper on relations between the European Union and the ACP countries on the eve of the 21st century: Challenges and options for a new partnership* (Brussels: European Commission, 1997), 39.
29. Christian Chavagneux, "Le FMI et la Banque mondiale tentés par la politique," *Esprit, op. cit.*, 111.
30. Marc Smyrl, "*Politics* et *Policy* dans les approches américaines des politiques publiques: effets institutionnels et dynamique du changement," *Revue française de science politique*, 52 (2002): 48.
31. "La gouvernance — Qu'est-ce que c'est? " *Courrier de la Planète* (Réforme de l'Etat et nouvelle gouvernance) 41 (1997).
32. Stemming from historians' works specialized in the study of the Middle Ages, the concept of governance has been introduced in social sciences by Anglo-Saxon university circles to organize and enrich the classic categories— henceforth considered unable to explain the increasing complexification of politics— and to indicate new processes and actors worth studying. It was resumed by the World Bank, at first as an analytical category, before giving birth to the notion of "good governance" which introduces a very strong normative

dimension. In the Cotonou Agreement, "good governance" is defined as "the transparent and accountable management of human, natural, economic and financial resources for the purposes of equitable and sustainable development" (article 9. 3).

33. Maxime Haubert, "Le risque idéologique," *Courrier de la Planète* (Société civile, la montée en puissance) 63 (2001).

34. "…the hegemonic discourse presents a vision deformed and even inverted of the reality of a postcolonial world where big masses of population are confined to exclusion, where the groups convened to participate in civil society are characterized by their relatively privileged social position, their relative weak importance and the extreme divergence of their projects, whereas only some of them are turned to the public sphere, organizations considered as representative of the civil society (notably "NGO") have often only a weak social legitimacy and a weak autonomy with regard to the actors of the public sector and the lucrative private sector, and the latter does not really show it willingness to have an effective dialogue on the actions undertaken, whether at a national level or at the international level. " Ibid.

35. Jean-François Thuot, *La fin de la représentation et les formes contemporaines de la démocratie* (Québec: Editions Nota bene, 1998).

36. Ibid.; see also Pierre Rosanvallon, *La démocratie inachevée: histoire de la souveraineté du peuple en France* (Paris: Gallimard, 2000).

37. Jean-François Thuot, *La fin de la représentation et les formes contemporaines de la démocratie, op. cit.,* 188.

38. In this Joint Declaration, it is clarified that "The parties agree that the definition of civil society may differ significantly according to socio-economic and cultural conditions of each ACP country. However they believe that this definition may include inter alia the following organizations: human rights groups and agencies, grassroots organizations, women's associations, youth organizations, child-protection organizations, environmental movements, farmers' organizations, consumers' associations, religious organizations, development support structures (NGOs, teaching and research establishments), cultural associations and the media."

39. Yolette Azor-Charles, "The partnership must be founded on mutual respect." *The ACP-EU Courier*, September 2000, 27.

Tripartite Social Partnerships in Small States: Barbados and Jamaica in Comparative Perspective

Philip D. Osei

Abstract

This paper attempts a comparative assessment of Barbados and Jamaica's experiment with a corporatist tripartite social partnership (TSP) strategy for development. The partners involved in the TSP are the government, private sector employers and representatives of the workers in each country. The benefits to be derived from the partnership included anticipated economic growth, protection of jobs, safeguarding of the existing parity of the rate of exchange of the local currency to the US dollar, and less inflation. From an initial assessment of the evidence, Barbados — the innovator — managed a successful policy, and has thus negotiated three other protocols since 1993 while Jamaica — the emulator — presided over a policy that failed despite all the resources committed and the initial enthusiasm with which the policy was received. An uncritical explanation that has been bandied about in the region suggests that the Barbadian success has been due to its possession of a huge outlay of social capital, whereas the opposite is true for Jamaica.

The author argues that the TSP, indeed, required a good amount of social capital, but that there are other equally important deep-seated, gen-

An earlier draft of this paper was presented to the annual conference of the British Academy of Management (BAM), London, 9–11 September 2002.

eral and idiosyncratic causes that contributed to the differing results. These include the nature of politics and the immediate circumstances of each country prior to the introduction of the policy, and each country's political culture, vibrancy of trade unions, policy style and state capacity for policy management.

Introduction

Since the early 1990s there has been a distinct move, under the rubric of public sector reforms, to search for alternative ways of delivering public services. This goal has been pursued for a number of reasons including the dwindling stock of public finance and the growing perception that public provision of social and infrastructural services have been ineffective; hence, the need to draw on the institutional strengths of the private sector. The move to public-private partnership (PPP) as an alternative policy delivery arrangement could be seen as just one strand among several delivery modes that have been adopted in contemporary public governance. Contracts, franchises, grants, vouchers, complete privatization of services, "agencification" and voluntary service are good examples of the diversity of delivery structures that have been adopted in recent times (Savas 2000, 105–6; Osei 2001, 73–83). Public-private partnership as an organizational concept is a divergent set of tools and organizational arrangements between public and private actors for the pursuit of public service goals. The definition by Bennett et al. (1999, 4) that the PPP is "a spectrum of possible relationships between public and private actors for cooperative provision of infrastructure services," can be considered as very restrictive in light of recent developments in the Commonwealth Caribbean where partnerships have been sought, not only for the provision and maintenance of infrastructure, but also for the perpetuity of entire economies. The British government's private finance initiative (PFI), instituted in 1992 under the Major administration and refined under the New Labor Government (Wakeford and Valentine 2001, 19–25) might fit the definition of Bennett and colleagues. Even when that is granted, other examples abound of low key partnerships at the decentralized governance level, in both developed and developing countries, for the delivery of environmental projects, water supplies, waste management and social care (UNDP 2000; World Bank 2000; Bennett et al. 1999).

In the Commonwealth Caribbean, an entirely different type of partnership arrangement has been pursued. The phrase "entirely different" is employed here to convey to the reader the fact that, whereas other PPPs proffer tangible quid pro quos such as dividends, returns and the sharing of associated risks that come with joint investment of physical capital and managerial resources, the Caribbean TSPs demand all the social capital that the partners can afford. Indeed, it offers intangibles for reward, and no immediate calculable personal benefits. In the cases dealt with in this paper — Barbados and Jamaica — those intangibles are couched in vague terms in the form of expected national economic growth, stable exchange parity of the local currency against the US dollar, and assurance of maintenance of high levels of employment. This arrangement accords with Mumford's (1998) categorization of partnerships as being an aspect of "relational contracting" (quoted in Wakeford and Valentine 2001, 23). However, the TSP for all practical purposes is only akin to a marriage contract, and less related to a sound business undertaking, because of the extreme emotional investments and the seemingly irrational expectations that are involved. This argument is based on a shrewd observation of the Caribbean economic scene and the tenuous basis of the forces that affect sustained economic growth. These vary from natural disasters such as volcanoes and hurricanes, to man-made disruptions in the form of street demonstrations against unpopular public policies; for example, the shootout between law enforcers and criminal elements in early July 2001 in Jamaica. A combination of these forces is able to shatter any predicted positive economic trends. For Jamaica, the latter scenario has the potential to thwart any growth expected in the tourism sector, the mainstay of the island's economy.

The Caribbean TSPs have been practice-led, and grew out of a perceived need to position the countries involved on a better footing to enable them to compete in an increasingly globalized and liberalized international market.

Theoretical Issues

Since the early 1990s there has been an interesting debate about the need for a shift from government to governance in the management of the affairs of modern complex societies, developing countries included (Stoker 1998; World Bank 1989, 1992). It has been recognized by academics and practitioners alike, that states do not have a monopoly on wisdom or indeed, the resources for policy making for socioeconomic development. In fact, in 1988 Joel Migdal noted that the state is just one player among a host of social forces who vie for the loyalty of society. It has been recognized also, in research on participation in the field of development studies since the 1970s, that the involvement of societal groups in policy formulation and delivery goes a long way in ensuring the sustainability of the benefits of development (Cooke and Kuthari 2001; Isham et. al. 1995; Midgley 1986; Oakley and Marsden 1984). By the 1990s it had become clear that state-centered development had not reached its objectives in developing countries (Wunsch and Olowu 1990). In light of this, in international development circles, attention began to be focused on NGOs (nongovernmental organizations) as partners in the implementation of public policies. This was so because the role of the state in development had begun to be attacked by the neoliberals who saw the activities of the state as having inhibited development. However, as the importance of the central role of the state as a development agent was rediscovered in the latter part of the 1990s (World Bank 1997), the overwhelming need for a state-society partnership was also recognized. Socioeconomic development is now posited to work well in a situation where states and citizens work together (Fiszbein and Lowden 1999).

The emerging pattern of governance now has to do with partnerships and networks for development, a key element of which is the interrelationship among a range of voluntary, private and public development bureaucracies. It is recognized that elected governments remain significant actors but that they have to collaborate with other organizations to achieve their goals (Maloney, Smith and Stoker 2000, 216). In fact, Maloney and colleagues also argue that "institutions in civil society do not simply underwrite the capacity for good government; they are incorporated into the processes of governing" (2000, 216). To achieve a high degree of efficiency in networks management of the type required by the new governance, the state needs to fundamentally rethink its modus operandi, overhaul its approach to leadership and look for a good supply of social capital (Klijn and Koppenjan 2000; Hyden and Bratton 1992). And even here, there are lots of caveats about social capital. The concept has been used in three different senses in the literature. First, it has been used to "connote the creation of civic associations, development of strong bonds of community reciprocity and the strengthening of social relationships" (Midgley 1995, 160). This is the view of Putnam et al. (1993). Second, it has been used to describe some efforts towards asset development among low-income groups, with a view to encouraging savings among the poor to accumulate the social investments that the poor require to meet their needs. This draws on the work of Michael Sherraden (see Midgley 1995), which was critical of the provision of income benefits in welfare states. Third, the term is used in a materialist sense to refer to the creation of physical infrastructure which communities and nations need to realize their developmental goals (Midgley 1995, 160). Examples of this include schools, hospitals, housing, and water projects. Fine (2001) observes that, indeed, capital can be social, due to the fluidity of capital. It is possible to have human capital, finance capital and other types of capital. Fine argues that "more generally, anything that can contribute to productivity or efficiency can be considered as capital, whether it be a physical factor" or one that is socially constructed — an efficient civil service, free from corruption, for example (2001, 36).

The Caribbean scholars whose works are reviewed in this paper adopted the Putnam definition of social capital and saw it in terms of a certain quality that inheres in human and interpersonal relations. But the concept so defined raises a number of questions. For example, what constitutes a useful social capital resource is said to compose of three strands: obligations, expectations and trustworthiness of structures. But we are reminded that while social capital can facilitate actions towards human well-being, it can also constrain it (Dasgupta 2000, 325; Maloney et al. 2000). This is made even more complex by the presence of certain attributes that are related to the distributive dimension of social capital — the closure of social networks, which supposedly creates the conditions for the emergence of effective sanctions that can monitor and guide behavior; and also the trustworthiness of social structures that allows for the proliferation of obligations and expectations (Maloney et al. 2000, 214)

From the foregoing discussion, therefore, it is possible to appreciate the existence of negative social capital, that is, the use of the social quality of cohesiveness and the availability of sanctions within social networks for purposes of achieving goals that run counter to public welfare. In Jamaica, the proliferation of gang culture and the existence of informal community leaders (area dons) who wield power in what are known as garrison communities (in local political parlance) give credence to how social forces can be organized for both good and evil.

General Background on Partnerships

Public-private partnerships have assumed a new salience in development policy in recent times. Ideologically, PPPs are being heralded as a temporary landmark for what is now called the "third way." To the pragmatist, they are regarded as a compromise solution and a replacement for the dogmatic pursuit of market economics and state led development. In effect, the partnership approach is seen as a suitable compromise between capitalism and socialism. Partnership, as a new form of governance, has many advocates in high places both bilaterally and multilaterally. The meaning of public-private partnership now encompasses "risk sharing relationships based upon a shared aspiration between the public sector and one or more partners to deliver a publicly agreed outcome" (Brittan 2001).

It is important to note that public-private partnerships have taken varied organizational forms, whether in Britain or the Commonwealth Caribbean. In the developing countries, in particular, the United Nations Development Program (UNDP) and the World Bank have been encouraging the use of joint ventures and quasi-private organizational forms as tools for overcoming identified capacity gaps in public service management. The UNDP has supported a number of projects in some of its member countries in the South, and established a Working Paper Series in 1999 to encourage further discussion of public-private partnerships for the urban environment. In addition to this, in 2001 a new Innovative Partnerships Grant was introduced to facilitate research (www.undp.org/pppue. Accessed 1 November 2001). Partnerships have been established in service areas such as water supply, sanitation and solid waste management. The World Bank has been interested in testing the use of private finance for road building and maintenance in developing countries. The assimilation of such a policy, and the question of who takes the glory for success and blame for failure, have been two of the attendant problems in this policy area. These are also related to the issue of ownership of policies. The Barbadian and Jamaican examples of TSP seemed to have circumvented the issue of ownership.

Methodology and Key Research Issues

This paper is an attempt to analyze the TSP experiments in two Commonwealth Caribbean countries: Barbados and Jamaica. It does so by examining the thoughts behind and outcomes of policies agreed to by the social partners. The views of civil society and academics on the subject are also analyzed. The partners include the business community (employers), public policy makers and the trade unions, as the main parties to the agreements, and academics and civil society on the periphery. The paper looks at the two countries' experiences because they have been the prime movers in this policy area in the Caribbean.

The sources consulted and analytical methods used include examination of public policy documents such as protocols of understanding; content analysis of newspaper articles; periodicals of the Caribbean Community (CARICOM); and the general scholarship on politics, social capital and development in the region. Perspectives from these are pulled together in order to fully appreciate the politics and technicalities of the policy formulation and implementation of partnerships.

An examination of the literature on TSPs threw up a number of questions that had to be pursued through context-specific research. These included the issue of incentives and what constitutes an adequate quid pro quo to motivate organizations (both public and private) and individuals to cooperate in a partnership of this complex nature. Some scholars have pointed to the abundance of social capital as being the main variable explaining the relative success in Barbados, and perhaps the lack of it as the determinant factor in the dismal failure of Jamaica's partnership experiment. This assertion constitutes the point of departure and the main contention that motivated me to undertake this study. The answer proffered by the social capital school seems too simplistic in my view. It is my belief that there are other important deep-seated, general and idiosyncratic causes, most of which relate to politics, political culture, policy style and policy management especially in the post-independence era, that need to be discovered.

The explanations for the differing outcomes of the experiments have been couched in terms of the abundance or lack of social capital and the relative docility of one society (Barbados) as opposed to the uncompromising pursuit of individualism of the other (Jamaica). An attempt is made to use the tools of policy analysis to assess the processes of policy adoption, emulation, policy management and outcomes. The author believes that a good amount of social capital, favorable social characteristics (excluding docility), a less adversarial political culture and a record of consistently effective policy management are salient in explaining the policy success of Barbados. Apart from all this, there is the most important research question of all to grapple with: the question of attribution or causality.

The paper also assesses the capacity of governments (in terms of cognitive, intellectual, fiscal, as well as managerial resources) to formulate appropriate development policy and manage complex partnerships and networks of organizations and individuals, both public and private, who have substantially different interests and agendas. In brief, this analysis looks at public strengths in sector policy management across the board, and draws inferences from previous performance in development policy and political management.

An examination of the nature of benefits and risks are also undertaken, and a number of interesting leads are followed in a bid to find plausible answers. Was policy made on impulse in Jamaica? How good was the fit between the partnership policy and the prevailing political/industrial relations culture? Who promoted the social partnership? What benefits were sought and how were these to be achieved? How were benefits going to be distributed? Who was going to own these benefits? Were there any winners and losers? Partnering, as we are told, is distinct from the first generation of privatizing efforts, and includes a sharing of both responsibility and financial risk (Linder and Rosenau 2000, 6; UNDP 1998). What then, were the risks, and how were these to be shared among the partners? Were the benefits to be derived so substantial as to induce and elicit the cooperation of the nongovernment partners? What lessons can we draw in designing workable public-private partnerships at both the local and national levels in Jamaica and beyond, and for the delivery of public policy in general?

Tripartite Partnerships in Jamaica and Barbados

The origins of the Caribbean TSP experiment can be traced to the experiences of Barbados in its initial attempt to implement a policy on prices and incomes for the country. This policy was evolved during the terminal period of an uneasy relationship with the International Monetary Fund (IMF) and its austere stabilization and structural adjustment loans in the early 1990s. Descriptively, the TSP as a partnership arrangement falls under a category of its own, quite different from the variants alluded to in the introduction to this paper. The Barbados experiment represents an innovation because it has been home-grown, whereas Jamaica's (discussed below) could be seen in the light of emulation of or diffusion from the former. The Barbadian experiment originated as a result of the country's rejection of IMF/World Bank conditions in the early 1990s. Similarly, Jamaica's experimentation came at the end of a borrowing round from the IMF. These partnerships were sought not only for the facilitation of better management of economic and social resources in disparate projects in the countries involved, but also for the effective management of growth and stability in the national economy. To be specific, in the Caribbean example, the emphasis has been on macroeconomic stability and exchange rate parity maintenance in a bid to secure sustained growth for the common good.

In terms of costs, workers and other citizens are called upon to make certain sacrifices behaviorally, by refraining from making unreasonable demands for pay increases. In the agreement, pay increases were linked to productivity. Similarly, people are required to give their commitment and loyalty towards the creation of a conducive environment and acquiescent industrial relations for achieving economic stability, growth and national competitiveness. In the Commonwealth Caribbean, the inherited truncated and hybridized Westminster system of political institutions and rules dictated that this kind of partnership had to be solicited through consensus building and not through coercion.

In a commentary on the kind of prices-and-incomes policy Barbados had adopted as a basis of its TSP, Downes (1994a) raised important questions regarding productivity, the distribution of productivity gains and the issue of price increases. Downes noted that these were very complex problems that depend on a range of factors. For productivity, some of the factors he considered were the use of modern technology, labor quality improvements or human capital investment (i.e. training and skills acquisition), improvements in managerial and organizational techniques, flextime work arrangements, changes in plant layout and increasing specialization due to a widening of market opportunities. His main arguments were that (a) the distribution of productivity gains could be a source of contention at the bargaining table. As such, the design of sharing schemes would become a priority issue in the collective bargaining process; (b) That if a short-sighted view of price increases was taken, it was likely to be limited to "legitimate cost increases," in which instance this would result in side market activity as shortages could develop for some commodities at the agreed controlled prices. Even so, he surmised that the management of price increases was going to be a daunting task. This is because he saw the monitoring of price increases as a "substantial information gathering exercise and the discussion of legitimate cost increases can be a time consuming process" (Downes 1994b, 35). One issue that was missing from Downes' otherwise interesting economic commentary was the question of transparency. In this voluntary agreement, how was honesty in cost declaration going to be ensured among the private players? Perhaps this is where trust as an essential aspect of social capital becomes crucial.

It is interesting to note that concern about enhancing productivity in the Caribbean had been on the policy agenda since the 1970s. National institutions of productivity were first established in 1982 in Trinidad and Tobago in the form of a National Productivity Board. This was later incorporated into the Trinidad and Tobago Management Development Centre. When Jamaica established a Productivity Centre in 1991, it was not initiated as an independent entity but rather as an integral part of the Jamaica Promotions Board (JAMPRO). However, in Barbados, a National Productivity Board was first established in 1992, and later reconstituted under an Act of Parliament in 1993 to raise national consciousness about productivity (Downes 1994a, 1) This reconstitution of the board was in preparation for the tripartite partnership that was in vogue at the time.

Barbados

The social partnership involved the government of Barbados, employers and representatives of workers. Three protocols have been agreed to and signed since 1993. The first one covered the period 1993–1995, the second 1995–1997 and the third 1998–2000. Barbados' TSP began in 1992 out of a deep-felt need for the country to do something drastic about its dwindling economic fortunes. This is because the partners recognized that there had been "gradual erosion in Barbados' competitiveness" which needed "to be reversed by resolute and coordinated action" (Protocol 1993–1995, 2).

Protocol One acknowledged that the country's prosperity over the years had been due, in large part, to its peaceful and harmonious labor-management relations. The parties accepted that tripartism was the most effective strategy by which a commitment to national cooperation and development could be realized. A firm belief in and commitment to the International Labor Organization's principles for the equitable development of labor and capital, particularly the Freedom of Association (Convention No. 98), was maintained.

The foundation blocks of the protocol for the prices and incomes policy included the following:

1. The Barbadians wished to safeguard the existing parity of the rate of exchange (BDS$2.00 to US$1.00). It was believed that a deterioration of this rate would lead to a significant reduction in the living standards of a majority of Barbadians.

2. There was a desire to expand the economy to satisfy the need for improved competitiveness. This was linked to the need to provide a right of access to employment in order to reduce the threat of social dislocation that can be caused by high levels of unemployment. The overall aim of this provision was couched in terms of the need to ensure the security and well-being of the community as a whole.

3. The Barbadians wanted to establish an environment which would help bring the country's goods and services into a more competitive position both at home and abroad.

4. Measures were sought to achieve restraint in wages and other compensation payments, as well as prices.

5. They resolved to strive for a restructuring of the economy on a sustainable basis, with opportunities being given to workers and employers alike to make a contribution to planning and redevelopment and also to share in the fruits of the improved economy.

6. Finally, a national commitment was required to improve productivity and increased overall efficiency, and to reduce waste by enhancing national performance. It was expected that this would make the country more attractive to investors and thereby further extend the opportunities for employment (Protocol One 1993–1995).

In order to achieve these developmental objectives a framework was to be established to protect workers' security of tenure and reduce labor disputes. A freeze on increases in wages and salaries was applied to all remuneration for all types of work that was performed wholly or substantially within Barbados. This freeze applied to salaries at all organizational levels, allowances, professional fees, payments in kind, fringe benefits and lump sums. There was provided in the protocol an important clause that bears an amazing resemblance to Tony Blair's "stakeholder economy," which he propounded in 1997 in time for the British general election. This promise held that increases in wages and salaries during the life of the agreement were going to be made only in terms of profit-sharing arrangements or productivity bonuses, based on an assessment of profitability or improvement in productivity. And this held only under the following qualifying circumstances:

1. Monopoly pricing was kept under review by a monitoring committee made up of the social partners. This was to ensure that increases were tailored to legitimate cost increases, and subject to the terms of existing agreements and regulatory arrangements.

2. The social partners would work together to consider and examine indexing wage adjustments and tax allowances in relation to increases in the cost of living.

3. The parties accepted and retained collective bargaining to address conditions of work, as well as the sharing of productivity gains.

4. A tax regime was established by government which supported the objectives set by the protocol (Protocol One 1993–1995, 6–7).

In this vein, the government undertook to establish a National Productivity Board by legislation, and mandate it to develop ways of measuring productivity within the public sector in order to avoid public sector workers being disadvantaged under the protocol. It was also envisaged that the new productivity board would assist in developing incentive plans and profit-sharing schemes for guidance and adoption in securing wages and salaries settlements (Protocol One 1993–1995). In order to cement this new relationship, the partners to the agreement decided that any decisions to further the objectives of the protocol should be unanimous. A minimum of four meetings a year was also agreed, and this was to be chaired by the Office of the Prime Minister. It is interesting to note that the coming into force of this protocol did not represent a blank slate, but retained all agreements entered into in the economy prior to April 1, 1993. The protocol was presented to parliament by way of a resolution for noting and approval. The first protocol was signed on August 24, 1993, under the leadership of Lloyd Erskine Sandiford, the then prime minister of Barbados.

Results

Very little academic assessment of the TSP has been done to date. From the available narratives (Gomes 2000), in the seven years of adoption of the protocol, that is between 1993 and 1999, the country's exchange rate remained constant at BDS$2 to US$1.00, and unemployment, which was 20 percent in 1992, fell to less than 10 percent in 1999 (Gomes 2000, 66). The success of the initial experiment produced a conducive environment for the negotiation of two other protocols between 1995 and 2000. What is also interesting to note is the fact that the Barbadian TSP survived a change of government, hence ensuring a continuity of the policy.

Protocol Two, formulated in 1995, placed emphasis on a search for a new mode of governance. It also identified important steps to be taken to effect a deepening of the social partnership. Subsequently, Protocol Three (1998–2000) sought to lay down the foundations for an effective tripartite mechanism. As a result of the last protocol, no major industrial dispute has been of a protracted nature, argues Gomes. It has been noted that the rate of growth of the economy in the last five years has ranged between 3.5 percent and 4.0 percent, and per capita GDP in 1999 was US$8,200 (UNPD Human Development Index 1999 as cited in Gomes 2000). With this recorded growth, Barbados is the only Caribbean country among the top 30 countries of the world on the UNDP's Human Development Index. This record of achievement was critical in inducing policy emulation by Jamaica.

The question to ask is how did the Barbadians do it? An important issue for further research is to assess the Barbadian case in detail since there is a paucity of critical investigation on the issue. One of the basic ingredients that can help us comprehend the Barbadian case is the issue of attribution or causality. One can immediately grasp the advantage of reduced industrial disputes and the savings in man-hours that can accumulate from this, as well as the ripple effect that this can have on overall growth. The relationship between exchange rate stability and a balanced macroeconomic management cannot be missed either. However, what has been the role of external factors?

Jamaica

Uppermost in the minds of the Jamaican policy elite, when they decided to attempt a social partnership experiment, was what the prime minister described in his public broadcast as the need "to create an economy with an ever expanding productive base, capable of competing with the developed countries of the world" (P. J. Patterson, Prime Minister, broadcast to the nation, 26 Feb. 1996, 1). This partnership was to be more than just an inter-organizational relationship among the public sector, private sector and the trade unions. This is because there seemed to be at stake the very survival of the Jamaican economy itself, and therefore there was a certain amount of urgency in making the partnership work. It meant achieving high levels of economic growth, an improved standard of living and a stable economy. Patterson believed that a social partnership scheme was the way to help the country achieve its economic objectives.

The broadcast to the nation in February 1996 came at a time when the country's borrowing relationship with the IMF was coming to an end. The government of Jamaica felt that this offered a unique opportunity for the country to chart its own developmental course, make its own mistakes and bear the consequences of self-governance. Understandably, the government was joyous about the country's graduation from IMF lending and with its substantial foreign exchange reserves that could pay for 13 weeks of the country's import requirements. The government's confidence in early 1996 was highly pitched; but was this confidence well founded or was it premature? The management of the economy, in historical perspective, eloquently suggests that this confidence was built on a sandy foundation. It could not stand the test of time as a financial sector crisis occurred in 1996–97 and the economy continued to experience negative growth. In 1995 the economy recorded overall growth of 0.7 percent; in 1996 the figure was –1.4 percent; and in 1999 –0.4 percent (Table 1). Correspondingly, the unemployment figures recorded over the same period indicated the following: 1995: 16.2 percent; 1996: 16.0 percent; 1999: 15.7 percent and 16.7 percent for 2000. However, within what seems like a gloomy economic

Table 1.
Jamaica: Poverty and selected macroeconomic indicators

Year	Population Below Poverty Line	Un-employment Rate percent	Growth Rate percent	Inflation Rate percent	Human Development Index
1989	30.5	17.7	6.8	14.4	0.722
1990	28.4	15.3	5.5	22.0	0.736
1991	44.6	15.4	0.7	51.1	0.749
1992	33.9	15.8	1.5	77.3	0.721
1993	24.4	16.2	1.7	22.1	0.702
1994	22.8	15.4	1.0	34.7	0.736
1995	27.5	16.2	0.7	19.9	0.735
1996	26.1	16.0	-1.4	26.4	0.702
1997	19.9	16.5	-2.1	9.7	0.736
1998	15.9	15.5	-0.7	8.7	0.735
1999	16.9	15.7	-0.4	6.8	-
2000	18.7	16.8		10.0	-

Source: Le Franc and Downes (2001, 178); Jamaica Survey of Living Conditions 2000.

forecast lie certain interesting developments that call for additional acumen in the interpretation of the Jamaican case. This includes developments such as the emergence of a thriving informal sector, a growing remittance economy resulting from the brisk emigration of Jamaicans, and an ironic reduction in absolute poverty in a period of continued negative economic growth (Le Franc and Downes 2001; Osei 2001). This situation seems to suggest that Jamaica was experiencing what the economists call the Dutch Disease (Osei 2002).

The formulation of a partnership policy in Jamaica involved taking stock of economic management. Prior to the agreement, the real cause for concern in the economy was noted to be inflation, fueled by salary increases that are not matched by increases in productivity. The suggestion here is that this is what sets into motion the unending spiral of inflation and devaluation, leading to a reduced standard of living, especially for those on fixed incomes. The ravages of these ills are noted to be particularly severe for the aged, the unemployed and the poor. To achieve the competitiveness desired, the government of Jamaica introduced a National Strategic Plan for development and economic growth.

The main goals that the Jamaican government sought from the TSP were outlined in a Memorandum of Understanding that issued out of the initial negotiations among the partners on September 20, 1996. These are as follows, to:

1. Stabilize the economic environment
2. Reduce interest rates
3. Raise domestic savings and investment levels
4. Increase productivity
5. Increase GDP growth
6. Increase employment levels
7. Improve real standards of living
8. Increase real wages and salaries
9. Increase exports of goods and services, and
10. Strengthen information provision services.

The "Stillbirth" of a Partnership

The challenge for the Jamaican government was how to emulate and adapt what has been touted as a successful social contract project in Barbados. A preliminary assessment of newspaper articles on the status of implementation of the Jamaican TSP project seems to suggest the policy received half-hearted support, and utter rejection from segments of the trade union. The president of the Private Sector Organization of Jamaica (PSOJ), Delroy Moses, was in full support of the partnership (*Observer*, December 20, 1996, 2). But as the Memorandum of Understanding was being finalized, there was an indication that the government could not hold to its side of the bargain. In August 1996 there was a hike in the local telephone rate announced by the Telecommunications of Jamaica. The National Workers Union called this "a breach of understanding which could impact negatively on the discussions which are now in its final stages" (*Gleaner*, August 3, 1996). This breach of faith meant that producers could not hold down prices. There were early signs of inertia and a loss of the initial enthusiasm with which the process was started, not to mention the loss of the resources that were expended in the process. The Jamaican TSP seems to have been a nine-day wonder. The momentum of implementation was not maintained in the face of initial opposition, especially from the Jamaica Teachers Association (JTA). This is because they thought only the government stood to benefit from the partnership. The JTA president argued that "whenever there was any disagreement only the worker *kept* his part of the bargain, while on the other hand, the high cost of raw material can force manufacturers to up prices or go bankrupt" (*Gleaner* June 3, 1996). What represents a requiem for the policy is the fact that the property at 36 Trafalgar Road which was designated as the Partnership Secretariat is where the Office of Utilities Regulation (OUR) is now housed.

The enunciation of the social partnership program by the government in 1996 initiated an appreciable level of public debate; it also led to new initiatives in terms of the formation in 1997 of what has come to be known as the Acorn group, intended to find common grounds in building trust between employers and trade unions. Its membership includes such significant figures as Neville Ying, a professor of Human Resource and Labour Studies at the Mona School of Business; Ward Mills, the director of human resource development and chief of public relations of the Grace, Kennedy Group; Trevor Monroe, a senator, professor of politics and representative of the University and Allied Workers Union; Douglas Orane, the chief executive of Grace, Kennedy; Christopher Bond and Clive Dobson of the National Workers Union; Hopeton Caven of the Trade Union Congress; Cliff Cameron of the Manufacturers' Merchant Bank; Joe Matalon of the Mechala Group and Novar McDonald of the Employers Federation. As could be expected of any dynamic group, some members dropped out and new ones were added including Peter Moses (president of the Private Sector Organisation of Jamaica), Karl James, Anthony Bell, Lambert Brown and Ruddy Spencer. What is interesting is that the Acorn group is a policy network that is independent of government. One of its main objectives was to stem the prevailing acrimonious industrial relations in the country (Peart 1999, 4). In addition to this, an important strategy the group adopted was to lobby the government to reconsider the issue of joint training. How were such civil society groups incorporated into the new governance arrangement that was evolving? How durable were such civil society initiatives going to be? And how inclusive have they been? The latter is a legitimate question to raise here, as a cursory look at the list of the initial membership of the Acorn group read like it was a men's club.

Ward Mill is reported to have said in 1999 that "there was still a feeling that perhaps the broad partnership may not be the answer and that the answer might be in building partnerships sector by sector" (Peart, 1999). Jamaica is touted as having more churches per square mile than any other country in the Caribbean region, yet the church was not included in the social contract. This was lamented by Reverend Ralston Nembhard, who had earlier suggested to the prime minister that any consensus forged should possess a moral underpinning in order to work effectively. Nembhard thought that it was a mistake for the government to think that the social contract only embodied economic paradigms such as general agreement on wage and price restraints and better fiscal and monetary behaviour. What he thought was at stake was the soul of the nation itself. He also believed that building a social contract was a matter of trust-building among contending factions, and therefore, an area of endeavour where the church could play a pivotal role in consensus building ("Where Is the Church" 1996). Nembhard's arguments suggest that the government of Jamaica made a mistake in its policy formulation by excluding such an important constituency as the church.

Explaining the Different Outcomes

Early in this discourse, I indicated that the differing policy outcomes in Barbados and Jamaica have been attributed to the possession of a huge amount of social capital by the former, and the paucity of it in the latter country. Two studies contributed to this conclusion. These are the works by Brewster (1996) and Gomes (2000), all of which were reported in the CARICOM Perspective and were therefore widely circulated within the Caribbean Community and read mostly by policy elites, academics and students. Gomes' work was reviewed in the section on Barbados in this paper. While Gomes espouses the social capital argument, it is Brewster's essay that raises the most controversial points.

Brewster does an interesting review of some of the political and policy questions that I have posited as the environment where explanations for the differing outcomes in the two countries should be sought. Brewster believes that Barbados' social cohesiveness and huge social capital outlay can be traced to the development policies pursued by the first two post-independence leaders of the country. This era spanned the leadership of Grantly Adams and Errol Barrow and lasted for nearly 40 years, from 1938 to 1976 (Brewster 1996, 59). That era was described as a period of relative stability and prosperity. Brewster further argued, "In Jamaica, however, there was nothing equivalent to the sustained program of social reform undertaken by Adams and accelerated by his successor Barrow, although Barbados lagged behind Jamaica in constitutional reform" (1996, 59).

In addition to this, Brewster suggested that the nature of politics following the Bustamante/Manley era in Jamaica "took a radically different turn, beginning in the 1970s." As a result of this the sort of social trust that the welfare program engendered or inspired in Barbados "was simply absent in Jamaica" (Brewster 1996, 59). In trying to substantiate the social capital argument, Brewster even goes further, submitting that "Political leaders in Jamaica in the 1970s inherited a substantial liability of social distrust, exacerbated by the more difficult economic circumstances of that time that set the scene for a cumulative process of class confrontation and defection from communitarian values in a society perceived as basically unjust and uncaring" (1996, 59).

These initial assertions in favor of social capital as the explanatory variable for the success of Barbados were tempered by the same writer, who indicated that he personally felt that there has been an erosion of the stock of social capital for which there was both qualitative and objective evidence. For example he cited unemployment in Barbados of 1996 to be a good 50 percent. There was also a rising incidence of crime and harassment of visitors; and the maintenance of infrastructure, buildings and social facilities was at a low ebb. Brewster also seems to suggest that there is a positive relationship between recent Western style modernization of Barbados and the dwindling stock of social capital at home. For example, "cynicism, passivity and spectatorship are on the rise, being stimulated by the increasing availability of American television; [and] the professionalization of non-profit and non-governmental organizations may be crowding out self-help communal efforts" (Brewster 1996, 60).

In my view, the above arguments make social capital as a possible explanation of policy success rather implausible. On its own, the social capital argument collapses and at best offers only a partial explanation of the goodwill that citizens have towards public action. It is in this regard that I think contemporary policy management, political and industrial relations culture, and policy style should be investigated. The collapse of the social capital argument also, by default, makes any suggestion of Barbadians being docile and easily led rather unattractive. Robert Buddan (2001) would have us believe that perhaps Barbadians are more gentle and less unruly than Jamaicans, and because of how rich and artistically gifted the latter society is, Jamaica could possibly be a more exciting home than Barbados. Buddan even panders to the hearsay that during the slavery period, the more docile people were off-loaded first in Barbados and the more unruly ones were shipped further, especially to Jamaica (Buddan 2001, 43, 45). Popular though this myth is, there is no record to substantiate the claim. Common sense would even dictate that the plantation owner in Barbados will choose the strongest and healthiest from among the new arrivals from Africa and perhaps the weaker ones would be sent farther afield to the Americas.

It is possible, therefore, to conclude that the abundant supply of social capital on its own does not offer a strong explanation for the success of the tripartite social partnership policy of Barbados as against the dismal failure of Jamaica. Further research is required to give us a better insight into how policy management, emulation and a good amount of social capital react together to produce a successful policy outcome. Last but not least, serious attention needs to be paid to the nature of trade union activity and dynamism in both countries. There are many more trade unions in Jamaica than in Barbados, and their vibrancy and organization have been very much part of the salient forces that have shaped Jamaican politics especially in the post-colonial era. The changing circumstances of unions since the country's adoption of neoliberal structural adjustment policies in the latter part of the 1970s, and recent extensive adoption of managerialism and its by-product in the form of contract employment, have laid a siege on the very relevance of trade unionism in Jamaica. This has brought an attendant insecurity and changed employment relations in the public sector. Some of these changes meant that transient poverty, low wages, and poor conditions of work formed the bedrock on which Jamaica was trying to build its tripartite partnership. From the arguments put forward against the partnership by the various unions, the bedrock of inequality could not form an acceptable basis for a lasting social dialogue among the parties. To explain the failure of policy adoption in Jamaica, therefore, one has to look closely at the reality of the social conditions of the country's political economy.

References

Bennett, E., P. Grohmann and B. Gentry. 1999. "Public-Private Partnerships for the Urban Environment: Options and Issues." *PPPUE Working Paper Series*. Vol. 1. New York: UNDP/PPPUE and Yale University.

Brewster, H.R. 1996. "Social Capital and Development: Reflections on Barbados and Jamaica." *CARICOM Perspective*, no. 66 (June).

Buddan, R. 2001. *The Foundations of Caribbean Politics*. Kingston: Arawak Publications.

Clifton, Segree. "The Social Contract." *Gleaner*. June 3, 1996.

Cooke, B., and U. Kuthari. 2001. *Participation: A New Tyranny?* London: Zed Books.

Dasgupta, P. 2000. "Economic Progress and the Idea of Social Capital." In *Social Capital: A Multifaceted Perspective*. Edited by Partha Dasgupta and Ismail Serageldin. World Bank: Washington, D.C. 325–424.

Downes, A. 1994a. "Enhancing Productivity in Barbados and the Role of the National Productivity Board." *Barbados Economics Society Newsletter*, no. 30 (May).

_____. 1994b. "The Prospects of Prices and Incomes Policies in Barbados." *Caribbean Labour Journal* 4, no. 1 (March–June).

Fine, B. 2001. *Social Capital Versus Social Theory: Political Economy and Social Science at the Turn of the Millennium*. London and New York: Routledge.

Fiszbein, A. and P. Lowden. 1999. "Working Together for a Change: Government, Civic and Business Partnerships for Poverty Reduction in Latin American and the Caribbean." *EDI Learning Resources Series*. Washington: World Bank.

Gomes, P.I. 2000. "Social Partnerships and New Modes of Governance." *CARICOM Perspective* (June): 65–69.

Hart, K. 1989. *Women and Sexual Division of Labour in the Caribbean.* Kingston, Jamaica: Consortium Graduate School of Social Sciences, University of the West Indies at Mona.

Hyden, G., and M. Bratton. 1992. *Governance and Politics in Africa.* Boulder: Lynne Rienner Publishers.

Isham, J., D. Narayan and L. Pritchett. 1995. "Does Participation Improve Performance? Establishing Causality with Subjective Data." *The World Bank Economic Review* 9, no. 2: 175–200.

Kannan, K.P. 1995. "Public Intervention and Poverty Alleviation: A Study of the Declining Incidence of Poverty in Kerala, India." *Development & Change* 26: 701–727.

Klijn, E-H., and J.F.M. Koppenjan. 2000. "Public Management and Policy Networks: Foundations of a Network Approach to Governance." *Public Management* 2, no. 2 (June).

Le Franc, E. and A. Downes. 2001. "Measuring Human Development in Countries with Invisible Economies: Challenges Posed by the Informal Sector in Jamaica." *Social and Economic Studies* 50, no. 1 (March): 169–198.

Linder, S.H. and P.V. Rosenau. 2000. "Mapping the Terrain of the Public-Private Policy Partnership." In *Public-Private Policy Partnerships,* edited by Pauline Vaillancourt Rosenau. Cambridge, MA.: The MIT Press.

Maloney, W.A., G. Smith, and G. Stoker. 2000. "Social Capital and Associational Life." In Stephen Baron, John Field and Tom Schuller, *Social Capital.* Oxford: Oxford University Press.

McPherse, Thompson. "Threat to Social Contract." *Gleaner.* August 3, 1996, p. 1.

Midgley, J. 1986. *Community Participation, Social Development and the State.* London: Methuen.

_____. 1995. *Social Development: The Developmental Perspective in Social Welfare.* London: Thousand Oaks. New Delhi: Sage Publications.

Migdal, J. 1988. *Strong Societies and Weak States: State-Society Relations and State Capabilities in the Third World.* Princeton, NJ.: Princeton University Press.

Mumford, M. 1998. *Public Project, Private Finance: Understanding the Principles of Private Finance Initiative.* Chesham: Griffin Multimedia.

Oakley, P., and A. Marsden. 1984. *Approaches to Participation in Rural Development.* Geneva: International Labour Office.

Osei, P.D. 2002. Comment on "Measuring Human Development in Countries with Invisible Economies: Challenges posed by the Informal Sector in Jamaica." By Elsie Le Franc and Andrew Downes. *Social and Economic Studies,* Vol. 51, No. 2.

_____. 2002. "A Critical Assessment of Jamaica's National Poverty Eradication Programme." *Journal of International Development* 14, no. 6: 773–788.

_____. 2001. "Executive Agencies: Intellectual Background to the Search for Appropriate Institutional Forms." *Caribbean Journal of Public Sector Management* 3, no. 1 (November): 73–83.

Peart, Cassandra. 1999. "Quiet Progress on Social Partnership." *Jamaica Observer.* Sunday, Jamaica November 21.

Planning Institute of Jamaica and Statistical Institute. 2000. *Jamaica Survey of Living Conditions.* Kingston, Jamaica.

_____. 2001. *Jamaica Survey of Living Conditions.* Kingston, Jamaica.

Premchand, A. 1997. "Public Private Partnerships: Implications for Public Expenditure Management." Prepared for the conference "Public Sector Management for the Next Century" University of Manchester, June 29–July 2, 1997.

"Private Sector Ready to Sign Social Contract." *Observer*. December 20, 1996, p. 2.

Putnam, R.D., with R. Leonardi and R.Y. Nanetti. 1993. *Making Democracy Work: Civic Traditions in Modern Italy*. Princeton: Princeton University Press.

Savas, E.S. 2000. *Privatization and Public-Private Partnerships*. New York and London: Chatham House Publishers.

Sherraden, M. 1991. *Assets for the Poor: A New American Welfare Policy*. Armonk, NY: M.E. Sharpe.

Stoker, G. 1998. "Governance as Theory: Five Propositions." *International Social Science Journal* 155: 17–28.

Stone, C. 1993. "Wages Policy and the Social Contract." *Caribbean Labour Journal* 3, no. 1 (January).

United Nations Development Programme. 1998. "Public-Private Partnerships." http://www.undp.org:80.

_____. 2000. "Public-Private Partnerships for the Urban Environment." www.undp.org/pppue.

Wakeford, J., and J. Valentine. 2001. "Learning Through Partnership: Private Finance and Management in the Delivery of Services for London." *Public Money & Management* 21, no. 4 (October–December).

Watt, P. 2000. *Social Investment and Economic Development: A Strategy to Eradicate Poverty*. Oxfam Insight Series.

Webster, A. 1993. "Comparative Advantage and Long-run Dutch Disease Effects: The International Trade of Trinidad and Tobago." *Development Policy Review* 11, no. 2 (Oxford): 153–165.

"Where Is the Church in the Social Contract." *Herald*, Sunday, February 18, 1996.

Witter, M., and C. Kirton. 1990. "The Informal Economy in Jamaica: Some Empirical Exercises." *Working Paper No. 36*, ISER. Kingston, Jamaica: University of the West Indies at Mona.

World Bank. 1992. *Governance and Development*. Washington, D.C.: World Bank.

_____. 2000. *Partnerships for Development*. Washington, D.C.: Creative Communications Group for the World Bank.

_____. 1989. *Sub-Saharan Africa: From Crisis to Sustainable Growth*. Long Term Perspective Study. Washington, D.C.: World Bank.

_____. 1997. *World Development Report 1997: The State in a Changing World*. New York: Oxford University Press for the World Bank.

Wunsch, J., and D. Olowu. 1990. *The Failure of the Centralized State: Institutions and Self-governance*. Boulder: Westview Press.

Government Policy Documents

Barbados Government. 1993. *Protocol for the Implementation of a Prices and Incomes Policy 1993–1995*.

_____. 1995. *Addendum to the Protocol for the Implementation of a Prices and Incomes Policy*.

_____. 1995. *Protocol for the Implementation of a Prices and Incomes Policy 1995–1997*.

_____. 1998. Protocol Three for the Implementation of a Social Partnership 1998–2000. Signed by the Social Partners at the Sherbourne Conference Centre, Barbados, on 21 May 1998.

Patterson, P.J., Rt. Hon. 1996. "The Social Partnership: Workers, Employers, Government, United for Stability and Growth." Prime Minister's broadcast to the nation, February 26, 1996.

Planning Institute of Jamaica. 1996. "Toward Developing a Social Partnership." March 4, 1996.

Social Partnership Secretariat, Jamaica. 1996. Draft Agreement for the Implementation of a National Economic and Social Understanding. Social Partnership, 1996–1997.

Globalization, Diversity and Civil Society in the Caribbean; Integration by Design or Default?

Jack Menke

Introduction

An important precondition for the regional integration process in the Caribbean is the existence of a strong democracy in the individual states, with civil society as the backbone of social democracy. Democracy can be perceived as a cutting edge between state, economy (market) and civil society, where these three spheres meet or attempt to meet. Here the decision-making takes place on national issues (such as the constitution, electoral system, and economic recovery programs) as well as on thematic or sectoral issues (such as poverty, inequality, gender, and human rights).

There are some basic characteristics in Caribbean societies that influence the democratization and development processes, many of which can be reduced to the openness, diversity and fragmentation of the region. These dimensions must be taken into consideration when designing strategies and mechanisms for integration at the national, regional and international levels.

This article seeks to assess the problems and the possible role of civil society in strengthening institutional capacity at the national and regional level, so that this sector can make a significant contribution to Caribbean integration. The article is divided into four sections: the Caribbean in the global restructuring process; conceptualization, problems and role of civil society; the goals and mechanisms of integration and finally the conclusion.

The Caribbean in the Global Restructuring Process

The various conceptualizations of the Caribbean, to a lesser or greater extent reflect the diversity and fragmentation of the region. Norman Girvan distinguishes seven definitions, based on different criteria (Girvan 2001). These range from a narrow geographical criterion to geopolitical, geo-economic, geo-social, historic, neocolonial and economic-cooperative criteria. Hence, whenever one is to discuss the collaboration between Caribbean societies that differ with regard to the former colonizing power and other crucial features, it is necessary to clarify the context and concept of the Caribbean region.

From the point of view of regional organizations and the affiliated member states, the Caribbean can be perceived to comprise the following concentric circles: The OECS, Organization of East Caribbean States; CARICOM, Caribbean Community and Common Market; CARIFORUM, which consists of the CARICOM members plus Haiti and Santo Domingo; CDCC, the Caribbean Development and Cooperation Committee of the ECLAC; and the ACS, Association of Caribbean States. Of these the OECS is the smallest and the ACS the largest circle. In this article "Caribbean" refers to the ACS conceptualization that includes the Greater Caribbean with 38 states and a population of 216,721 million.[1] In this conceptualization the diversity and fragmentation between the political entities is reflected in the (former) colonizing power, language, culture, ethnicity, economic development, political status and population size, and external relations.

Like the wide diversity and fragmentation underlying the many conceptualizations of the region, Caribbean social science is also characterized by a broad spectrum of ideological viewpoints and rival paradigms (Sankatsing 1989). From a methodological point of view it is suggested to take the "unit of analysis" rather than the traditional social science discipline for a better understanding of the various scientific conceptualizations. Based on the unit of analysis Sankatsing distinguishes two dimensions for classification of the various social science conceptualizations that were developed in the past century in the Dutch and English speaking Caribbean: the "social sphere" and the "level." The levels of analysis to be distinguished are "enclave," "sub national," "national," "regional" and "international." The relevant social spheres to which the unit of analysis can belong are the economy, the social structure, culture and politics (Sankatsing 1989). Next we take a brief look at the four social spheres.

In considering the economy, the main contributing factor is the foreign domination, which resulted in various theoretical perspectives to conceptualize the Caribbean model of development in terms of the historically determined external dependence (Girvan 2001; Grugel 1995; Thomas 1988). Among the most important characteristics of this model of development are:

- Openness and high vulnerability of the economy;
- The location on the periphery of the international capitalist system;
- The excessive influence of foreign capitalist centers and external institutions;
- A high concentration of power internally.

The external dependence greatly influences the many attempts to redefine the Caribbean in the course of history. Taking also into consideration the role of internal developments, the Caribbean has continuously been redefined as a response to both external and internal factors (Girvan 2001). A great heterogeneity, informalization and inequality is generally characteristic of the social and economic structures.

In the cultural sphere, diversity and fragmentation are not limited to the differences between the states, but are also features of the distinct national states and the subnational level. At the national level a great cultural diversity is found, particularly as regards the ethnic composition, religion and the linguistic structure. For example, Suriname is characterized by a rich sociolinguistic structure with 16 languages spoken. This linguistic diversity is closely related to the ethnic composition and the social structure.

Fragmentation and diversity also characterize the political sphere of the official political democracy. There are, for example, political parties coinciding with ethnic divisions and internal splits (fragmentation) or parties "representing" various ethnic or cultural groups (diversity) (Menke 2002). Here again, one is faced with different conceptual and ideological viewpoints as well as rival paradigms as regards politics and the political system.

Global restructuring[2] (the popular term today is globalization) originally was a proactive policy response of West European countries and other developed countries to slow growth, increasing instability of the international capitalist system, and the rise of the newly industrializing countries and Japan since the seventies. The global restructuring affects Caribbean societies in a systemic way, and has a profound impact on the distinguished social spheres — the economy, the social structure, culture and politics — at the different levels of analysis. Within the sphere of the economy, global restructuring affects service economies and non-fuel primary commodity economies in a systematic way. The latter type of economies that are dependent on primary products such as bauxite, rice and bananas experienced the negative effects of falling terms of trade, delinking of production from employment, or pressure on their preferential position. This resulted in a decline of economic activities and income in the respective economic sectors. For example, the decline of the bauxite mining and processing in the Caribbean (Jamaica, Suriname and Guyana) since the 1980s is largely due to the fall of primary aluminum on the world market and new technologies (such as recycling) to reduce the production costs. In the case of Suriname, from 1980 to 1987 the contribution of bauxite to GDP decreased from 16 percent to 8 percent, while employment decreased by 50 percent, from approximately 6000 to 3000 (Menke 1998). Changes in the social structures of Caribbean societies are closely linked with the impact of globalization on the economy. There is remarkable increase in self-employment, a systemic growth of the informal and illegal sectors, and a higher participation of females in the economy.

As regards the political system and the political democracy, globalization had a negative impact on electoral and political stability in many Caribbean societies that were already struggling to manage their diversity and fragmentation. A key issue relates to the model of development in Caribbean societies with their high diversity and fragmentation and the role of civil society.

The impact of globalization on Caribbean culture is felt particularly in the "one-dimensional" packages of the American way of life through modern telecommunications technologies and the Internet. Finally, the already existing persistent poverty, inequality and social injustice were aggravated during global restructuring.

Given the profound impact of global restructuring on Caribbean societies, a principal question is how to redefine the role of civil society in the ongoing regional integration process of the Caribbean, in the context of its economic and social vulnerability, fragmentation and high diversity.

Civil Society

Civil society may be described as the intermediate realm between state and family, populated by organizations that are separate from the state, that enjoy autonomy in relation to the state, and are voluntarily formed by members of the society to protect or extend their interests or values (IDB 2001, 141). This definition by the IDB contains important characteristics of civil society. However, the latter needs to be delineated from other sectors and specified in the wider developmental context of the society. Civil society needs to be distinguished from the state and private sectors with their respective political and economic elites, who are often interconnected. It can then be described as the wide range of formal activities and informal networks of people in their role as citizens, and the way they promote or protect their interests and voluntarily organize themselves with certain autonomy from the state and the private sector. Civil society consists of formal organizations and informal networks such as professional associations, NGOs, community groups, academic institutions, research centers and political parties, religious organizations, cooperatives, labor unions, foundations and the independent press.

Origin and Role of Civil Society

From a developmental perspective, the emergence and evolution of civil society in the Caribbean was different from Europe, as was the case with the formation of the State. An important indicator for the growth of Caribbean civil society from the eighteenth to the twentieth century is the expansion of civil rights. This was achieved by means of movements and organizations that were strong enough to compete with the state for power, or that at least had some success in increasing civil rights (Schalkwijk 1994). Prior to abolition of slavery in the nineteenth century, civil society was solely connected with the elites, since slaves had very limited civil rights. The elite associations of planters and the colonial administration were concerned with promoting their own interests and civil rights and not with those of the wider society of slaves and free people. Some religious denominations became the main vehicle for civil society in Colonial Caribbean. This differed from the European experience, where the State had to wrest itself from religious control. In the Caribbean the Church had to get rid of State control, and provided education and opportunities for social mobility to mulattos, blacks and other groups. "After Emancipation gradually other organizations became actors in Civil Society and we see social and religious life becoming disentangled. The growth and diversification of Civil Society can be reconstructed also from the growth of Non Commercial Private Organizations (NGO's), since these represent specific interest groups" (ibid.). The diversity of civil society follows logically from the diversity in Caribbean societies. This diversity has been recognized as a critical potential for development by CARICOM. This is formalized in the Charter of Civil Society (CARICOM Secretariat 1997).

In the Caribbean of today, civil society is present at different forums through a variety of individual and umbrella organizations that cut across language, culture, ethnicity and nationality. To mention a few: the Caribbean Council of Churches (CCC), the Caribbean Development Policy Center (CPDC), CAFRA, CRIES, academic associations such as the Association of Caribbean Economists (ACE), and the Caribbean Studies Association (CSA).

Civil Society Functions

Civil society can be considered from another perspective than the formal political democracy with its related institutions and leadership. Civil society has its own organizations and institutions and related representatives or leaders, and is of growing importance because of its moral, social, democratic, and development functions.

Civil society fulfils a watchdog function by means of the promotion and protection of values such as social rights, equality, freedom, democratic procedures, peace, justice, transparency and consensus-building. It operates in the field between the market, state and private households. In this field, citizens take the initiative in the interest of the community. Civil society thus aims at the creation of a moral order. To this end its function is to limit the power of the state and the market, and serve the community by guarding over values such as civil freedom and democratic procedures, and if necessary opposing authoritarian tendencies.

Another important function of civil society is the development function. From the perspective of broad diversity — among others the religious and cultural diversity and the rights of indigenous people — the sustainable economic development and protection of the environment are of great importance. These are all dimensions addressed in the CARICOM Charter of Civil Society. Civil society can also provide indicators to measure or evaluate the thrust in the institutions of political democracy, whereby influence is being used to control the political democracy, including values of good governance, the electoral process and the democratic system in operation. Another important task of civil society is developing and promoting social democracy. Here civilians have a voice and act in society's interests against citizens who, as members of a political body, have a vote, which they exercise primarily through how they perceive their own interests (A Po Lim 2001, 10).

When the conceptions of social democracy versus political democracy are being considered from a dynamic developmental perspective, these two approaches will be more complementary. The political democracy and its leadership can be perceived as a top-down approach of democracy, while social democracy and the civil society in an ideal situation can be considered a bottom-up approach.

Problems and opportunities

The distinction often made between southern and northern NGOs coincides with donor and receiving organizations. Partly due to the negative socioeconomic implications of globalization, many southern NGOs have become dependent on northern donor organizations, particularly in terms of financing their exploitation. However, it is a misconception that the relations between these NGOs are restricted to finance and funding. The relationships also comprise advice and information on development and policy related matters. In terms of development cooperation between North and South the relationships are generally positive, which opens opportunities for exchange of experiences and collaboration in the area of regional integration.

Another major problem of many southern NGOs is their poor policy implementation and low absorption capacity. Such is the case in Suriname where a low absorption capacity linked with a shortage of qualified human resources was identified, while at the same time there is an overutilization of actual human resources. NGOs are the backbone of civil society. Like the overall civil society, the NGO sector shows a great diversity. This is reflected in the principal policy issues and the target groups but also in the type of NGO. In the latter case, one could make a distinction between grassroots NGOs (linked directly with the target group), intermediaries (providing services and contributing to strengthen grassroots NGOs); and service providers (providing services to NGOs that the state doesn't deliver, without strengthening grassroots organizations). Regional organizations do not sufficiently utilize the potential of some types of NGOs. Apart from policy oriented NGOs or umbrella organizations, there is an opportunity to mobilize and take advantage of NGOs in two major areas: those with the capacity to strengthen social democracy and those with the capacity to enhance social justice and equity. These are areas where traditional policy making and political democracy has demonstrated its inability to respond adequately and provide solutions to these persistent problems.

The implication of the statement "think global, act local" is that community-based organizations and local democracy are crucial mechanisms to realize and institutionalize democratic participation, development and social justice. However, in some Caribbean states the realization and institutionalization of democratic participation, development and social justice by means of formal local democracy and/or civil society seems to be less than expected. First, there are countries where the central government appoints local government members and where citizens don't have the right to vote for their local government representatives. Such is the case in Antigua, St. Lucia and St. Vincent.

Second, in most states with local government elections there is a participation crisis in terms of the facility to vote in local elections, but also in citizens' capacity to associate in organizations that, in turn, allow them to become effective participants in processes (Ragoonath 2002). This is the case in many Caribbean countries with local government systems. There is evidence that voters' turnout was less than 50 percent in the Bahamas, Belize, Dominica, Guyana, Jamaica and Trinidad and Tobago. In some countries the participation was extremely low in certain regions. For example in Belize, in 3 of the 8 municipalities in the 2000 elections, the turnout was less than 12 percent, while in the capital city of Dominica in the turnout in the 1999 elections was a 16 percent (ibid.). In Suriname local government elections have been held since 1987. In this country voters' turnout is relatively high at over 65 percent, which is due to the fact that these elections are held simultaneously with the central government elections.

However, there are opportunities to realize institutionalized democratic participation, development and social justice by means of a combined effort of civil society and formal local government institutions. One could take advantage from experiments in Caribbean societies with good practices in this field (Ragoonath 2002). Finally, language and culture, to a certain extent, is an impediment to regional integration. This stems from the colonial past and heritage, which largely explains the strong links of the various language and cultural areas in the Caribbean with their European colonizing countries. Illustrative are the strong links of the Spanish speaking Caribbean with Spain, the English speaking countries with their Commonwealth links, the French speaking countries with their department status, and the strong ties of the Dutch Antilles and Suriname with Holland. These cultural identities are also reflected in the composition and character of many umbrella NGOs and other civil society organizations in the region. Complaints are often heard that one linguistic group of countries or persons have traditionally dominated many of the supposedly linguistically diverse organizations. However, the good news is that there are some regional civil society organizations that attempt to cut through the language and cultural barriers, among them the ACE, the CPDC and the CCC. Illustrative is the Constitution of the ACE, founded in 1987, in which it is established that the Executive Committee shall consist of four vice presidents, respectively from the English speaking, Spanish speaking,

Dutch speaking and French speaking Caribbean. The problem is that most of these organizations are not structurally involved in the decision-making of already existing regional institutions such as the OECS, CARICOM, CARIFORUM, the CDCC and the ACS.

Goals and Mechanisms of Caribbean Integration

There is some humor in a story of a development worker who stayed a few months on the border of two Caribbean mainland states, Guyana and Suriname. Smuggling across the Corantyne, the Border River, had become a tradition of close collaboration in the daily life of Guyanese and Surinamese people. At a certain point in time a policeman appeared on the smuggling scene and tried to prevent the act of smuggling. The development worker, who had such a good time with the people, exclaimed: "Why the hell is this beautiful tradition of integration condemned as an act of smuggling!"

This piece of humor sheds some light on a critical question: should civil society embark on Caribbean integration by default or by design? The default option refers to the approach that policy officials of regional and intergovernmental organizations mostly give reactive responses to externalities and the rules of supranational institutions. The other way is that civil society and regional organizations take a "people at the center" and proactive "integration by design" approach by utilizing their existing social capital and human resources to deepen, strengthen and hasten the integration process.

In the context of the latter approach, the principal goals of civil society involvement in Caribbean integration are:

1. To improve the institutional capacity, particularly the policy formulation and the implementation capacity through greater cooperation among civil society and private and state related academic institutes, across linguistic, cultural, social and economic diversities in the Caribbean.

2. To increase solidarity and democratic participation among the Caribbean citizens and improve the quality of political, social and economic democracy across linguistic, cultural, social and economic diversities.

These goals are justified by a growing interaction between people and institutions in the Caribbean as a result of the many networks, umbrella organizations and regional organizations at the state level. This creates a need for improving collaborative policies and actions.

Which are the mechanisms to achieve these goals?

a. Mobilize public opinion and exchange information on success stories of civil society organizations in the sphere of economy, culture and politics across the member states of the Caribbean and utilize the social capital at the regional institutional level.

b. Civil society and local democracy institutions in a combined effort should encourage citizens' participation and enhance the quality of democracy.

c. Institutionalize cooperation between academic and policymaking institutions across the region in the area of policy formulation, implementation and evaluation.

d. Develop a Caribbean agenda for research, training and awareness building, focusing on the ideas of integration, development and the transformation of political democracy into a broader concept that includes social democracy at the national and regional level.

Mobilizing public opinion and utilizing the social capital at the regional institutional level

In the global restructuring process there is a decreasing thrust in political institutions and its leaders (Misztal 1996). There seems to be a great need for more thrust and solidarity in modern societies. One reason the need for thrust is emphasized has to do with the disintegration of traditional values based on nuclear family, a fixed employer and the nation state. Civilians, amidst increasing uncertainty, tend to stress culture, ethnicity and territory.

In the process of a decreasing thrust in the political institutions and increasing poverty, females appear more sensitive to socioeconomic issues and are more supportive of national cooperation in order to restore thrust. Illustrative are opinion polls held in Suriname showing that a significantly higher proportion of females opt for national cooperation coalitions to cope with socioeconomic and political problems (INDEST 1997). Recently there has been wide international interest in the issue of thrust and social capital. This perspective focuses on tight, horizontal networks of organizations that are willing to cooperate with others (Putnam 1995). This widens their ability to act collectively as well as increasing the amount of thrust and attachment to norms of reciprocity. Cooperation, thrust and reciprocity are notions underlying the idea of social capital. Communities differ in the way they have access to social capital.

The international mushrooming of civil society organizations is an expression of the social capital, and is a critical factor in the democratization of Caribbean societies. Here is an important role for civil society: to reestablish and increase the thrust, solidarity and cohesion in institutions, and give priority to organizations (such as credit unions) where thrust and solidarity are high on the agenda.

Increasing Caribbean democratic participation and improving the quality of democracy

This mechanism utilizes both civil society and local government in the Caribbean to encourage citizen participation and improve the quality of democracy. Focus should include participation in elections and policy decision-making at the micro, meso and macro levels. There could be a combined effort of civil society and community based activities in order to facilitate local government. Lessons could be learned from experiments in other Caribbean societies. There are instances of good practices in various parts of the Caribbean (Ragoonath 2002). Illustrative are the local Participatory Observatories in which representatives from civil society and the community collaborate to discuss what local government is going to do, as was the case in St. Lucia and Dominica. The advantage of the Participatory Observatories is that they serve as a pressure group, to push the local government authority and making sure that they function (ibid.).

Institutionalizing cooperation between academic and policymaking institutions in policy formulation, implementation and evaluation

A principal mechanism is at the level of collaboration between academic and policymaking institutions across the Caribbean. Illustrative for this type of collaboration is the initiative by the Association of Caribbean States (ACS) based on a study "The Virtual Institute of Caribbean Studies" (ACS 2002). An important finding of the study is the idea to establish a virtual network of universities, departments, institutes and centers devoted to Caribbean studies through the implementation of a master's degree in Caribbean studies delivered through the Internet. This initiative could allow participants to transcend the traditional disciplinary approach and acquire an integrated perspective of the political, economic, social, and cultural forces shaping the greater Caribbean.

The rationale of this master's program is included in the general missions of the ACS, as stated in their Constitutive Convention: "The Association is an organization for consultation, cooperation and concerted action, whose purpose is to identify and promote the implementation of policies and programs designed to harness, utilize and develop the collective capabilities of the Caribbean Region to achieve sustained cultural, economic, scientific and technological advancement."

The ACS's "Virtual Institute" report assumes that a wide interest in Caribbean studies responds to a number of interlinked developments. First, as a consequence of the globalisation and regionalization processes there is increasing interaction among Caribbean states and territories across linguistic and political affiliations, which is reflected in the new pan–Caribbean intergovernmental organisations (the ACS and CARIFORUM) and NGOs such as CRIES. A second development is "the growing cultural awareness of populations of Caribbean ancestry in the mainland countries of Central and South America. This has led to recognition of the need to take account of cultural diversity and the cultural aspirations of the ethnic minorities in these societies" (ibid.). A third development is the Caribbean Diaspora in North America and Europe that shows a steady growth accompanied by the interest of scholars and students in the cultural, social and political heritage of the Caribbean. The fourth development is also linked with globalisation and regionalization in a way that these processes "have generated a need for increasing supplies of graduates with specialised skills in trade policy and in economic and social policy that are relevant to the local and regional environment" (ibid.).

Developing a Caribbean agenda for sustainable development and the transformation of political democracy to include social democracy

This mechanism is to develop a comparative pan–Caribbean agenda for research, training and awareness building with the aim to enhance development and transform social democracy (civil society) and political democracy into a complementary and wider conception of democracy. It is recommended to design an agenda for research training and awareness built on key integration issues. The research and training agenda should include the following main topics: basic values of democracy and governance; watchdog of integration and democratic participation; and policy decision-making.[3]

BASIC VALUES OF DEMOCRACY AND GOVERNANCE

The basic values of the people should be reflected in social democracy (civil society) and the system of political democracy as well. These values are shaped by internal and external (historical) forces. Some of the important themes are listed below.

Values and conceptions of democracy and leadership. This theme is important to get insight in the moral dimension and democratic standards of civil society vis-à-vis political democracy and its leadership.

Good governance. The culture of governance can be related to the moral values of civil society and the political democracy. In the global restructuring process, the criteria for good governance in Caribbean societies are determined primarily by international finance organizations or donor countries. The values underlying these criteria are often controversial. In addition to international finance institutions and the formal institutions of the political democracy, civil society should be involved to determine and keep the standards for good governance in the Caribbean.

Consensus building and conflict resolution. Consensus building and conflict resolution and the way these are perceived by civil society and the political democracy, are of great importance for the Caribbean, which consists of societies with a diverse population. Comparisons can be made between the various systems of political democracy (Westminster majoritarian versus the non-majoritarian model) and social democracy, and lessons can be learned in terms of weak and strong points. Among the important issues are the representation of ethnic groups and minorities in the democratic system and public sector; and the perceptions, requirements and strategies for institutionalization of consensus and harmony between the different groups in Caribbean societies.

WATCHDOG OF INTEGRATION AND DEMOCRATIC PARTICIPATION

To guarantee a strong political democracy, the active involvement and proper functioning of key civil society groups— such as the intellectuals and media workers— is necessary. These groups have an important role in protecting and maintaining moral and political values, and are a critical watchdog in the development of democracy.

Functions of civil society for integration and democracy. Here focus is on the relevant social capital and the function of civil society to cushion against nondemocratic developments in the Caribbean region.

Intellectuals. Participants in the political and social debate (among others academics, lawyers, journalists and writers) have been playing a role in critically guiding social, economic and political developments in different historical periods. A key question is how these intellectuals survive and adapt in the global restructuring process, and what should be their contribution in Caribbean integration.

The media. The media includes newspapers, radio broadcasting stations and television. Some relevant questions are how the media survives and adapts in the global restructuring process with the mega-media corporations of the North, and what should be the media strategy for civil society to promote and protect social and political democracy in the Caribbean.

POLICY DECISION-MAKING

This topic relates to the functioning of Caribbean democracies, and the role of the various groups in decision-making on strategic issues. It deals with the reasons behind decisions of strategic importance, the way decision-making take place, how the decision-making is legitimized, and the implications for the population. An important issue is the decision-making process in the political and social democracy, respectively. Another issue relates to public sector organization and culture. Political decision-making and political appointments as well need to be characterized by transparency of procedures and the institutionalization of standards, a proportionate distribution of resources between ethnic groups that enables an efficient and effective functioning bureaucracy.

Conclusion

The ongoing global restructuring affects Caribbean societies in a systemic way, with a profound impact on the economy, the social structure, culture and politics. Most Caribbean states are experiencing the negative implications of falling terms of trade, delinking of production from employment, or pressure on their preferential position; this results in a decline of economic activities and income in the leading economic sectors as well as the people's economic sectors. Changes in the social structures are closely linked with the impact of globalization on the economy and are accompanied by an increase in self-employment, expansion of the informal and illegal sectors, and an increase of the already existing persistent poverty, inequality and social injustice. At the political level, globalization has a negative impact on the electoral and political stability in many Caribbean societies that were already struggling to manage diversity and fragmentation. The impact of globalization on Caribbean culture is felt particularly in the "one-dimensional" packages of the American way of life through modern telecommunications technologies and Internet. Given the profound impact of global restructuring on Caribbean societies, a principal question relates to the role of civil society in the ongoing regional integration process of the Caribbean, in the context of its economic and social vulnerability, fragmentation and high diversity.

Civil society is present in the Caribbean at different forums through a variety of individual and umbrella organizations that cut across language, culture, ethnicity and nationality. This diversity is recognized to constitute a critical potential for development. The key role that civil society could play includes the watchdog function, the development function and the promotion of social democracy. The watchdog function includes the promotion and protection of values such as social rights, equality, freedom, democratic procedures, peace, justice, transparency and consensus-building. It aims also to limit the power of the state and the market, and serve the community by guarding over values such as civil freedom, democratic procedures. The development function, amidst the religious and cultural diversity and the rights of indigenous people, aims at achieving sustainable economic development and protection of the environment. The promotion of social democracy could guarantee that civilians have a voice and act in society's interests against citizens who, as members of a political body, have a vote.

Civil society should take a proactive "integration by design" approach rather than an "integration by default" approach by utilizing existing social capital and human resources to deepen, strengthen and hasten the regional integration process. This is the context in which civil society can strengthen the institutional capacity at the national and regional level, and make a significant contribution to the Caribbean integration. Civil society has already made many attempts to redefine the Caribbean in the course of history as a response to both external and internal developments. There are good practices already in place in existing regional civil society organizations. The problem is that these organizations are not structurally involved in the decision-making of existing regional institutions such as the OECS, CARICOM, CARIFORUM, the CDCC and the ACS.

The principal goals of civil society involvement in Caribbean integration are the improvement of the institutional capacity through greater cooperation among civil society, private and state related academic institutes; enlargement of solidarity and democratic participation among Caribbean citizens; and improvement of the quality of political and social democracy across linguistic, cultural, social and economic diversities. The mechanisms to achieve these goals could be most effective in an "integration by design" approach, one that combines a top-down with a bottom-up approach: a deep and broad participation of Civil society and its resources.

Endnotes

1. Also included are the three French dependent territories, which are non-certified members of the ACS. The G3 countries (Mexico, Columbia and Venezuela) with their 147.852 million people contribute 68 percent of the total population and 78 percent of the total GDP of the ACS in 1995 (Girvan 2001).
2. "Global restructuring" refers to the policies adopted by OECD and other developed countries in the 1970s. This concept has three dimensions: first, lowering the break-even point of industry by driving down costs; second, enhancing competitiveness through a dynamic technological process of creative destruction; third, developing the most cost-efficient international sourcing of raw materials and products. The faltering growth in the developed world was being experienced in developing countries in the drop in the relative prices of most primary commodities (Foster 1989).
3. Some of these topics were raised from the perspective of the elites in a project "Elites, Democracy and Society in the Caribbean" at the University of Suriname in 2001.

References

ACS. 2002. "The Virtual Institute of Caribbean Studies: Report of a Feasibility Study." May.

Barber, B. 1984. *Strong Democracy: Participatory Politics for a New Age*. Berkeley: University of California Press.

Charter of Civil Society, CARICOM Secretariat, 1997.

Dew, E. 1978. *The Difficult Flowering of Suriname: Ethnicity and Politics in a Plural Society*. The Hague: Martinus Nijhoff.

Foster, John Bellamy. 1989. "The Age of Restructuring." In Arthur MacEwan and William K. Tabb, *Instability and Change in the World Economy*. New York: Monthly Review Press.

Girvan, Norman. 2001. "Reinterpreting the Caribbean." In Brian Meeks and Folke Lindahl (eds.), *New Caribbean Thought*. University of the West Indies, Jamaica.

Grugel, Jean (ed.). 1995. *Politics and Development in the Caribbean Basin*. Bloomington, Indiana: Indiana University.

INDEST. 1997. Post-election opinion poll in Paramaribo, Surinam.

Inter-American Development Bank. 2001. *Governance in Suriname: RE3-01-001 Economic and Sector Study Series*.

Lim, A Po. 2001. Hans Samenlevingspatronen en Democratie (Syllabus Course Democratie, Bestuur en Besluitvorming, University of Suriname).

Menke, Jack. 2002. "Democracy and Governance in Multi-Ethnic Societies: The Case of Suriname." In Selwyn Ryan and Ann Marie Bissessar. 2002. *Governance in the Caribbean*. SALISES. Trinidad and Tobago: The University of The West Indies.

_____. 2001. "Skin Bleaching Practices and Implications in the Multi-ethnic and Multi-colored Surinamese Society." *COLOR Foundation*.

Misztal, B. 1996. *Trust in Modern Societies: The Search for the Basis of Social Order.* Cambridge: Polity Press.

Lowenthal, D. 1972. *West Indian Societies: London: Oxford University Press.*

Lijphart, A. 1977. *Democracy in Plural Societies: A Comparative Exploration.* New Haven: Yale University Press.

Putnam, R. 1995. *Making Democracy Work: Civil Society in Italy.* Princeton, New Jersey: Princeton University Press.

Ragoonath, Bishnu. 2002. "Embracing Civil Society in Local Governance: Challenges and Prospects for the Commonwealth Caribbean." Paper presented at the round table "The Changing Relationship Between Political Democracy, Social Democracy and the Market," 8–9 November 2002, University of Suriname, Paramaribo.

Ryan, S. 1999. *Winner Takes All: The Westminster Experience in the Caribbean.* ISER. St. Augustine.

Sankatsing, G. 1989. "Caribbean Social Sciences: An Assessment." Caracas: UNESCO.

Saward, M. 1994. "Democratic Theory and Indices of Democratization." In D. Beetham (ed.), *Defining and Measuring Democracy.* London: Sage.

Schalkwijk, M. 1994. *Colonial State-Formation in Caribbean Plantation Societies: Structural Analysis and Changing Elite Networks in Suriname, 1650–1920.* Ph.D. thesis, Cornell University.

Smith, M.G. 1965. *The Plural Society in the British West Indies.* Berkeley/Los Angeles: University of California Press.

Young, I. 2000. *Inclusion and Democracy.* Oxford: Oxford University Press.

The Digital Divide: A New Imperialism?

Gale Rigobert

Information and communication technologies (ICT) have been a core driver of the phenomenon of "globalization." In this new environment, information has new value and generates new power.
— S. Dutta, B. Lanvin and F. Pau, 2002

Introduction

The neoliberal version of globalization promises the trickling down of the burgeoning wealth in the North to the underprivileged of the South. The hyperglobalists contend that what we are witnessing at this conjuncture is unprecedented, hence revolutionary. However, the evidence suggests that much of the developing world is still far from realizing the kind of economic and technological convergence that was envisaged. This gap is evident in the socioeconomic disparities between the haves and the have-nots, and is mirrored in the technology divide.

The ability of countries in the periphery to harness information and communication technologies (ICTs) for growth is restricted by the position those countries occupy in the international division of labor. Their primary role is still that of producing raw material for export to markets in the North, and importing manufactured goods from the North. The asymmetrical trade relations continue to be a feature of international trade. In the emerging techno-economic paradigm, competitiveness in the new economy is determined largely by investments in knowledge and information, research and development, and intellectual capital. The developing world can ill afford to ignore this reality. However, financial and human resource constraints hamper their best efforts to correct this. Or is it that the international political economy is so heavily influenced by the impe-

73

rialistic agenda that the world system itself has not evolved beyond a Wallersteinian conceptualization of core, semi-periphery, and periphery and all that this connotes?

This prompts the following question: To what extent is it possible for countries in the periphery to escape the dependency syndrome? Is it that one form of dependency is being replaced by another, or that the ICT revolution has valid transformational potential? None of these can be understood completely without a thorough deconstruction of the dynamism of imperialism itself. The paper questions the notion that the ICT revolution has introduced a new dimension to the concept of imperialism. Are the emerging technologies new vehicles for affecting the imperialistic agenda?

Measuring the Income Gap

Dramatic new developments in communications technology have ushered in new techno-economic realities, but not everyone stands to gain. Some will be marginalized in this process. Already, developing countries of Africa and the Caribbean are reeling under the pressures of globalization and the technological implications. There is no panacea in sight. In fact, the concern is that what we are witnessing is an exacerbation of inequality and a polarization of the technological haves and have-nots. This is reflected in income gaps between the countries of the core and the periphery. The 2000 United Nations Development Program (UNDP) Human Development Report states that there has been a phenomenal increase in the income gaps between the richest and the poorest nations.

In 1820 the income gap between the richest and poorest country measured 3 to 1; in 1973 it was 44 to 1 and in 1992 it rose to 72 to 1 (UNDP 2000, 6). Intra-nationally, too, the income gap is widening, and remains disturbingly high in much of the developing world. The polarization of world incomes has widened over the last few decades. The combined wealth of the top 200 billionaires reached $1,135 billion in 1999, up from $1,042 billion in 1998. This is in stark contrast to the combined income for the 582 million people of the developing world, which totaled $146 billion (UNDP 2000, 82).

The hope of reducing poverty is overshadowed by the fact that 1.2 billion people live on less than US$1.00 a day. Countries in the Organization for Economic Cooperation and Development (OECD) dominate the worldwide production of ICT goods and services, and a yawning technology gap exists between the developed nations of the North and the peripheral South. A cursory survey of the Network Readiness Index (NRI) tells the story plainly. A study of 75 countries revealed that the OECD countries secured the top 20 places while Caribbean countries such as Trinidad and Tobago and Jamaica ranked 46 and 57 respectively (The Global Information Technology Report 2001–2002, xiv).

The implication is that while the Bretton Woods Institutions and UN agencies bellow the gains to be had by the spread of ICTs, the reality is that we are generations away from a global society of states that are digitally connected. The patterns of exchange have remained essentially the same over the last 500 years, with the peripheral countries lagging far behind those of the core. A large majority in the South is yet to enjoy the fruits. Perhaps it is because the international division of labor has not gone through any structural shifts to facilitate the ascent of peripheral nations. Fundamentally, it is still characterized by the socioeconomic stratification of core, semi-periphery and periphery. The evidence suggests that it remains remarkably difficult for graduation from one stratum into the next to take place.

Imperialism, Globalization and ICTs: The New Conjuncture?

The intellectual evolution of imperialism spans several centuries beginning at the end of the fifteenth century when it was narrowly conceived as European overseas expansion (territorial annexation). However, *imperialism* is broadly conceived as the exercise of control or domination over another. Marxist perspectives on imperialism suggest that capitalist expansion necessitated imperialistic ambitions. Lenin contended that imperialism is the monopoly stage of capitalism.[1] However I am more sympathetic to Amin's notion that "Imperialism is not a *stage*, not even the *highest stage*, of capitalism: from the beginning, it is *inherent* in capitalism's expansion."[2]

And so we ask, has there been a definitive shift away from the imperialism that characterized European expansion? Or, are we seeing an alternative defined, not by the colonial exploits that began with Columbus' fifteenth century voyages, but by technological and scientific potential? Globalization is thus perceived as an embodiment of postmodern or twenty-first century imperialism in new guise, tangential with Johan Galtung's eclectic use of the concept. Imperialism, he contends, "is a species in a genus of dominance and power relationships.... Dominance relations between nations and other collectivities will not disappear with the disappearance of imperialism; nor will the end of one type of imperialism (e.g. political or economic) guarantee the end of another type of imperialism (e.g. economic or cultural)."[3]

In identifying five types of imperialism — military, political, economic, cultural and communications— Galtung suggests that imperialism "does not presuppose the *primacy of economics*. Attention is given also to political, military, communicative, cultural and social imperialism."[4] And it is here that the heuristic utility of his concept of imperialism is evident, and is particularly useful in ascertaining whether what we now perceive as globalization is but a new form of imperialism. More specifically within the context of this paper — how one form of imperialism has been replaced by another, that is— we have moved away from a purely military form of imperialism to one that finds resonance in the communications sphere. This is not to suggest that the imperialistic powers-that-be have ceased to use other types of imperialism; rather, the imperialistic agenda is being facilitated through a new medium.

An analysis of the political economy of ICTs, with a particular focus on technological diffusion intellectual property rights, and copyrights (the latter two being the main source of power and wealth in the new techno-economic paradigm), emphasizes the distinction between the techno-rich countries and those that are technologically bereft. In the case of the English speaking Caribbean, telecom company Cable and Wireless still enjoys monopoly rights in many of the islands. However, it is heartening to note that the OCES territories and Jamaica have begun to liberalize the telecommunications sector. Already in Jamaica there has been a notable decrease in the price of telecommunications goods and services, particularly with regard to mobile telephones and services. A similar trend is evident in the OECS territories.

Galtung's conceptual matrix of imperialism does not presuppose the artificial liberal distinction between politics and economics. What is captivating about the different types of imperialism is their convertibility: in other words, how one form of imperialism can be converted into another. Political imperialism, for example, can be combined with or converted into economic imperialism by dictating the terms of trade, where the latter are not seen so much in terms of trade composition.[5] Galtung recognizes that via a similar process, communication imperialism may be converted into cultural imperialism by regulating the flow of information, not only in the form of news, but also in the form of cheaply available books, etc., from the dominating country.[6]

The critical question to be asked is whether the phenomenon that we are currently witnessing is new, or whether it is a continuity. What is new in the current conjuncture is the extent to which the various types of imperialism are being bridged and connected by communications technology. Those who control the flow of information are able to shape the way in which the world is presented, disseminating images of "reality" which condition the way the world is seen and interpreted.[7] I will stretch the analysis further, beyond traditional media, to incorporate the burgeoning electronic media, which is essentially the main vehicle for conducting the imperialistic agenda — not simply in terms of the content that Galtung alludes to, but also in terms of the production of hardware, software and, of course, content.

And perhaps it is this techno-reality which has redefined the landscape of international political economy, triggering a paradigm shift, one which finds resonance with Perez' and Freeman's concept of a new techno-economic paradigm. The United Nations has often lamented the failure of firms to transfer technology, and have been critical of the practice of transfer pricing and, by extension, the lack of commitment to the economic development of developing countries. Nowhere is this more evident than in the amount spent on research and development by OECD countries versus that spent by the developing world. If we are to take patenting as an indicator of the level of activity in research and development, the data suggests that the developing world lags far behind. In 1998 Japan and the USA granted 994 and 289 patents per million people respectively, compared with two from Brazil and Uruguay, and one from Botswana and Estonia.[8]

Investment in research and development of appropriate technology is one of the key indicators for ascertaining readiness for take off in the e-conomy. The figures for the Latin American and Caribbean region in this respect tell a frightening tale. Expenditure on research and development over the period 1996–1997 was very low, and accounted for only 3.1 percent of the world total, compared with Europe and North America, which accounted for 28.8 percent and 38.2 percent, respectively. The disparity is clear, and is also reflected in earnings from royalties and license fees. It is here that we identify the yawning gap between those who shape and inform the dimensions and content of that technology and all that it embodies, and those who are mere consumers.[9] But even more critical is the weight assigned to this very same technology, as a key variable in the development formula.

Similarly, we should become duly concerned that only a few companies own and control the media output in the world. There are no more than five global, vertically integrated media companies: News Corp., Disney,

Time Warner, Viacom and TCI, which make films, books, recorded music, and TV programs and own newspapers, magazines, radio stations, cable companies, and TV networks.[10] The socio-technical and cultural implications are obvious—what we know and how we come to know it and understand it is controlled by a few. Moreover, we are being charged a premium for it. Therein lies the crux of the digital divide. There is also an underlying cultural divide, in that there is little indigenous content for the majority of the world's people. It has been argued that 80 percent of the world's news, films, and television originate in the North, which controls the media in the developing countries as well.[11] Compare that with the 0.02 percent of global Internet content emanating from Africa.[12]

Globalization and the Evolution of Information and Communications Technologies

Globalization— the process through which an increasingly free flow of ideas, people, goods, services, and capital leads to the integration of economies and societies— has brought **rising prosperity** *to the countries that have* **participated**. *It has* **boosted incomes** *and helped* **raise living standards** *in* **many parts of the world**, *partly by* **making sophisticated technologies available** *to* **less advanced countries** ... **greater integration** *has promoted* **human freedom by spreading information and increasing choices**.[13]

The aspect of globalization that provokes perhaps the least controversy is the extent of the information and communications revolution. The technological revolution continues to fuel the globalization process; deepening and widening economic relations, dissolving time lines and geographical boundaries. Cheap information networks, real-time communications and significantly reduced travel costs facilitate the intensification of human and corporate interactions across geographical and cultural boundaries. These developments may have generated and shaped those currents and the course of globalization.

Dollar and Kraay claim that the increased trade that has come about as a result of globalization has "encouraged growth and poverty reduction and has contributed to narrowing the gaps between rich and poor worldwide."[14] These miracle solutions to social, political and economic problems of the periphery promised by globalization seem slow in coming. Much of the data suggests that while global income has increased, this growth has been concentrated in the Triad (the US, Japan, and the European Community) and has not resulted in the narrowing of the income and development gap. Rather, it has widened the gap between rich and poor. In 1900, average income per head in the richest country was about 15 times that in the poorest, but by 1990 it had pulled away to a level more than 50 times higher.[15] In 1960 the 20 percent of the world's people who lived in the richest countries had 30 times the income of the poorest 20 percent — in 1997, 74 times as much.[16] This is not to deny that there is some evidence of economic growth; but it is very slight.[17]

On the contrary, Dollar and Kraay would argue that "the real losers from globalization are those developing countries that have not been able to seize the opportunities to participate in this process."[18] While there is much talk of the intensification of political and economic relations among nation states and other major actors, the power dynamics and international division of labor remain essentially the same. The global political arena is still characterized by the interplay of power politics, between the advanced powerful nations of the core (the Triad) and the poor, weak nations of the periphery. The global disparity in income, resource endowment and wealth remains a burning concern, and appropriately so. How then can globalization alleviate the woes of the millions who live in poverty? Can globalization deliver on its promise of leveling the playing field and increasing the wealth of all?

Promises of global prosperity ring hollow to the majority of the world's people. The entire economic fabric, bridging the old economy and the new, is no less than a global paradigmatic shift towards a knowledge economy. The frightening reality is that the new technologies have been a new source of exclusion instead of inclusion. The implementation of the TRIPs (Trade-Related Intellectual Property Rights) regime only serves to pour salt onto an already bleeding wound. Arguably, the new law serves as the handmaiden of imperialism in an age of globalization. The same argument can be advanced for the stringent structural adjustment programs prescribed by the International Monetary Fund and the World Bank. It is critical that some positive measures are taken to ensure that some of the fruits accrue to the less fortunate, promoting growth and efficiency.

The Digital Gap

The gap between the technology-savvy and the technologically bereft is staggering and belies any notion of an emerging new paradigm of justice and equality. Hence the increasing concerns about an emerging and widening digital divide. The digital divide connotes a disparity between the developed countries of the North and the developing countries of the

South in their respective capacities to develop, access, and use information technology for productive purposes. In much of the developing world
Internet usage is below 1 percent.[19] Sub-Saharan Africa and East Asia have
the lowest percentage of Internet users: only 0.4 percent of their populations, compared with 54.3 percent in the USA.[20] The digital divide mirrors the existing social and economic inequalities, which exist both within
and between countries, thus debunking the most benign hopes that "ICTs,
if applied properly, cease to be luxury items for the rich, and become
enabling technologies, to empower the poor. Instead of creating a digital
divide, the very same technology *can* create a digital 'bridge.'"[21] What is
even more concerning is Mansell and Wehn's pessimistic observation that
in the case of the Caribbean, for example, technological convergence will
take 15–20 years.[22]

    If Susan Strange is correct in her assertion that the life span of tech-
nology is shrinking, then given the existing technology gap, what we are
witnessing and can anticipate is that rather than narrowing, the gap is
likely to widen over the coming years. In this regard Mansell and Wehn
make the frightening assertion that for countries of sub-Saharan Africa,
convergence is out of sight; 50–100 years away.[23]

    Wallerstein himself, however, recognized that there were certain in-
built limitations in the pursuit of global CIT growth, where what we have
seen emerging is a new form of dependence. This assertion is substanti-
ated by the heavy reliance of the South on the North for technological
products, both hardware and software.

Economic Implications of the Digital Divide

    The rapid growth in technological advancement over the last few
decades has been accompanied by *"widening North-South gaps in all key
economic indicators: income wealth, production, consumption, investment,
savings and trade. Unfortunately, nowhere are the gaps wider than in science, technology and knowledge. The North-South gap in scientific and technological capacity is widening at a faster rate, and 'catch up' has become an
even more distant prospect than before"* (Thomas 2000, 55).

    The UNDP report in 2001 captured the reality of the digital divide in
its warning that "policy not charity, will determine whether new technologies become a tool for human development everywhere" (UNDP 2001, 6).
It goes further still in asserting that "the digital divide need not be permanent if technological adaptations and institutional innovations expand
access" (UNDP 2001, 35). The challenge we face is to learn how developing

countries can bridge the divide. But before we can embark upon this Herculean mission, we must understand why the divide exists at all.

A new development paradigm is emerging, one that reeks of techno-determinism. However, the idea that technology determines the level of economic growth and development is not a new one. Moreover, the technology gap itself is a historical problem: "the digital divide mirrors the technology gap separating the rich countries from the poor ones—a gap that opened up during the industrial revolution and has yet to be fully bridged."[24] What is new, presumably, is the overarching role of technology not only in the productive enclaves, but in every aspect of modern life. The extent to which ICTs have become commonplace is unprecedented.[25]

The critical issue here is not so much that we in the periphery should gain access to the tools of ICT, but rather how ICTs can be used to enhance productivity and increase economic gain. Bridging the divide, therefore, is not confined to only the technical hardware or software. The real gain is measured by the value of economic flows into that sector and the foreign exchange earnings generated by the use of ICTs. Until there is a significant generation of real value, technological convergence, and by extension bridging the divide, remain an illusion.

A Way Forward

Bridging the digital divide constitutes the greatest challenge of the ICT revolution. Historically, technology has not had a positive or necessarily significant impact on increasing the quality of life in the developing world. The problems are captured in the debates surrounding the transfer of technology to the South and the miserable failure of proposed strategies to achieve that goal. Not least among these is the fact that technology transferred to the South has either been obsolete by the time it gets there or inappropriate for the economic structures of these economies.

The emerging technologies can only play a decisive role in resolving the socioeconomic problems of the periphery by selectively picking the elements that are historically, socially, economically and politically conducive to growth. A failure to do this means that even our most Herculean efforts at development of the classical neoliberal version will yield little success. It requires a dynamic engagement with the particularistic issues of development in the region, similar to what Addo referred to as a *nouvelle engagement*. This is the new imperative.

The current conjuncture necessitates a break with the classical developmentalism that has yet to trigger economic growth and development in the developing world. Pragmatic growth strategies that break with linearity, and engender a more creative and proactive role for peoples of the South, selectively arriving at a cocktail approach to development, should be the preferred option.

There is a burgeoning body of literature that suggests that the developed world did not get to where it is now by following the neoliberal prescription that it now advocates.[26] However, the West has imposed a neoliberal order on the world evangelized by the Bretton Wood Institutions à la the Washington Consensus. We in the developing world should be instructed by these postulations. Though we are marginal players and have suffered a daunting series of setbacks, we are still in a position to take advantage of the emerging opportunities. However, it will be necessary to reiterate the call for good governance and the development of national e-development strategies.

The current techno-economic paradigm demands that ICT strategies for development assume a primacy of place on the development agenda along with the traditional concerns of poverty reduction, health, housing and other development imperatives. Having access to the tools of ICTs and using these tools productively are two completely different things. Moreover, the goal is to harness these tools to engage in higher value-added production. Peripheral countries ought to be mindful of the potential dangers. In this vein the example from Jamaica in instructive, where it was observed that "High volatility characterizes the development of [the IT] sector ... the industry has grown in leaps and bounds but has failed to produce sustained growth."[27]

Harnessing ICTs for development is a complex activity. Fundamental to the success of an e-development strategy is the incorporation of stakeholder and sectoral interests. Government, the private sector and civil society must engineer a partnership that is premised on a win-win strategy. Moreover, the realities of an increasingly globalized economy dictate that macro-organizational policies of the various actors have to become increasingly correlated with those of other actors in the global economy. Additionally, whereas classical economists often speak of diminishing returns, this techno-economic conjuncture may very well enable investors to realize the law of increasing returns.[28]

I will join in the chorus calling for better management of the interface between the national and the global economy in order for the tangible benefits of globalization to accrue to developing countries, and to prevent further marginalization and domination of developing countries in the globalization process.

Conclusion

Though the precise economic and developmental impacts of employing ICTs in the short term are still unclear, there is enough evidence to suggest that these impacts are becoming ubiquitous and do have some positive impact, however difficult it may be to compute. However, the saying "catch up or lose out" has a frightening resonance with the economic reality of the day.

Further inquiry into the extent to which promising signs may lead to a reversal of fortune for peripheral states now entering the information economy is necessary, if not urgent. These include the falling prices of communications hardware and services. Some writers have argued that between 1995 and 2000 the price of PCs has dropped by an average of 22 percent per year.[29] Liberalization of telecommunications, which promises cheaper connectivity and reduced service costs to the customer and an increasing e-wareness on the part of governments and other key stakeholders in the region are encouraging.

Already governments of the developing world are exhibiting their political will to build the physical infrastructure and provide the regulatory framework required for admission into the global information society. Peripheral countries will of necessity have to embrace IT and sophisticated information systems in their existing economic activities to ensure survival.[30] But the gains are directly related to the e-readiness of the country, and that depends partly on its human resource capacity. This will also have implications for the kind of foreign direct investment the country can attract.

The 1999 UNDP report points to the examples of Egypt and India as success stories in the implementation of appropriate ICT strategies.[31] With reference to the small islands of the Caribbean, those factors that were traditionally perceived of as constraints can very well serve as advantages. According to Henry Alamango, "Their geographical containment and single level government makes for a flexible, responsive administration," making the implementation of seamless infrastructures an achievable strategic advantage compared with larger, more developed countries.[32]

Notions of a sustained structural crisis should, therefore, not discourage us. We must be guarded in our expectations, yet creative in our response.

Endnotes

1. V.I. Lenin, *Imperialism, the Highest Stage of Capitalism: A Popular Outline*, (International Publishers, 1939).
2. Amin, *Monthly Review*, 13
3. Galtung, "A Structural Theory of Imperialism," 81.
4. Galtung, "A Structural Theory of Imperialism,"184.
5. Galtung, 1971.
6. Ibid.
7. Ibid.
8. UNDP, *Human Development Report 2001*.
9. http://www.panos.org.uk/home/summary%20Study1.doc.
10. McChesney, "Global Media, Neoliberalism and Imperialism" *Monthly Review*, March 2001. Since the AOL/Time Warner merger these conglomerates have further consolidated their stranglehold.
11. Didsbury, "The Economic Impact of the Emerging Global Information Economy," 158.
12. Oyinle, "Africa and the Global Information Society"; He argues that Africa risks further marginalization if the digital divide goes unchecked.
13. Aninat (Deputy Managing Director of the IMF), "Surmounting the Challenges of Globalization," 4.
14. Dollar and Kraay, Trade Growth and Poverty" *Finance and Development*, 16.
15. Coyle, *Paradoxes of Prosperity*.
16. See UNDP, *Human Development Report 1999*, 36.
17. Paul Streeten (*Finance and Development*, June 2001) argues that globalization is neither unprecedented nor irreversible. Moreover only very few developing countries have benefited from the gains of globalization. It is the more advanced countries that seem well positioned to gain from the process of globalization. Countries like Japan, Korea, Malaysia and Singapore arguably realized improvement in living standards, which can be attributed to free trade and access ready access to capital markets, all features of a globalised economy. See authors such as A. Goto & B. Barker for similar arguments.
18. Dollar and Kraay, *Finance and Development*. 19.
19. http://www.ecpd-eu.org/e_zine_six.pdf. Similarly, of 280 million Arabs, only 1percent use the Internet.
20. UNDP, Human Development Report 2001.
21. Nielsen, *Empowering the poor: the future for information and communications technologies in development*, 34.
22. Mansell and Wehn, *Knowledge Societies*, 24.
23. Ibid.
24. Ishaq, "*On the Global Digital Divide,*" 45.
25. It has been argued that the Internet is the fastest growing information medium when compared with early technologies such as the radio and the television. For example see Nazli Choucri, "Introduction: CyberPolitics in International Relations," *International Political Science Review* 21, no. 3 (2000): 243–263.
26. See Chang, *Kicking Away the Ladder*.
27. United Nations Commission on Science, "The Science and Technology Innovation Policy Review: Jamaica" (Geneva: United Nations, 1999), 61.
28. Compaine and Gomery, *Who Owns the Media?*
29. See Paula De Masi et al., "Who Has a New Economy" *Finance and Development*, June 2001, 38.
30. Hall and Benn, *Contending with Destiny*, 136.
31. UNDP, *Human Development Report 1999*.
32. Alamango, "Information and Communication Technologies," 72.

References

Alamango, Henry. 1999. "Information and Communication Technologies: An Initiative for Islands and Small States." The Commonwealth Ministers Reference Book 1999/2000. London: Kensington Publications Ltd. and Commonwealth Secretariat.

Amin, Samir. 2001. *Monthly Review*, "Imperialism and Globalization." June 1.

Aninat, Eduardo. 2002. "Surmounting the Challenges of Globalization." *Finance and Development*, March, 4.

Chang , Ar-Hoon. 2002. *Kicking Away the Ladder: Development Strategy in Historical Perspective.* London: Wimbledon Publishing.

Coyle, Diane. 2001. *Paradoxes of Prosperity: Why the New Capitalism Benefits All.* New York: Texere Publishing.

Compaine, Benjamin M., and Douglas Gomery. 2000. *Who Owns the Media? Competition and Concentration in the Mass Media Industry.* 3rd ed. Mahwah, NJ: Lawrence Erlbaum Associates.

Didsbury, Howard F. (ed.). 1985. "The Economic Impact of the Emerging Global Information Economy on Lesser Developed Nations." *The Global Economy: Today, Tomorrow and the Transition.* Bethesda, Md.: World Future Society.

Dollar, David, and Aart Kraay. 2001. "Trade Growth and Poverty." *Finance and Development*, September.

Dutta, S., B. Lanvin and F. Pau (eds.). 2003. *The Global Information Technology Report 2002–2003.* New York: Oxford University Press for the World Economic Forum.

Edoho, Felix Moses (ed.). 1997. *Globalization and the New World Order: Promises, Problems, and Prospects for Africa in the Twenty-First Century.* Westport, CT: Praeger Publishers.

Galtung, J. "A Structural Theory of Imperialism." *Journal of Peace Research* 8, (1971).

Goto, A., and B. Barker. 1999. "Small Open Economies in an Increasingly Connected World." *International Social Science Journal* 60 (June): 194–202.

Hall, Kenneth, and Dennis Benn. 2000. *Contending with Destiny: The Caribbean in the 21st Century.* Kingston, Jamaica: Ian Randle Publishers.

Ishaq, Ashfaq. 2001. "On the Global Digital Divide." *Finance and Development*, September.

Kirkman, G., P. Cornelius, J. Saens. *The Global Information Technology Report 2001–2002: Readiness for the Networked World.* New York: Oxford University Press for the World Economic Forum.

Korbin, Stephen. 1998. "Back to the Future: Neomedievalism and the Postmodern Digital World Economy." *Journal of International Affairs* 52, no. 2 (spring).

Mansell, R. and U. When (eds.). 1998. *Knowledge Societies: Information Technology for Sustainable Development.* Oxford, UK: Oxford University Press.

McChesney, Robert W. 2001. *Monthly Review*, February.

Nielsen, P. 2002. *Empowering the poor: the future for information and communication technologies in development.* The ACP-EU Courier. 192: 34–36.

Oyinle, Ajibola Maxwell. 1999. "Africa and the Global Information Society." In *Commonwealth Ministers Reference Book 1999/2000.* London: Kensington Publications Ltd. and Commonwealth Secretariat.

Streeten, Paul. 2001. "Integration, Interdependence and Globalization." *Finance and Development*, June.

Thomas, C. 2000. *Cooperation South*, Nal, pp. 49–59.
UNDP. 1999. *Human Development Report 1999*. New York: Oxford University Press for UNDP.
UNDP. 2000. *Human Development Report 2000*. New York: Oxford University Press for UNDP.
UNDP. 2001. *Human Development Report 2001*. New York: Oxford University Press for UNDP.

Internet Sources

http://www.ecpd-eu.org/e_zine_six.pdf. Accessed December 2002.
http://www.panos.org.uk/home/summary%20Study1.doc. Accessed 10 December 2002.

Governance in a Small State

Ann Marie Bissessar

During the 1980s, there was a concerted attempt to replace systems of government with new and improved systems of *governance*. Essentially, governance involved the reform of the structures, tools and processes of government administration. Not unexpectedly, a number of challenges emerged during this period; one of the most important being that this type of reform had to fit into or be supported by the political systems and cultures of the various countries. Reform of the systems of government has been explored in various countries and a number of lessons have been drawn. For instance, it was found that in the United States the federal government had few state-owned enterprises to privatize so it relied on public-private partnerships and contracting. The Nordic countries, however, presented a hybrid approach and relied modestly on market mechanisms, while the Westminster reformers relied on privatization (Kettl 2000). In the case of small states, however, the literature on the challenges involved in governance is sparse. This article attempts to explore some of the challenges that emerged or are likely to emerge in the movement from government to governance in a small country: Trinidad and Tobago, West Indies. Whereas the World Bank has developed a number of benchmarks for evaluating governance such as public expenditure management, tax policy and administration, administrative and civil service reform, legal and judicial reform, and anticorruption measures, this discussion is confined to the policies of the Trinidad and Tobago government with respect to measures such as divestment, privatization and contracting out.

Governance in a Small State

The term *governance* is now part of a global vocabulary. It involves a fundamental reshaping of service delivery by governments. In many countries, governments have attempted to root out the traditional bureaucracies and the pathologies that some reformers suggested flowed from them, and have sought to replace them with more competition-driven market strategies including privatization of state-owned enterprises and outsourcing tactics. While organizations such as the World Bank and the Organization for Economic Cooperation and Development have compiled comparative data for the developed countries and the OECD countries, the challenges of introducing new systems of governance in small states have been inadequately addressed. This article therefore attempts to fill a gap in the existing literature. Specifically, it examines and evaluates the attempts by the government in Trinidad and Tobago to divest, privatize, and contract out some of its key services.

Since the 1980s, World Bank ideology has increasingly shifted from what was perceived as government to what today is its defining mantra, namely governance. For the World Bank, the shift in emphasis from government to governance represents a clear paradigm movement and a disenchantment with the statist policies of politicians and bureaucrats of the '60s and '70s; this can also be seen in some of the structural adjustment proposals they followed. That paradigm shift found expression in the now familiar policy of rolling back the state, reducing opportunities for rent-seeking, and embarking on market-friendly policies. The shift from import-substitution technologies to market-influenced policies was no doubt facilitated by the international collapse of communism. Yet, the disappointment with and resentment generated by structural adjustment programs almost everywhere had eroded confidence in them, leading to calls for "structural adjustment with a human face." By 1989, however, the Bank's concern for the quality of governance in the resolution of social and economic problems had been clearly expressed. By 1992, but more so in 1997, the Bank made clear its thinking on the importance of governance and the state (World Bank 1992).

The conversion of the World Bank directorate to the new philosophy of governance also committed it to policies such as civil service reform, legal reform, accountability, budget discipline, anticorruption initiatives and deregulation. These in turn implied institutional reform to enhance the capacity of institutions to bring about change (North 1996). The term *government* had generally meant an emphasis on a large agency, controlling society largely by command and economic forces clearly demarcated from civil society. In such a conception, government was a tool for the management of the society and the economy. Its techniques included laws, elections, political parties, legislatures and an independent judiciary.

Governance, by contrast, entails an entirely new set of premises. It rejects the notion of an opposition and clear demarcation between society and state. Instead, it views state and civil society as involved in a partnership. Indeed, to understand the state one needs to recognize that it rests on civil society and can therefore rise or fall on the nature of the society on which it stands. It must also be recognized that, as globalization theorists have pointed out, borders are becoming increasingly porous. International organizations, both state and private, now impinge on the powers of domestic policymakers. The narcotics state, money laundering, and new policing measures all dictate a new approach to the management and government of societies. This also entails new and more cost-effective ways of delivering public services whether through partnerships, incentives or disincentives.

From the standpoint of public administration, the term *governance* thus suggests a shift from line bureaucracies to fragmented service delivery. While the traditional use of *governance* and its dictionary entry define it as a synonym for government, a number of writers contend that it signifies a change in the meaning of government, referring to a new process of governing, or a changed condition of ordered rule, or a new method by which a society is governed (Rhodes 1996; Stoker 1998). Writers also argue that while *government* implied a system of ordered rule, governance is ultimately concerned with creating conditions for ordered rule and collective action. In essence, therefore, while the outputs of governance are not different from those of government, both apply different processes to achieve the same objectives.

Reviews of the literature generally conclude that the term *governance* is used in different ways and has a variety of meanings. There is, however, some consensus that it refers to the development of governing styles in which the boundaries between the public and private sectors have become blurred (Stoker 1998). Writers also point out that the concept of governance points to the creation of a structure or an order that cannot be externally imposed but "is the result of the interaction of a multiplicity of governing and each other influencing actors" (Kooiman and Van Vliet 1993, 64). In some cases, the term *governance* undoubtedly means "strong government"; as used by the World Bank, however, it refers to efficient and accountable government.

There is no doubt that, like the concept of New Public Management (NPM), the changing terminology for governance emerged in the 1980s. As Hood (1991) had pointed out in the case of NPM, several interrelated trends seemed to have promoted the shift from government to governance. Minogue (2000) and others have suggested that governance was rooted in the sudden collapse of socialism in the former Soviet Union and some

Eastern European countries. Yet, what Hood (1991) had termed mega-trends were also critical factors. For example, the first trend he identified emerged out of the need to slow down or reverse the growth of government, particularly in areas such as staffing. The second trend was the shift towards privatization and semi-privatization, while the development of automation was cited as the third trend. According to Hood, the development of a more international agenda increasingly focused on issues of public management, policy design, decision styles and intergovernmental cooperation represented the fourth trend.

In a sense, then, the term *governance* was the broad umbrella under which NPM took root. Indeed, the tenets of NPM and governance were remarkably similar. NPM was based on a reduced role for the state and endorsed the move towards contracting out and privatization. NPM reformers were also advocates of accountability, private sector style management, and the introduction of performance measures and standards. Both governance and NPM were thus based on neoliberal doctrines that stressed the blurring of the boundaries between the public and private domains and favored more market-oriented approaches to public sector management.

While these factors were all important, as Ferguson (2002) in his examination of public service reform in the Caribbean pointed out, the fundamental catalyst leading to the call for good governance was the serious and protracted economic crisis that began in Guyana and Jamaica in the 1970s and Trinidad in the 1980s. With rapidly declining revenues, these countries were forced to approach international financial institutions and, more precisely, the Bretton Woods (International Monetary Fund/World Bank) organizations. The IMF, of course, had certain stipulations governing the loans that were allocated to the various governments. The conditions governing the loans were packaged in what was intended to be a coherent policy framework including structural adjustment. According to Ferguson (2002) the major policy measure was the conscious downgrading or minimizing of the role of the state in the national economy.

The reduction in the role of the state was not only part and parcel of the NPM movement but it also was implicitly tied in to the notion of good governance. It should be recalled that during the era of state-led development in the Caribbean, the public sector was criticized for being too large. With the advent of structural adjustment measures, the strategy proposed by governments was to effect significant reductions in the public sector utilizing various mechanisms. These mechanisms varied from forced layoffs and retrenchment to voluntary separation. In the case of Trinidad and Tobago, it also involved a ten percent reduction in salaries along with the suspension of other allowances. In addition to the reduction of the wage bill, there was a concerted move by governments in both the developed and developing countries to privatize state-owned enterprises.

Yet, as Nettleford (2002) pointed out, privatization, deregulation and liberalization were mere means to an end rather than the ends in themselves. He observed:

> To have them make sense against the background of the region's history, politics, culture and current perceptions of ends of government, they must serve the ends of empowerment of the mass of the population along with all others, whether by way of promoting worker share ownership, broadening the economic base of ownership in the society, instituting land reform, or releasing the creative potential of a far larger number of private citizens to have them participate on a "level playing field" once dominated by the state. (Nettleford 2002, 15)

Nettleford is quite right in his assessment. No doubt while factors such as economy and transparency were important, the basic tenet of good governance involved the blurring of the spheres between the civil society, the public sector and the private sector. Indeed, in principle, good governance is what can rightly be described as stakeholder government. The latter half of this paper will accordingly evaluate the extent to which the familiar principles of governance have been introduced in Trinidad and Tobago. It will examine and evaluate the attempt by government to privatize or contract services. Some historical review will be necessary given the critical importance of historical processes in the move toward a system of governance.

Government in Trinidad And Tobago: 1956–1986

Trinidad and Tobago is a small island republic with a population of 1.3 million persons. The size of the population, the size of the territory and the GDP per capita all suggests that this country can be categorized as a small state. It should be recalled that the following characteristics have important implications for development and are shared by many small states:

- Remoteness and insularity
- Susceptibility to natural disasters
- Limited institutional capacity
- Limited diversification
- Openness and the reliance on external trade and foreign investment
- Access to external capital
- Poverty

It should be noted, however, that while these are essential characteristics of small states, there is great diversity among small states themselves. Small states may differ as a result of their historical experience or the natural resources that are available in these countries. In other words, within small states many policy options and approaches will need to be tailored to regional and country circumstances (Bernal 1998; Commonwealth Secretariat 2000).

Like a number of countries in the Anglophone Caribbean, Trinidad and Tobago was formerly a British dependency, part of the wider British Empire. Consequently, these islands had been subjected to a Crown Colony system of administration. The method of government introduced during the 1920s to 1950s was based on a simple administrative arrangement that placed reliance on rules, regulations and procedures. Although the British public services were geographically independent at this time, the rules and regulations governing this establishment were based on the guidelines of the wider colonial service. Jeffries (1938), for example, observed that the services of the colonies were not independent but were an aggregate group of dependencies with varying constitutional status and wide variations in culture, geography and racial groups linked together by a common dependence on the British Crown. As a result, little or no attempt was made to relate systems of administration and later government to the sociocultural environment of individual societies (Kanungo and Jaeger 1992).

By 1950, following an outbreak of disturbances in the colonies in 1938/39 and subsequent recommendations of the West India Commission, a quasi-ministerial system of government, which consisted of elected members of the Executive Council, was introduced. The Colonial Secretariat in the islands was reorganized so that it included divisions that roughly corresponded to areas assigned to the new ministers. By the late 1950s and the early 1960s many countries were granted independent status. It should be noted, however, that even though independence was granted, these former colonies still adhered largely to the rules, regulations, and behaviors that were essentially British in orientation. Indeed, the colonial administrators left a lasting legacy, which included a Westminster style model of government along with a major personnel agency, the Public Service Commission.

With independence, however, the goals and objectives of the country underwent profound changes. While law and order and security were still important, the more pressing need was to foster national development by way of economic growth. It was also important to set up links with developed countries as well as Caribbean neighbors. Independence

therefore brought dramatic changes to the political, social and administrative spheres. In order to improve these utilities and develop an infrastructure that had been largely neglected under colonial rule, many
countries embarked on an expansion in the number of ministries and
agencies. In Trinidad and Tobago, for example, the number of ministries
increased from ten in 1958 to 18 by 1973. Statutory authorities were also
established and assigned responsibility for the provision of water, elec-
tricity and public transport. The establishment of these ministries subsequently called for an increase in the size of the workforce. For example,
the number of positions in the public services of Trinidad and Tobago
increased from 12,556 in 1962 to 21,000 in 1973. The number of persons
employed at this period, however, suggest that apart from acquiring the
necessary labor force, giving employment in public service positions was
in fact a means of rewarding party stalwarts for their support and a method
of wooing support for the ruling party.

It was evident, during the period 1956–1969, that the state in Trinidad
and Tobago was in fact practicing a method of government very similar
to the system that they had inherited from the British. The state had in
fact been transformed into a paternal welfare state, which provided a variety of services for the population. In addition, the state was the only actor,
since the role of the private sector was limited. Like its British predecessors, however, service delivery by the now independent government was
governed largely by rules, regulations and procedures. This was understandable since numerous constraints would have faced the newly independent nations, such as the lack of properly trained staff with the capacity
to formulate policies, the lack of resources and the lack of vision on the
part of the political directorate.

In terms of economic growth, while Trinidad had as early as 1857 discovered oil deposits in La Brea, the state had taken a hands-off approach
to both drilling and refining. Again, this reaction could have been due to
the absence of financial or human resources. It was understandable, therefore, when the policy makers embraced the model that was proposed by
the St. Lucian economist, Arthur Lewis. The model of Industrialization
by Invitation proposed by Lewis suggested that introducing an inward-
looking program of industrial growth would not be viable in a small state
mainly because of the size of the domestic market. He went on to argue
that for islands with small populations, "Neither their own growing
demands nor the replacement of imports can provide a large enough market. The domestic market for manufacturers is too small to support more
than a fraction of what is needed" (Lewis 1950, 14).

In 1957, then, the government of Trinidad and Tobago, on the prompting of Lewis, established an Industrial Development Corporation (IDC). The task of the IDC was to assist the government in setting up its production platform and to assist investors (including foreign investors) with their investment problems. The government also introduced a number of incentives by way of encouraging exporting firms. The state also embarked on numerous development projects including forays into the health sector, the education sector, and the agricultural sector.

By 1963, however, Lewis' model would come under attack and by 1970, propelled by a number of factors, the state embarked on the introduction of a new economic model which involved taking over the "commanding heights of the economy." By 1974, the government had fully embraced the notion of public ownership under the guise of localizing the economy, accelerating the development process, rationalizing the provision of public services and aiding the development of nontraditional production sectors. Adam and others (1992) observed that the changes in the economic policies of the state somewhat fortuitously coincided with the rapid expansion of government revenues consequent on the 1974 increase in the price of oil and the discovery of new natural gas reserves. By the late 1970s and the early 1980s through a policy of both nationalization and government-backed creation of new industries the state was able to expand its state-owned sector, so much so that by 1973, the total expenditure on the acquisition of assets and public participation amounted to TT$24.4 million; the principal payments included were:

(a) 50 percent shareholding in the telephone company formerly held
     by a foreign company $14.8 M
(b) 52 percent government participation in the flour mills $ 2.1 M
(c) 21 percent in the National Fisheries Company $ 0.6 M
(d) Payment of interest and annual installment on the acquisition
     of 51 percent of the shares in Caroni Ltd. $ 1.5 M
(e) 10 percent participation in Maritime Life Caribbean Ltd. $ 0.6 M
(f) Part payment in respect of the acquisition of the petrol
     filling stations formerly owned by British Petroleum $ 0.5 M
(g) Part payment in respect of the acquisition of 50 percent of
     petrol filling stations formerly owned by Esso Oil Co. $1.3 M

Source: The Budget Speech of Trinidad and Tobago, 5 January 1973, 563.

These assets were all vested in state companies, which were expected to operate under commercial criteria and were regulated by the White Paper on Public Participation. It is not clear why the state did not at this point invite private sector companies to participate in the economy. Some have suggested that the justification for entry by the state into the economic arena was that they had participated in certain companies during the prior two years and thus had gained considerable experience. Yet, it was an experiment that would be costly. By the end of 1972, the gross public debt of the country was estimated at $536.1 million, locally held debt amounted to $344.0 million, and foreign-held debt amounted to $202.1 million. At the end of 1971 the net public debt stood at $466.1 million. The cost of servicing the debt in 1972 amounted to $506 million; local debt service cost $30.7 million and external debt service amounted to $19.9 million (*Budget Speech of Trinidad and Tobago*1973, 567).

By 1974, a number of developments and changes had taken place in the domestic and international market including an increase in the price of petroleum, increasing prices of essential imports, an increase in the wage bill and a drought that affected agricultural production. To combat these challenges, the state proposed a number of policies including the introduction of licensing procedures. In other words, the state turned to regulations and regulatory policies in order to increase economic growth. Substantial assistance was also provided through subsidies to farmers; construction activity and jobs in construction were given a boost through incentives proposed by the establishment of Property Development Companies. Yet the government continued to defend its position by suggesting that it was doing what was best for the country. In his Budget Speech of 1974, the minister of finance explained:

> Mr. Speaker, the Government's policy of securing meaningful participation in apex industries and in the resource-based industries in particular has been fully endorsed by the population. The policies which we have announced and which we have assiduously followed, are now being adopted in most of the developing world, particularly in those countries with resource-based economies. Some citizens have urged the Government to extend the limits of current policy which was fully described in the White paper published in 1972. However, in taking decisions in these and other matters, Government will always have regard to the total national interests in both the short and long term and select the instruments which are appropriate to the country's needs and circumstances. Above all, we seek as far as possible to secure and safeguard the national goals through consultation and dialogue. (Budget Speech 1974, 621)

In other words, rather than retreating, the state had not only become involved in taking over the commanding heights of the economy but it also perceived itself to be protecting the interests of the citizen as well. It was clear, though, that at this time the state did not view the private sector as a possible partner. It was not surprising, then, that in 1985 the state was a majority shareholder in 48 firms, in 37 of which it owned 100 percent equity. By 1986, the total value of the government's shareholding had reached over TT$4 billion (excluding the utilities) and some of the companies were significantly larger than the largest in the private sector. The state owned sector also accounted for a substantial proportion of GDP. In 1985, for example, the total value of the state owned enterprises and the public utilities was TT$2.9billion or some 16 percent of the GDP. (Adam et al. 1992, 182). This sectoral distribution of the majority-owned state owned enterprises indicated that the government had achieved its aim and had indeed taken over the commanding heights of the economy.

It was evident that during the period 1956–1986, the state was largely a welfare state and there was little or no participation by the private sector in the economy. Also apparent was that in the drive towards a state-driven economy, what had been put in place to ensure some measure of accountability were a number of regulatory institutions or regulations. For instance, a Public Utilities Commission (1986) along with a Hospital Authority (1981) were established. Yet, what continued to plague government were excessive cost over-runs by the state owned enterprises and even the public services; this suggests that the regulatory bodies themselves were not effective in curbing inefficiencies in the system.

Some suggest that "taking over the commanding heights" of the economy was an ideological position by Williams. There was no doubt that during his research on capitalism and slavery, Williams had come to the conclusion that economic development could only be led by the state and that indeed the state had played a critical role during the Industrial Revolution in Britain. As Ramsaran (1999) and others have observed, though, it was not the ideological position alone that was responsible for the decline of the state. A number of factors were equally important including gross mismanagement of the state enterprises, patronage and corruption, lack of accounting mechanisms and tolerance by the government. Whatever the reasons, it was clear by 1986 that the government policy had to undergo significant changes.

The Movement to Governance 1987–2002

It was more than obvious that during the period 1970 to 1989 the state had adopted strategies in which it assumed that it had unlimited capacity to intervene in the economic arena. However, the failure by the state to carry out its assigned development role was all too apparent, and it was clear that the experiment of taking over the commanding heights of the economy had failed. The state adopted a new approach generally referred to as Resource Based Industrialization (RBI). The focus of this strategy was to invite investors to participate in the economic activities of the country.

It should be noted that RBI was one mechanism that emerged out of neoliberal ideology, which suggested that the introduction of market forces would lead to cheaper and more efficient delivery of services. It was felt that society would be better off if the market or analogous competitive institutions were allowed to determine policy decisions. Yet, as Guy Peters (2001) pointed out in another context, the retreat of the state was due to other contributory factors as well. He argues that while market forces were important, factors such as demographic change, income inequalities and the decline of stable organizations were also important considerations. There was also the perception that private-sector methods were almost inherently superior for managing activities and that the traditional bureaucracies did not provide sufficient incentive for individuals working within them to perform their job efficiently.

By the end of 1980s therefore, many countries including Trinidad and Tobago, pushed no doubt by the international lending agencies, embarked on a comprehensive reform exercise. The first decision taken by all these countries was to reduce the size and complexity of governmental organizations. As Peters (2001) recalls, "the market approach assumes that the principal problem with the traditional structure of the public sector is its reliance on large, monopolistic departments that respond ineffectively to signals from the environment" (Peters 2001, 32).

In order to do this, a number of prescriptions were employed. A fundamental mechanism used to break down large government monopolies was privatization or the use of private or quasi-private organizations to deliver public services. In the case of Trinidad and Tobago, by 1993/4, the state had divested a number of state-owned companies. Table 1 provides a list of some of the larger companies.

Apart from privatization or divestment of these enterprises, the government of Trinidad and Tobago also embarked on a number of shareholder projects. For example, in 2002, it commenced several gas-based downstream investments such as the LNG Trains 2 and 3 which when completed is expected to have a production capacity of 9.6 million tons of gas per annum. The stakeholders in this project included BPTT, British Gas, Repsol and the National Gas Company. Discussions by the National Gas Company were also held with prospective investors including Noranda, Pechiney and Suray with respect to the establishment of an aluminum smelter plant. Another major initiative was the proposal by British Gas to develop a cross-border field jointly with Petroleos de Venezuela on the north-eastern coast of Trinidad (Republic of Trinidad and Tobago

Table 1.
Divestment of State Enterprises in the Energy Section

Company	Date Divested	Principal Investor	Value (US$M)
Fertrin/TTUC—100 percent	March 1993	Arcadian	132.1
Trinidad and Tobago Methanol — 31 percent	January 1994	Ferrostal/Helm	47.0
Trinidad and Tobago Methanol — 24 percent	January 1994	Ferrostal/Helm	18.0
Petrotrin Oxygen Nitrogen Plan—100 percent	August 1994	Caribbean Ispat	1.2
Petrotrin Urea Formaldehyde Plant—100 percent	August 1994	ARESTECH	9
Iron and Steel Co. of Trinidad and Tobago—100 percent	December 1994	Ispat	70.1

(Compiled from a number of financial documents and budget speeches.)

2001, 24). In addition to the petrochemical industry, the government was also involved in stakeholder ventures in the airline industry with the continuation of the British Airways Flight to Tobago and the introduction of a Caribbean Star between Barbados and Tobago and between Trinidad and Tobago.

The arguments for and against privatization are numerous. In the case of Trinidad and Tobago, the justification for privatization was that it led to a significant reduction in the current account deficit. However, while in the short term the revenue from the sales was employed constructively for funding general infrastructural developments, in the long run the government was severely criticized for selling valuable assets to foreigners and also retrenching workers in these enterprises and industries. For example, when the Tourism Development company was closed, 110 employees became unemployed; similarly, the closure of the Trinidad and Tobago Printing and Packaging Company resulted in the laying off of 250 workers.

In addition to divestment and stakeholder participation, another mechanism commonly employed by many governments including the government of Trinidad and Tobago was to employ private contractors in areas such as housing, construction, the paving of roads, janitorial services, maintenance and security. In other words, the state was retreating from a number of activities that it had formerly monopolized in the past. Yet, it was a retreat that was costly. Indeed, data taken from various fiscal reports indicate that the total expenditure for contract workers, and services such as janitorial and maintenance services in government ministries and departments for the year 2001 was phenomenal — amounting to TT$61,712,254 million. This expenditure, however, did not reflect the total costs incurred for projects such as road paving, road construction, or other short-term national activities (Republic of Trinidad and Tobago 2000/2001).

The introduction of contracts as part of the broader program of governance raises a number of fundamental issues. Kettle perhaps defines it appropriately. He explains: *"Public reliance on private markets is far more complex than it appears on the surface. In these relationships, government inevitably finds itself sharing power, which requires it fundamentally to rethink not only how it manages but how it governs"* (1993, viii).

The challenge facing most governments, however, was not only confined to the issue of sharing power, but also the difficulty of writing down complex services in specifications. Deakin and Walsh (1996) argue, for example, that it is easier to operate market-based contracting approaches for simple repetitive services than for complex professionally based activities. It has also been suggested that the formalities of the contract system do not easily capture custom and practice and informal modes of adaptation.

It was to be expected, also, that as the level of contractual labor increased, there would have been a corresponding reduction in civil service employment. However, there was little or no reduction in either the size or the expenditure of the public sector. Apart from expenditure that was incurred as a result of contracting out, it has been alleged — and perhaps this is one of the pathologies of small states— that many contracts awarded during the period 1986–2001 were awarded to family members or friends of the ruling political party. Unfortunately, these allegations seemed to have some basis. Commissions of Inquires into projects such as the construction of the airport in Trinidad have revealed that the award of contracts was not in keeping with regulations governing such contracts, and charges were consequently leveled against a number of private contractors. What perhaps was most damaging for the government, however, was a number of disclosures where managers and ministers were later charged for fraud; in one particular case, a former Prime Minister was charged with failing to disclose his accounts as required under law. The issue, however, was not merely the breach of the law but the amount that had been deposited in the account: ten million Trinidad and Tobago dollars.

During the period 1986–2001, the government of Trinidad and Tobago also attempted to decentralize some of its operations. In many countries, decentralization had been achieved through the splitting up of large departments into smaller agencies or through assigning functions to lower levels of government. The main objective of decentralization, however, was to create multiple, competitive organizations to supply goods and services. In the case of countries such as the United Kingdom, New Zealand and the Netherlands (Davies and Willman 1991; Boston 1991), large departments were divided into smaller segments.

In the case of Trinidad and Tobago, decentralization occurred primarily at two levels. The first level involved the decentralization of the health sector into regional authorities. The second level involved the decentralization of responsibilities from the central personnel agencies to the line agencies. Unlike her Caribbean neighbor, Jamaica, however, there was no proposal on the part of the Trinidad and Tobago government to introduce executive agencies, which, it should be recalled, had been introduced in Britain.

Yet, as writers observed, implementing a system of market-oriented organizations assumed a capacity to monitor effectively and to measure adequately the performance of the decentralized bodies that had been created. In the case of Trinidad, there was little monitoring and no monitoring agency had been set up. This lack of evaluation and monitoring had serious consequences. For example, after numerous costs overruns, it was found that at the end of first year of introducing the Regional Health Authorities there had been little or no improvement in the standards or delivery of health care. Similarly, so far as the central personnel agencies were concerned, little or no effective delegation had taken place. Indeed, Peters (2001) was quite prophetic when he noted, "the breaking up of the departmental structure, if anything, has tightened the grip of each organization in its policy area. Further, the entrepreneurial element and the loss of civil service rules means that growth in the budget of the agency is more directly linked to the perquisites of office than ever before" (Peters 2001, 35).

Peters was quite right. There was no doubt that in almost all governmental agencies in Trinidad and Tobago, expenditure had increased significantly. In 2002, for example, TT$179 million was allocated to the health sector to bring about improvements in public health facilities and health services delivery. Of this, TT$86.9 million was employed to advance the implementation of the Inter-American Development Bank–assisted Health Sector Reform Programme. (Public Sector Investment Programme 2003, 18). Problems, however, continued to plague the health sector, including strikes by doctors and nurses, lack of beds, the inability by the hospitals to provide meals and medication, outdated equipment, and more recently the closure of the emergency department. Because of these myriad and ongoing problems, members of the public have been forced to seek health care services from private agencies. In essence, then, while there has been decentralization as outlined by the Act governing the Regional Health Authority, to date there has been little or no improvement in the delivery of health care.

Some have suggested that the decentralization exercise had failed because there had been little or no monitoring on the part of the government. This diagnosis is partly true. Other factors were also responsible, including the laxity or perhaps even the deliberate disregard of the regulations and procedures by the chief executives and the managers. It should be recalled that NPM had advocated that "managers should be given the power" to manage. What was demonstrated during the period 1986–2002 in Trinidad and Tobago was that managers, recruited from outside the public sector, openly flouted the procedures and regulations governing public service activity. Perhaps, as some have suggested, private sector managers wanted to circumvent the delays that were part and parcel of large bureaucracies. This was understandable. What was not understandable in the case of Trinidad and Tobago was that managers compensated themselves handsomely by way of bonuses since they claimed they "surpassed performance standards."

White had argued that "*democratic virtues of participation, as well as the chance of developing innovative ideas about how to solve policy problems should be seen as justifying the extra expenditure of time and energy*" (1988, 70–71). However, in the case of Trinidad and Tobago, what White had termed the "virtues of participation" did not only involve time and energy, it also involved expenditure that was borne principally by the tax-paying public. The question, then, is whether participatory government is the solution to better governance. An even more pressing question is, what or who was allowed to participate?

It is true that a central theme of the government of Trinidad and Tobago during the period 1986–2001 was the emphasis on improved systems of governance. Accordingly, as part of the new paradigm a number of mechanisms was introduced, including the divestment and privatization of state-owned enterprises along with the contracting of janitorial and maintenance services and other activities. Yet, in the case of a small state such as Trinidad and Tobago, while some of the measures for promoting good governance had been introduced, it was found that that other attendant measures such as regulations and regulatory institutions to allow for the requisite checks and balances were not put in place. This was a serious shortcoming on the part of the government, since there were a number of ethical lapses in which employees and politicians sometimes disregarded organizational or legal rules for personal gain, preference and power. The problem, though, was not only one of ethical practices. What actually occurred was a reconstruction of the state, where power became concentrated in the hands of a few. In the absence of clearly defined regulations or statutes defining conduct, it was to be expected that good governance as broadly defined by the World Bank became no more than a slogan.

Conclusion

What this article has demonstrated is that in the move for better governance, pushed it is true by external factors, the government of Trinidad and Tobago embarked on a pattern of policy making that appeared to involve greater participation by way of privatization and contracting out. Yet, the objective of less involvement by the state was not realized. The traditional, large, monolithic bureaucracy remained intact and the government subsidized a number of major activities that were undertaken by the private sector and nongovernmental organizations.

The problem was not, however, simply one of funding. Rather, there were criticisms of excessive mismanagement and in a number of cases what emerged suggested that there was corruption in public office. It is true that the government sought to put in place legislation to prevent such occurrences, but as with many small states, implementation of legislation appears to be one of the major constraints facing policy makers. While, therefore, some of the major tenets of governance were introduced, other tenets of governance or principles that were equally important such as accountability, legitimacy and transparency were neglected.

While in the case of the United Kingdom, the United States and other developed countries contracting out has led to the increased accessibility of certain services and made the public more aware of the nature of the services they receive, this has not been the experience in Trinidad and Tobago. It should be recalled that in the case of the developed countries, the private sector and nongovernmental agencies are well established. Therefore, one would expect that with the introduction of market forces there would be a number of private competitors bidding to deliver a service. Because of this kind of competition, prices offered to the public would be lower.

In the case of small states such as Trinidad and Tobago, however, as the historical discussion which followed before would have indicated, the private sector was always weak; this had been largely responsible for the government during the period 1962–1986 becoming the prime mover in the economy. The development of the internal market in the 1980s in the case of small states like Trinidad and Tobago thus took place against a background of a very underdeveloped private sector, which was highly monopolistic. In addition, the private sector was largely involved in buying cheap and selling dear; involved mostly in retailing activities and lacking a history of creative entrepreneurship, they would have been unable to fill the vacuum left by the retreat of the state. With this kind of background, it was understandable, as Schmitter (1974), Micheletti (1990) and others have pointed out in another context, why contracts were awarded to selected groups largely for patronage purposes. While privatization, contracting out and decentralization may have improved the quality of governance in countries like the United States, the United Kingdom, Australia, New Zealand and elsewhere, in the case of Trinidad and Tobago, because of the absence of the necessary infrastructure and culture, measures such as these served to make the problems of governance even more difficult.

References

Adam, Christopher, William Cavendish and Percy S. Mistry. 1992. *Adjusting Privatization*. Jamaica: Ian Randle.

Bernal, Richard L. 1998. "The Integration of Small Economies in the Free Trade Area of the Americas." *CSIS Policy Papers on the Americas*, Volume IX.

Boston, J. 1991. "The Theoretical Underpinnings of State Restructuring in New Zealand." In J. Boston and others, eds. *Reshaping the State*. Auckland: Oxford University Press.

Commonwealth Secretariat/World Bank Joint Task Force. 2000. *Small States: Meeting Challenges in the Global Economy,* Report of the Commonwealth Secretariat/World Bank Joint Task Force on Small States, Washington, D.C. and London, April 2000.

Davies, A., and J. Willman. 1992. *What Next? Agencies, Departments and the Civil Service*. London: Institute for Public Policy Research.

Deakin, Nicholas, and Kieron Walsh. 1996. "The Enabling State: The Role of Markets and Contracts." *Public Administration* 74 (spring): 33–48.

Ferguson, Tyrone. 2002. "External Influences on Caribbean Public Administration." In *Policy Transfer, New Public Management and Globalization: Mexico and the Caribbean*. Edited by Ann Marie Bissessar. Bostonway, Maryland: University Press of America Inc.: 1–32.

Hood, Christopher. 1991. "A Public Management for All Seasons?" *Public Administration* 69: 3–19.

Jeffries, Charles. 1938. *The Colonial Empire and Its Civil Service*. Cambridge: Cambridge University Press.

Kanungo, Rabindra N., and Alfred M. Jaeger. 1992. "The Need for Indigenous Management in Developing Countries." In A. Jaeger and R.N. Kanungo, *Management in Developing Countries*. London: Routledge.

Kettl, Donald F. 2002. *The Global Public Management Revolution: A Report on the Transformation of Governance.* Washington D.C.: The Brookings Institution.
_____. 1993. *Sharing Power: Public Governance and Private Markets.* Washington: The Brookings Institution.
Kooiman, J., and M. Van Vliet. 1993. "Governance and Public Management." In K. Eliassen and J. Kooiman eds. *Managing Public Organizations.* 2nd edition. London: Sage Publications.
Lewis, Arthur. 1950. "Industrial Development of the British West Indies." *Caribbean Economic Review* 2: 1–61.
Michiletti, M. 1990. "Toward Interest Inarticulation: A Major Consequence of Corporatism for Interest Organizations. *Scandinavian Political Studies* 13: 255–76.
Minogue, Martin, Charles Polidano and David Hulme (eds.). 2000. *Beyond the New Public Management: Changing Ideas and Practices in Governance.* Cheltenham, UK: Edward Elgar Publishing Ltd.
Nettleford, Rex. 2002. "Governance in the Contemporary Caribbean: Towards a Political Culture of Partnership." In *Governance in the Caribbean.* Edited by Selwyn Ryan and Ann Marie Bissessar. St. Augustine, Trinidad: SALISES: 11–22.
North, Douglas C. 1996. *Institutions, Institutional Change and Economic Performance.* Cambridge University Press.
Peters, B. Guy. 2001. *The Future of Governing.* 2nd edition. Lawrence, Kansas: University of Kansas.
Ramsaran, Ramesh. 1999. "Aspects of Growth and Adjustment in Post-Independence Trinidad and Tobago." *Social and Economic Studies* 48 no.1 and 2: 215–286.
Republic of Trinidad and Tobago. 1999. *Annual Statistical Digest,* 1998/99 no. 4. Trinidad and Tobago: Central Statistical Office, Government Printery.
_____. Budget Speech. 5 January 1973. Trinidad and Tobago: Central Statistical Office, Government Printery.
_____. Budget Speech. 21 January 1974. Trinidad and Tobago: Central Statistical Office, Government Printery.
_____. 2001. House of Representatives. *Budget Statement 2002.* One People, One Nation: Leaving No One Behind. Presented by Senator the Honorable Gerald Yetming, Minister of Finance. September 14, 2001.
_____. 2002. *Estimates: Details of Estimates of Recurrent Expenditure for the Financial Year.* Text prepared by the Ministry of Finance. Printed by the Government Printer, Port of Spain, Republic of Trinidad and Tobago.
Rhodes, R. 2000. "The Governance Narrative: Key Findings and Lessons from the ECRC's Whitehall Programme." *Public Administration* 78, no. 2: 345–363.
_____. 1996. "The New Governance: Governing with Government." *Political Studies* 44: 652–657.
Schmitter, P. 1987. "Still the Century of Corporatism?" *Review of Politics* 36: 85–131.
Stoker, Gerry. 1998. "Governance as Theory: Five Propositions." *UNESCO.* 17–28.
White, S. K. 1988. *The Recent Work of Jurgen Habermas: Reason, Justice and Modernity.* Cambridge: Cambridge University Press.
World Bank. 1992. *Governance and Development.* Washington, D.C.: World Bank.

Globalization, Governance and Integration: The Case of Health Care Service as a Predictor of Social Stability

Ronald Marshall

Introduction

In this paper I begin by describing globalization, governance and integration from a health care perspective. Then I move on to an interpretation of health care within a framework of economic and social discourse and discuss how the quality of health care can lead to stability or instability through governance. Finally, I provide some general comments, predictions and consequences for global health care, particularly in developing countries. In the end, I question the responsibility of those charged with the delivery of health care within the social, cultural and political domains against the ever-present reality of globalization.

In the 1980s the buzzword was privatization. In the 1990s and in the 2000s it was and still is globalization. Globalization represents a significant departure from past economic philosophies. Globalization promises to bring the developing and developed countries together with the intention of building strong economies that eventually will strengthen the world economic system. Whether this will benefit the poorer countries is questionable. To achieve the benefits of globalization, the assumption is that various national economies must be integrated. Integration requires the easy movement of trade and finances across the various international borders facilitated by the changing or redrafting of policies within the principles of globalization.

Globalization is not only about economies; it has to do with changes in traditional values. Old trading methods are marginalized and erstwhile trading arrangements that do not find favor with globalization are given short shrift. A staggering array of education, goods and persons circulate across countries and is moving us towards greater homogeneity (Stromquist 2002). The effect of this is no small matter. It impacts on the individual; it has both positive and negative effects.

Globalization in its radical sense must be taken to mean the development of a new economic structure and not just conjunctural change toward greater international trade and investment within an existing set of economic relations (Hirst and Thompson 1996).

According to Hirst and Thompson (1996) the globalization of economic activity and the issues of governance were thought to have appeared since the Second World War; in particular, since the 1960s. They point out that globalization really took off following the collapse of the Bretton Woods semi-fixed exchange rate regime in the 1971–73 period. This was when capital markets rapidly internationalized and international economic relations became predominant. This, according to the authors, heralded the genuine globalization of an integrated and interdependent world economy. According to Nayyar & Court (2002), however, globalization is nothing new; but in the past there were no international transactions in foreign exchange because the gold standard created fixed exchange rates.

It is the contention in this paper that the internationalization of economic relations raises the question of governance and integration, particularly as it relates to developing countries. Further, the effects of globalization on health care systems cannot be overlooked. As a public sector reform strategy, globalization holds implications for changes in governance, integration and economic and social stability. Since some aspect of rationing in health care is inevitable (Ham and Coulter 2000), regulation of financing, health care access and provision becomes necessary.

Governance

According to the literature, *governance* means adopting policies that would facilitate good economic management and sustainable growth. Good governance stresses accountability and transparency, a sound banking system and an independent judiciary. Governance can take five forms:

(1) Governance through agreement between major nation states.
(2) Governance through the creation of international regulatory agencies.

(3) Governance through large economic areas by trade and investment blocs.

(4) Governance by balancing national policies with those of firms and major social interests.

(5) Governance through the offering of protection through economic competitiveness.

Globalization forces nations to come to terms with and scrutinize their own economic policies so that they can better take advantage of and be prepared for any shocks from the international world economy.

Integration

Integration is related to equality between different national financial markets. A fully integrated capital market ensures a single international rate of interest on short and long-term loans and on single share on bond price. However, this does not always materialize. There are ever-present obstacles to this integration. If economic integration is the end product of globalization, then its impact on health care services must be addressed through good governance. Unless this is recognized, globalization could foster increased marginalization and inequality. Thus, the question of integration must be addressed, not only from equity in exchange rates, but also from a social perspective. Consider how the health of some groups may be affected by policies that are out of sync with the realities of globalization.

Health Services as a Predictor of Economic Stability

Any measure of a country's development in real terms must take into consideration the part that health plays in it. Maternal health care is considered the barometer of a nation's quality of health care. Equally important are the health facilities or resources that are aimed at maintaining the health of the nation's working population. In this respect, the international economic benefits of globalization must be harnessed to health care services that address heart diseases, diabetes, cancers, AIDS and many other diseases. At the lower levels of society, the benefits of an improved health care system must be felt by those for whom it matters most — those who have difficulty accessing health care for economic, situational and social reasons. The positive effects of globalization must be brought to bear on the productive energies released by improved public health.

Direct and Indirect Effects on Health Care

In examining the issue of globalization and health care, Woodward et al. (2001) see globalization as a key challenge to public health, particularly as it relates to developing countries. However, they have discerned that the linkages between globalization and health are complex. Adopting a conceptual framework for globalization and health, the authors take into consideration the following: there are both indirect and direct effects on health, operating throughout the national economy and the household economies. These affect health related sectors such as water, sanitation and education. In addition, there are more direct effects on the level of the population, the health care system and the individual risk factors for health.

The authors point out that globalization is one of the key challenges facing health practitioners, since there is no consensus on how globalization affects the health of the population or what policies are adequate responses to it. They are certain, however, that there are new rules, new actors and new markets that affect the ability of countries to protect and promote health.

Criteria for Getting Benefits from Globalization

There are several criteria for getting the maximum benefits of globalization, according to Woodward et al.:

(1) The economic gains of globalization must extend to all countries, particularly low-income ones. In this respect, changes in the international rules and institutional arrangements must reflect the needs of developing countries.

(2) The economic benefits of globalization should be translated into health benefits. This can be accomplished through the national economy, to the health care system, the health-related sectors, and the household economy.

(3) The adverse effects of globalization on a population's health must be minimized. Tobacco marketing and cross-border transmission of infectious disease are cases in point. In short, governments must take the necessary measures to protect public health.

(4) A genuinely health-centered process of globalization can be achieved only by ensuring that the interests of developing countries and vulnerable populations are fully represented in international decision-making forums (Woodward et al. 2001, 6).

It is argued that we need an active response to globalization rather than speculating whether it will be beneficial or not. But there are general areas of concern: international volatility of capital; and migration, disease surveillance, famine and oppression.

The key concern for the majority of persons is the question of equity or partnership in the resources that would be realized from globalization. One strategy is to empower groups to demand accountability.

Globalization — Accessibility and Dominance

The movement of a great mass of people, technology and resources across borders has raised concerns over health and health care access. The good news is that a patient can get medication or medical attention in any part of the globe. On the other hand, it can mean the quick transmission of diseases over distant geographical boundaries. The SARS virus, originating in China and quickly spreading to Canada by air travel, is a case in point. It threatened fragile economies and health systems, particularly in developing countries. China and Canada's resources were stretched, amidst growing concern of increasing infection and the urgency of locating a cure.

Like any other system, national health systems must be reformed or reorganized to face the challenges from the global realities.

Globalization tends to override the sovereignty of nation states. Unless policies are put in place to ensure the protection and the democratic distribution of rewards or public goods, including health care, then globalization can exacerbate a social situation. Governments, therefore, must be charged with the responsibility of bringing together the various players in the arena, namely, corporate actors such as international private organizations and those concerned with building civil society.

Good governance is about ensuring prosperity for everyone. However, with globalization, it is questionable whether in a democratic capitalist society there would be any differences in the structure and behavior of various groups within society. As the rich countries become richer, so too will their economic elites. The elites in poorer countries of the world will continue to have a greater say in the distribution and allocation of resources. The object is "to provide more countries with opportunities to improve their development prospects and more people within those countries to improve their living conditions" (Nayyar and Court 2002, 7).

Health Care, Class and Development

It is instructive to know that most health issues are born out of class positions. The lower classes have insufficient resources to pay for quality health care, are affected more severely by stress, work in hazardous and unhealthy conditions, and are poorly paid. Twenty percent of those in the high-income countries account for 86 percent of private consumption. On the other hand, the poorest 28 percent consume 1.3 percent of the world's resources (Glyn cited in Navarro 2002).

How does health become tied to the economic vagaries of a country? How does health move from a public good to a private good with public implications? The health sectors in various counties have a long history commencing with helping the poor and going on to establishing health care as a right (for every citizen) that must be paid for. At present, health care is linked to development. Health is both an end in itself and a means of fostering development. From the purposes of globalization, investment in the health sector can be justified on strictly economic grounds (Laurell and Arellano 2002).

In the 1980s with privatization on everybody's lips, health care shifted from being treated as a public good to a private good. With globalization the transformation was completed. We moved back from the idea of a private good to a public good. Globalization has the power to totally transform public goods and place them into the hands of private international investors.

Globalized Health Care

However, health is not a commodity one can easily walk away from. In this respect it remains a public good or at least has public features. Herein lies the conflict and the challenge. How far can governments under the influence of the international world economy bow to the dictates of private influence to transform their health sector?— the benefits are enormous. On the other hand, what social risks are governments courting?— the risks are tremendous.

> [A]s income differences widen people suffer not only the health effects of increased relative deprivation and low status but probably poorer social relations as well. Social status, rank or pecking order is, after all, about power, coercion, and access to resources without regard for the needs of others.... Measures of income inequality and the quality of social relations ... are measures of the extent to which the social order is based on

power or mutuality, coercion or socially, antagonism or cooperation, reciprocity or competition, order-giving and order-taking or a more inclusive pluralism (Wilkinson 2002, 350–351).

Cockerham (1992) makes the point that although Medicare and Medicaid have opened doors of accessibility denied by the relationship between poverty and lack of access to quality medical care in the United States, lower-class people still are treated on welfare medicine. They still live in poor environments and have poor opportunities and shorter life spans. This is a situation that can spin out of control. The social breakdown and conflict, barring a revolutionary period, tend to take place or are concentrated in the most deprived areas (Wilkinson 2002). It behooves us to appreciate that health is truly wealth and that a wealthy individual will have little cause to challenge the social order.

Trading Places

There is a great, almost pressing need at the turn of this century for integration in all major aspects of an individual's life. The Bretton Woods Conference of 1947 highlighted the need for parity by the formation of the General Agreement on Tariffs and Trade (GATT), now the World Trade Organization (WTO). But, according to Nayyar and Court (2002) integration under GATT was shallow. Under the WTO it is more expansive. It seeks harmonization or deeper integration, meaning better domestic economic policies, investment, competition, technology, taxation and labour standards (Nayyar and Court 2002).

Navarro (2002), however, is not convinced of these "neo-liberalist measures." As far as he is concerned, globalization has not delivered to the developing countries as the globalization theorists had claimed. He identifies a number of areas of concern: the overwhelming majority of imports to the OECD countries came from OECD countries and not from less developed countries. As a matter of fact, only 5.5 percent of imports into developed countries came from the less developed countries, namely, the South Eastern countries; the rate of growth of all manufacturing imports has declined during the 1950s; and manufacturing represented only 18 percent of all employment in the OECD in 1994. Further, that percentage is declining in all OECD countries. Navarro argues that it is questionable "whether the lowering of wage levels and social protection can be attributed to the globalization of economies since exports have been increasing rather slowly and even declining in most developed capitalist countries and manufacturing imports from low-wage countries represent a very low percentage of overall employment" (2002, 85).

How then does globalization provide equity for everyone, including access to health care? To answer this we turn to Nayyar and Court (2002, 7): "It is clear that markets are not sufficient and may, in fact, exclude a significant proportion of people. The endeavor should be to make the market driven process of globalization conducive to a more egalitarian and broad-based development pattern."

Governments must not only be the facilitators but the providers. According to Nayyar and Court (2002) governments must provide the necessary goods at the global level. These include global security, global economic stability, global environment, global health and knowledge.

In fact, globalization should lead to good governance, which in turn would lead to economic and social integration. Global integration feeds back into or reinforces good governance. Good governance, it is to be noted, feeds directly into the provision of adequate health services, without which economic and social instability can follow.

The Global Health Pie

The desire of enabling developing countries to get a slice of the global pie is very strong. At best, these countries must prepare their economies by removing trade barriers and putting legislation, where necessary, in place. At worst, they could be isolated and left behind. Either way instability may follow. When globalization benefits are felt, they must be evenly distributed; otherwise the inequity could lead to restiveness among the less fortunate. When the globalization train passes by without anyone getting on board, the middle and upper classes may cry foul and charge that bad governance is responsible.

It is argued that one can embrace globalization and in the process be a member of a world integrated economy. However, in addition to the attention that must be paid to each individual country's economic and social conditions, good governance must be a necessary feature of the global integration package. Good governance must ensure that the gains from globalization do not remain in the hands of the few; good governance must ensure that fragile but culturally significant aspects of a country are not traded on the international market, where public goods could be transformed to global goods. Good governance must be wary of privatizing health care and putting it into the hands of international and local investors and out of the reach of the vast majority of the poor.

Impact of International Investments

The removal of international investments from the national economy courts a serious risk of this happening and in the process creating a downward spiral of economic and social conflict that may lead to political instability. The collapse of the health care system could hurt not only the social classes but the government as well.

Caution is necessary when entertaining, assessing and realizing the effects of globalization on the health care sector. As happened with colonialism, imperialism, and modernism, those who bore the burden of inequities were the less developed countries. It was left for the theorists and the analysts to draw the final curtain on what might be considered a provocative period for those who were attempting to catch up.

Whose Health Priorities?

The health priority dilemmas in developing countries, to use a phrase from Bryant (2000), can be put in the following way: Whose priorities? In whose interest? Linked to whose policies? According to which criteria? To be decided by whom? Implemented by whom? At what cost? With what expected impact?

The author was specifically observing health priority dilemmas in developing countries, but his views are pertinent to the nature of the discussion here. His contention is that the question of health is not only a technical challenge, but a social, cultural, economic and political challenge as well. It is to this that I will now turn. Technically, health care is mired in expanding far into the rural areas while attempting to concentrate within the city centers. This is where the demand for specialists are. The city center is also a meeting place of convenience. You can do a large variety of things, including shopping, seeking dental care and seeking employment. Yet, it is problematic to get health care access in far-flung areas. Here is where home health care is beginning to emerge. Home health care deals with providing care to the aged, the persistently ill, and those with complexities of illness. These individuals may be caught in a web of social circumstances and increased risk while the real issue is accessibility. On the other hand, it may be difficult for members of the community to exercise any degree of control over their situation or their lifestyle. It has been found that the issue of control over one's lifestyle is significant to the extent that one is not environmentally vulnerable to the circumstances in which the behavior takes place (Blaxter 1990 cited in Nettleton 1995). In these regions also the effect of poor health in women and children cannot go unnoticed or undocumented.

The life expectancy of women in developed regions is, on average, 6.5 years longer than that of men (United Nations 1991). This is also true in other parts of the world, but this varies from five years in Latin America and the Caribbean to 3.5 years in Africa and 3 years in Asia and the Pacific (United Nations 1991 cited in Nettleton 1995).

Rural Health

It is interesting to note that with all the focus on globalization and global health care, very little is said about rural health care. Rural health care is very significant for countries like China, Guyana, Costa Rica, Mexico and Cuba. Mexico, in particular, is among only a handful of nations in Latin America that have seriously attempted to provide basic primary and secondary care to rural population (Sherraden and Wallace cited in Sherraden 1995). It has been pointed out that this was made possible by the concept of "integrating rural health care into a broader rural development agenda" (Gallagher and Subedi 1992). It is therefore likely that concentration on globalization and economic integration misses the part that these might play in alleviating health inadequacies. Further, the omission of health care from any discussions on globalization signals that such debates are incomplete from a development perspective.

Culture and Acculturation

To talk about health care without recognizing the cultural linkages is to wantonly ignore the behaviors of various subpopulations across national boundaries. Simply put, culture determines how we eat, drink, smoke, and how we perceive health overall. Culture remains a powerful explanation for linking practices across cultures (see Marshall 2001) and it explores why, in the face of mounting information, certain cancer-causing foods remain a staple in some countries. With the removal of trade barriers and the movement of people across international frontiers, a process of acculturation is high on the agenda of most, if not all, permanent immigrants. This brings us to the issue of migration. Migrants, like refugees, are faced with types of health access that may be uncomfortable or alien compared to their manner of accessing health care in the home country.

Migration is a characteristic of the world today. For example, the globalization of multinational companies has increased the demand for migrants' labor between various countries in different stages of modernization (Shuval 1995). This means that a host country can "import" a number of diseases depending on the surveillance apparatus that the country has in place. But more importantly is that the migrant may be forced to acculturate or risk disease and injury. Some examples of the obstacles to health care access in another country are language, ethnicity, race, doctor-patient communication, status, and class. However, some of these difficulties have been overcome by the open-door policies of some countries, notably the USA and Israel. In this regard health care takes on a multicultural outlook, from diagnosis to treatment.

Global health care take little notice of this and instead concentrates on the cost of and access to health care, employing improved technology with economic investment. It assumes homogeneity of populations, if not homogeneity of differences. This clearly is a paradox for the relations between globalization, governance, integration, health care and stability.

Conclusion

Globalization, governance and integration present a naturally occurring phenomenon of capitalist societies that permits us to see the impact of these forces on health care, the inalienable right of every individual. The relentless drive of technology and information have placed this development squarely on our doorsteps. It involves the layperson, the state, the professionals and the investors.

According to my observations, the advent of globalization poses a new challenge to the processes of governance, accountability and integration. The question to be raised is this: Does globalization impede quality health care access to the vast majority of people in the developing countries? This is a very difficult question to answer. Various governments may act differently and at different levels where the lines between overall global benefits interface with global health.

Inequality in health care means poor school performance based on inadequate nutritional levels; it means absenteeism due to illness of various types; and it means poor social relations between groups. One of the most troubling issues surrounding globalization of health care is the question of equity, particularly in multiethnic, multicultural countries. The developing world cannot be compared to the United States, Britain, Germany or any of the other major industrialized countries. In those countries globalization may work wonders through technological innovations, but for developing countries it may spell uncertainty and fear.

References

Bryant, John H. 2000. "Health priority dilemma in developing countries." In *Global Challenge of Health Care Rationing*. Edited by Angela Coulter and Chris Ham. Philadelphia: Open University Press.

Cockerham, William. 1992. *Medical Sociology*. New Jersey: Prentice Hall.

Gallagher, Eugene B., and Janardan Subedi. 1992. *Global Perspectives on Health Care*. New Jersey: Prentice Hall.

Ham, Chris, and Angela Coulter. 2000. "Introduction: International Consequence of Rationing (or Priority Setting)." In *Global Challenge of Health Care Rationing*. Edited by Angela Coulter and Chris Ham. Philadelphia: Open University Press.

Hirst, Paul, and Grahame Thompson. 1996. *Globalization in Question*. Cambridge: Polity Press.

Laurell, Asa, and Cristina Olivia López Arellano. 2002. "Market Commodities and Poor Relief: The World Bank Proposal for Health." In *The Political Economy of Social Inequalities. Consequences for Health and Quality of Life*. Edited by Vincente Navarro. New York: Baywood Publishing Company, Inc.

Marshall, Ronald. 2001. *Alcoholism: Genetic Culpability or Social Irresponsibility? The Challenge of Innovative Methods to Determine Final Outcomes*. New York: University Press of America.

Navarro, Vincente. 2000. "Neoliberalism, "Globalization," Unemployment, Inequalities, and the Welfare State." In *The Political Economy of Social Inequalities: Consequences for Health and Quality of Life*. New York: Baywood Publishing Company, Inc.

Nayyar, Deepak, and Julius Court. 2002. *Governing Globalization: Issues and Institutions*. Finland: United Nations, University World Institute for Development Economics Research (UNU/WIDER).

Nettleton, Sarah. 1995. *The Sociology of Health and Illness*. Cambridge: Polity Press.

Sherraden, Margaret Sherrard. 1995. Development of Health Policy and Services for Rural Mexico. In *Global Perspectives on Health Care*. Edited by Eugene B. Gallagher and Janardan Subedi. New Jersey: Prentice Hall.

Shuval, Judith T. 1995. Migrants, Refugees, and Health: Some Policy Implications of Israel's Experience. In *Global Perspectives on Health Care*. Edited by Eugene B. Gallagher and Janardan Subedi. New Jersy: Prentice Hall.

Stromquist, Nelly P. 2002. *Current Issues in Comparative Education* 4:2. Available at: http://www.tc.columbia.edu/cice/volu.5nr2/all52.htm.

United Nations. 1991. *The World's Woman, 1970–1990. Trend as Statistics*. New York: United Nations.

Wilkinson, Richard G. 2002. Income Inequality, Social Cohesion and Health: Clarifying the Theory—A Reply to Muntainer and Lynch. In *The Political Economy of Social Inequality: Consequences for Health and Quality of Life*. Edited by Vincente Navarro. New York: Baywood Publishing Company, Inc.

Woodward, David, Nick Drager, Robert Beaglehole, and Debra Lipson. 2001. *Bulletin of the World Health Organization* 79.

Rethinking Globalization's Discontent

Sadia Niyakan-Safy

Introduction

Globalization is one of the most important watchwords of the twenty-first century, yet it is one of the least understood concepts and perhaps the most feared process of our time. Particularly for small developing island economies, globalization appears to be a great evil usurping the power of nation-states, overriding cultural diversity, and increasing debt, inequality and poverty (McDonald 1998; Pantin 1998 and 1999; Ryan 1998; NATUC 1998).

The argument is that the characteristics of small island states, such as smallness, insularity and remoteness, limited natural resources, small domestic markets, highly open economies, export concentration on a few (commodity) products, and a small range of local skills make human development very difficult (Haitink 1998).

In this paper, the discontents of globalization will be revisited. The paper argues that while globalization has undoubtedly aggravated the socioeconomic, political, and cultural problems of the poorer countries of the world, globalization itself (defined as a process of global political, economic, social and cultural integration) is by no means responsible for these problems. That it has aggravated the social, political and economic ills of poor countries is perhaps due to the fact that for the most part, the policy responses of these countries have been inadequate to deal with the challenges of the process. In the words of prominent thinker and economist Lloyd Best, "We rationalize it in terms of islands small and open. However, many small countries show that what is decisive are not God-given size and resources but human agency and business management" (Best 1998).

The first section of this paper will discuss the issue of terminology and the emergence of globalization in order to provide a working definition of the concept. In the second section, the discontents of globalization will be revisited paying particular attention to the issues of the nation state, inequality and poverty, globalization and the feminization of poverty, global acculturation, and lastly, globalization and the environment. The main premise of this section is that it is not globalization but weak governance and the lack of political will to institute necessary policy reforms that are responsible for the many ills attributed to globalization.

Having said that, it is recognized that globalization can in fact exacerbate existing social, political and economic ills. The third section discusses the imperative that the globalization process be properly managed if the potentially positive effects of the process are to manifest themselves.

Definitions and Emergence of Globalization

Many have now come to the conclusion that the process of globalization is not a phenomenon of the 1990s, but is a process that has been taking place for over 500 years (Arrighi 1997; Wallerstein 1999; Schaeffer 1997). Yet, while many seem to agree about when the process began, not many agree as to exactly what globalization is.

Writing for the Human Development Report, Watkins (1997) associates globalization with the resurgence of laissez faire economic theory. He states that the elements of globalization include the expansion of free trade, foreign investment, unregulated financial markets, speculation, issues of distribution, and regionalism. Globalization, therefore, is synonymous with neoclassical economics.

Several other authors define globalization as the increasing integration of the world's economies (Ghai 1992; Hoogvelt 1998; Sklair 1994). This integration is facilitated by the growth of a global market discipline, increasing specialization of production around the world through the spread of TNCs (transnational corporations), and the emergence of a financial economy that is facilitated by economic deregulation and neoliberalism.

Other thinkers, particularly those of the postmodernist school, have suggested that globalization also encapsulates a process of acculturation. Cultures and tastes become "global" with the globalization of production. As the world is molded into a single market, tastes, entertainment, fads and fashions become very similar. To these thinkers, globalization represents a triumph of the culture of consumerism (Barber 1995; Durning 1995; Sklair 1994).

For some, globalization represents a political process yielding the triumph of capitalism and democracy over socialism and authoritarian rule. This became most evident with the breakup of the Soviet Union and the dissolution of its international socialist empire. The new global order has three centers of economic and political power: North America, Western Europe and Japanese spheres of influence (Preston 1996; Klak 1998; Brown 1993). Others see the breakup of the Soviet Union, the demolition of the Berlin Wall and the reunification of Germany as signs of increasing political integration (Boyles 1996).

Whatever the views, it is clear that globalization is a multifaceted phenomenon manifesting the signs of increasing global integration technologically, politically, economically, and culturally. The rapid development of telecommunications and air transportation have transformed the world into a "global village." It is now possible to fall asleep in one continent and wake up in another, or to sit in one corner of the world, and with the click of a button, communicate with someone at the opposite end.

Economically, the rise of certain East Asian countries has challenged the economic hegemony of the United States, causing us to question the concepts of "First," "Second" and "Third" worlds (Guy 1993; Harris 1987). Furthermore, it is clear now that these rigid divisions of the world are no longer applicable, inasmuch as there are class differences *between* and *within* countries in both developed and developing countries.

Signs of political and economic integration are also evident in the blossoming of regional trading blocs such as the North American Free Trade Agreement (NAFTA), the General Agreement on Trade and Tariffs (GATT), the Caribbean Community (CARICOM), and the European Union. More recently, the launch of the "Euro" currency has deepened the process of economic integration. The birth of international institutions such as the United Nations and its agencies—the Red Cross, Amnesty International and the World Health Organization—has meant improved efforts at international cooperation (Kilminster 1997).

Culturally, globalization represents a transnationalization of cultures. The movement of peoples across countries and continents has also meant the movement of cultures globally. Globalization represents, therefore, not only a "McDonaldization" of the world, or the institutionalization of a Western culture of consumerism, as some have argued (Sklair 1994, 178), but it has also meant the transportation of cultures from the developing world to European and American centers where migrants congregate.

Hence, globalization is not simply trade liberalization and financial deregulation. When it is seen as simply a resurgence of neoclassical economics, it is easy to blame the process for the woes of developing countries.

Most certainly, globalization is a complex phenomenon, involving both integrative and disintegrative tendencies (such as facilitation of the international drug trade, kidnapping rings, pornography trade, and terrorist activities through the spread of communications technology). This process will only intensify in the years ahead, but whether the positive or the negative tendencies will be allowed to predominate rests squarely on the shoulders of our leaders.

Globalization's Discontents

The Nation-State

One of the often talked about consequences of globalization is its effect on the nation-state. Some have argued that globalization has forced nation-states to surrender their sovereignty and autonomous decision-making powers to supranational authorities (Brown 1993; Luard 1990; Gilpin 1987; Ghai 1992). This is interpreted, on the one hand, to be the result of stringent structural adjustment policies (SAPs) imposed on developing countries in the face of rising debt. Since rising debt and structural inefficiencies in the economy have been blamed on overinvolved states, the result has been that the terms of SAPS in many developing countries reduce the role of the state to a mere facilitator rather than the driving force of the economy (Ghai 1992).

Others attribute the declining role of the state to the increasing economic powers of TNCs, whose operations states need to help further economic growth within their borders. The constant threat of trade boycotts, or of reduced economic activity as a result of TNCs pulling out of the host country, act as a constraint on the decision-making powers of governments, particularly those in the developing world (Brown 1993).

Without doubt, the globalization process has meant some reductions in the powers and roles assigned to the state. However, one must not exaggerate the loss of sovereignty of the nation-state. If anything, increasing global integration requires strong states, and while the roles of nation-states are being redefined in the emerging global economy, this by no means means an emasculated state. On the contrary, global capitalism needs the state for successful functioning (Wallerstein 1997).

According to Wallerstein, the purpose of global capitalism is the accumulation of capital, and one of the core concerns of the capitalist is to protect the capital he has accumulated. For this, he needs a "night watchman state." The night watchman state protects the capitalist from those intent on pilfering his property (financial, intellectual or otherwise); it protects him from high taxes and other "inefficiencies" in the system; and it protects him from the vagaries of the free market by not making it free for those who do not have the means to compete equally on the market. In other words, the state will refrain from subsidization. That the sovereignty of the state is on the decline is not due to globalization, says Wallerstein, "but because of a transformation of the geo-culture, and first of all, because of the loss of hope by the popular masses in liberal reformism" (14).

This view is supported by others who lay the blame for the decline in national sovereignty squarely on the shoulders of people's unhappiness with their governments and their policies. One author states, "Governments all around the world have been subverted by internal strife, corruption, public dissatisfaction, recalcitrant military forces, and by their own ineptitude" (Boyles 1994). Indeed, it is no secret that one of the underlying reasons many developing countries found themselves in debt in the eighties was the continued presence of a feudal-type elite class who borrowed excessively from foreign banks, mismanaged the loans by not investing wisely in the productive capacities of the country, and siphoned off monies to their foreign bank accounts (Baran 1982).

The power of TNCs over states is also a result of the fact that states have a vested interest in satisfying these large companies, who are the main sources of funding for the states' election campaigns (Brown 1994).

Many governments lack the political will necessary to initiate just and lasting reforms within their country. The power to redistribute resources lies in the hands of governments, but not many are willing to exercise this power inasmuch as it goes against their own political interests and the interests of the political and economic elite. While other factors of geopolitical significance contributed to the success of East Asian countries,[1] the "East Asian Miracle" is perhaps the most glaring example of the continuing powers of nation-states in this era of globalization. The tiger economies of Singapore, Taiwan, Korea and Hong Kong aptly demonstrated that the public and private sectors can work together for successful national development.

Some have argued that what has been called the East Asian Miracle is no miracle at all, but the hard work of governments committed to development objectives (Wade 1990; Fairbank 1993; Chang 1993; Chu 1997). These authors argue that the right mix of policies of protection and openness, government and market control, import and export-led policies, and the strengthening of institutional capacity succeeded in producing phenomenal growth rates and macroeconomic stability in East Asia for three decades, from the '60s to the '80s. It was strong governance that facilitated the process. The current global concern with promoting knowledge as the

chief means to development, can be said to have been inspired by the East
Asian example, where governments invested heavily in the development
of their human resources. This development of human capital has been
recognized as one of the main causes of the unprecedented economic success of the region.

Ironically, it was the onset of weak governance (corruption and mismanagement) coupled with financial crisis that led to panic on the part of
the international investment community, causing a massive withdrawal of
foreign capital that led to a full-fledged crisis in East Asia by the early
1990s (Radelet and Sachs n.d; McKibbin and Martin 1998; Battu 1998,
DeLong 1998).

Even Cuba has shown us what a national government can achieve in
the face of unrelenting international pressures. Despite decades of trade
embargos against Cuba, the government has invested strongly in education and health care such that their educational and health statistics are
well above developing countries' average (Corbridge 1995). Oscar Lewis
has commented on the absence of a "culture of poverty" in Cuba in comparison to its existence in the urban slums of Western countries (Lewis
1998). This can be said to be a direct result of the government's investment in the well-being of its people.

Hence, governments need not conform to the image of the toothless
tigers they have been purported to be. Perhaps now more than ever, the
roles of national governments are increasingly important within the global
economy (Giddens 2002; Harding and Le Gales 1997; Kassim 1997; Stewart and Garrahan 1997; Bowker 1997). Bowker best captures the position
in which the nation-state finds itself:

> The pressure on state sovereignty has increased in this more interdepen-
> dent world. However, the state retains a monopoly right to legislate, raise
> taxation and implement policy. Therefore, the individual still looks
> towards the state for the provision of his or her basic welfare. It is also
> worth bearing in mind that sovereignty has an external aspect as well. For
> the state has the right, in international law, to represent its citizens in the
> international system. The state concludes treaties with other states, and
> has the exclusive right to sit on international bodies, such as the UN and
> the EU. As a result, the state provides the best opportunity for representa-
> tion on the international scale for individuals whose lives are increasingly
> affected by global forces. (252)

Inequality and Poverty

Among the many arguments of anti-globalizers is that globalization
is responsible for deepening poverty and increasing inequalities both *within*

and *between* nations (Hewitt de Alcántara 1994; Ghai 1992; Wade 2001; UNCTAD 1997; Schaeffer 1997). Whereas it previously was believed that poverty and inequality were characteristics of developing countries, it has now been amply demonstrated that poverty and inequality also are on the rise within developed nations (Lens 1971).

The argument is that the ability of TNCs to transfer their operations to countries where labor is cheap is creating unemployment and increasing poverty in First World countries. At the same time, however, their presence in developing countries is creating unfair competition for infant industries and small businesses whose operations are not of the scale required to compete equally with the multinationals (Schaeffer 1997). Because of this, the only true benefactors of free trade are the TNCs, who are able to reap most of the profits from free trade agreements (Hewitt de Alcántara 1994; Ghai 1992). More recently, some authors from the Caribbean have pointed out that economic globalization via the loss of preferential trading agreements has had dire negative effects for banana products from eastern Caribbean countries (Pantin 1998; Express Editorial 2000). These unfair trade practices are believed to have exacerbated inequalities both between and within countries.

While rising inequality is a global concern, the research on inequality around the world has not provided uniform results from which to draw general conclusions. Wade (2001, 5), for instance, considers the distribution of income inequality between countries, by considering the average income of each country, measured in Purchasing Power Party terms. He found that globally, there has been a widening of income inequality between the richest and poorest countries. For instance, Africa, India, Indonesia and rural China were at the bottom of the scale with an average annual income level below \$1,500, while countries such as the US, Japan, Germany, France, the UK and Italy were at the top of the scale with an average annual Purchasing Power Party income above \$11,500.

However, while inequality is on the rise between countries or regions of the world, it is on the decline within some countries. The time factor is another crucial variable since within any given country, inequality may be on the decline at certain times and on the rise at other times. This is demonstrated below in the case of Malaysia:

Year	Gini Coefficient	Year	Gini Coefficient
1957–1958	0.421	1984	0.480
1970	0.499	1990	0.446
1976	0.529	1995	0.464

Sources of data: (a) Bowman, K. (1997); (b) Department of Statistics, Malaysia (1996).

The data indicate that while inequality has been consistently low in Malaysia overall, there has been slight increases and decreases during certain periods. Hence, inequality increased from 1957 to 1976, declined between 1976 and 1990, and increased again in 1995. As Knowles (2001, 1) points out, "Inequality can be measured using data on gross income, net income or expenditure. In addition, the unit of measurement can be the individual or the household. A priori, we would expect to obtain quite different measures of inequality, depending on which of these classifications are used."

Globalization has been blamed for increasing global poverty. Estimates are that half of the world's population, almost three billion people, live on less than $2 a day (Shah 2002). The causes of poverty are complex and multifarious, but the unequal trade relations that are part and parcel of economic globalization have been known to exacerbate poverty (Wade 1990). Notwithstanding, we must be cautious about throwing the baby out with the bath water. Consumers have more to gain than lose from economic globalization, as increased competition between transnationals and local businesses will drive prices down, making consumer goods more affordable for the poorer classes (Schaeffer 1997). Take, for example, the concerns expressed by Robert Farah, the managing director of MDC-UM, a furniture making company in Trinidad. In an interview with the Trinidad Express newspaper, Farah lamented that trade liberalization has allowed furniture of "more aesthetic appeal" to be imported into the country at much lower retail prices than locally produced products. He argued that "MDC-UM has been forced to bring its prices down by 30 per cent just to keep up with the lower prices the importers are able to charge" (Rampersad 2002).

Hence, trade liberalization might be a sore on the skin of local business and capitalist interests, but it is certainly a welcome move for consumers who now have a greater variety of goods and services within their reach, and at lower prices. Also, the competition created by economic globalization can encourage local producers to improve their own standards and services to compare with internationally acceptable standards. Again, this will be better for consumers who will be getting more worth for their money.

Globalization has produced economic growth in some countries like Trinidad and Tobago, where the growth rates have averaged between three and four percent for the past five years. Trinidad's exports to the US grew by 5.4 percent in 2001, while the country ran a trade surplus with the US of over US$1.2 billion (Austin 2001).

Increasing growth rates and falling prices for consumer products do not automatically translate to equality, though. In fact, a fall in the prices of consumer products may well happen at a time when the power to consume is weakened by high unemployment rates. Hence, whether or not the poor stand to benefit from economic growth and falling prices has to do with the policy decisions that governments make. Economic growth has to be matched by redistribution efforts. In Costa Rica, for example, a welfare state was created after the civil war, and more money was spent on poverty reduction, social services, education and employment generation. The government also reduced military spending in order to have funds to pursue its social program. As a result, the income of the poorest almost doubled by the early 1990s (Bowman 1997).

Globalization and the Feminization of Poverty

Some critics have pointed out that globalization is leading to a "feminization of poverty." Many traditional areas of women's work, such as agricultural labor, are now taken over by big multinationals, exacerbating women's unemployment. Also, the flexible specialization of labor has relegated many women to the most menial and least paid jobs in factories. Others argue that the workings of global capitalism have increased women's workloads both inside and outside the home, without a corresponding increase in salaries (Goldberg and Kremen 1990; Khoury 1994; *Women* 2000; Tsikata 1995).

However, a report from the Swasti Miller, of the UN's Women Watch Online Working Group on Women's Economic Inequality, reveals that globalization has in fact brought new opportunities to women, but that women without education or updated skills have not been able to take advantage of the new opportunities. In China and Vietnam, for example, globalization has brought new opportunities for young women with familiarity with English in new service sector jobs. However, many women have been made redundant because they do not have the skills to match the new jobs (Sandrasagra 2000).

In the Caribbean, educational and political leaders are now realizing the importance of developing human resources in order to take advantage of the globalization process. Dr. Bhoe Tewarie, principal of the St. Augustine campus of the University of the West Indies and pro-vice-chancellor, says the education sector is fundamental to the transformation of the region. According to Tewarie, "Education is in fact the critical bridge even if telecommunications will provide the highway. Higher education needs a dedicated focus if we are to at all match the pace of development which is required in this region in order to gain the best benefits of the globalization process" (Maharaj 2002).

In like manner, Sir Dwight Venner, governor of the Eastern Caribbean Central Bank in St. Kitts, emphasizes the importance of developing knowledge and skills to reap the potential benefits of globalization. According to Venner, "In small regions, in order for us to succeed in the global environment, our small populations must possess the highest levels of education and skill" (Maharaj 2002).

Programs that seek to empower women through investment in education and skills training, the availability of micro-credit to encourage entrepreneurship, and investment in physical infrastructure and social services can go a long way in helping women to reap the benefits of globalization.

The Acculturation of the World

Another fear regarding globalization is that it is overriding the indigenous cultures of the world. This acculturation is possible because of the rapid growth of the mass media in developing countries. American or Western culture permeates the film, television and music industries globally. The global culture is a consumer culture where everyone is encouraged to consume Western products—even those who cannot afford to do so (Barber 1995; Durning 1995).

Fears about the spread of consumerism are valid, yet some have pointed out positive effects of this process:

> The rise of a mass consumption society produces political, economic and cultural side-effects that are troubling. But surely, the criticism of this world and of the liberal capitalism which created it, must first recognize its accomplishments. The political and economic changes that have created Mc World are, on the whole, admirable ones. Giving people the ability to live longer, to move where they want, own a house, to enjoy such pleasures as vacations and restaurants and shopping is good, even noble. (Zakaria 1996, 30)

Hence, globalization has the potential to improve the standard of living for more of the world's peoples, but this requires just and equitable rules to ensure that everyone can enjoy the fruits of the process. Local, national and international agencies all have important collaborative roles to play in this regard.

The fears that globalization will promote Western culture while oppressing indigenous ones also are often exaggerated. Globalization implies unity, not uniformity. The process, if properly managed, will produce greater local cultural diversity, not homogeneity (Giddens 2002). The increasing movement of people between countries and continents as a result of the globalization process provides countless opportunities for the export of developing countries' cultures to the developed regions of the world. Migrants act as cultural ambassadors of their home countries, hosting art, drama and musical shows in their host countries (Thomas-Hope 1985). Prominent among these is the Notting Hill Carnival in London, which promotes a fabulous display of Trinidadian music, dance, and art forms in the heart of a European center. Transmigration has in fact facilitated the formation of Caribbean centers in key areas in Western cities such as New York, Toronto and London. Any visitor to Leffers in New York, or Sheperds Bush in London, is easily transported to the sights, sounds and tastes of the Caribbean.

Globalization and the Environment

The global commons is another common concern of postmodernist society. Global warming, the destruction of forests, and the pollution of water, air and land are all justified concerns. Some see the process of globalisation as the reason for our present environmental woes.

Once again, structural adjustment and globalization are linked in a web of controversy. With the yoke of debt around their necks, many Third World governments are forced to adjust by increasing their incentives to foreign investors. Often, these incentives include the lowering of environmental control policies, which opens up these countries to pollution-generating industries and the illegal dumping of wastes by transnational corporations (Brown 1994). The proliferation of these industries in Third World cities poses a very real threat of chemical leaks and accidents—the one often but sadly remembered is that in Bhopal, India, in 1984, when a chemical leak from a Union Carbide pesticides factory killed more than 2,000 people and maimed another 200,000 (Smith 1992).

In the defence of globalization, much of the environmental degradation that takes place in developing countries can be curbed by strict government legislation and implementation. However, the desire for economic growth overrides the need of many Third World governments for environmental preservation. With stricter pollution controls in developed countries, many Third World governments are finding that without strict pollution legislation, they can achieve a competitive advantage over industrialised countries. Hence, many industries are allowed to pollute without restrictions. Pollution, therefore, has become a hidden subsidy for Third World countries (Adams 1990).

Because many governments are dependent on big companies for financial resources, they are less likely to restrict their operations. But this need not be the case; governments in developing countries collect exorbitant taxes, and better management of these revenues could yield some much-needed finance. However, globally, governments are spending more on the military than they are on social services; many do not keep campaign promises of providing more housing, schools, better sanitation and more efficient public services; and many governments are guilty of instituting highly inflated salaries for themselves as soon as they assume leadership, rather than revamping social services and upgrading public infrastructure. Hence, many become dependent on big corporations to do their jobs for them, and fall prey to the machinations of big companies.

To say, then, that globalization is the cause of the world's environmental woes is to simplify the issue by ignoring the political economy behind environmental degradation. Governments of small island states can reject environmental degradation as the Bahamas did in 1986, when a barge of 3,000 tons of trash from a Philadelphia incinerator arrived at its port for disposal. The government of this small island gave a resounding "no" to the trash being dumped on its soil. The barge, which travelled for 16 years in the search for a country to be dumped on, was forced to make a return journey to Philadelphia where it was finally disposed off in a landfill (Williams 2002).

Managing the Globalization Process

Properly managed, globalization as a process of increasing political, social, economic and cultural integration can work for the benefit of both developed and developing nations. While it brings with it many challenges for small developing nations, it also brings with it many opportunities. The contradictions of globalization are eloquently captured in the words of Smith and Naim (2000):

> Globalization surrounds us all in turmoil, and propels our lives through its confusion of contradictions. It empowers some people while it impoverishes others. It celebrates the market and jeopardizes economic growth. It is an engine of invention, a machine of destruction. It liberates and defeats. It invites us to share the pleasures of a common culture while it menaces heritage, tradition, and belief. Globalization mocks the state and demands more of it, validates democracy and subverts it.

Reaping the potential benefits of the globalization process requires a greater, more effective management of the process by both national and international institutions. As argued in this paper, globalization does not negate the role of the state, but rather calls for a more effective response by the state. This paper has attempted to show that the states that have found ways of participating more effectively in globalization are the ones reaping the most benefits from the process. At the same time, there is need for greater accountability in the functioning of international institutions such as the World Bank, International Monetary Fund, and the World Trade Organization. Weak states must be given stronger, not weaker, representation in international institutions to ensure that the scales of power balance equally. Effective governance is needed not only at the local and national levels but also at the international level.

In 1924, President Theodore Roosevelt called for a new international organization to replace the League of Nations, whose responsibility would be to defend life, liberty, independence, religious freedom, and to preserve human rights and justice internationally (Beck 1986). He believed that such a universal organization of nations should mark the end of methods of unilateral action, exclusive alliances, spheres of influence and balances of power that had failed for centuries. Roosevelt believed that peace must rest on the cooperative effort of the whole world. On June 25, 1945, the United Nations was born.

The United Nations and its subsidiary organizations are perhaps the closest we have come to effective global governance. Yet, unilateral action by powerful states is still the name of the game after more than five decades of the United Nations. Clearly, there is much reformative work to be done to ensure that the United Nations works effectively in achieving its objectives, and to secure global peace and security. This will be a challenge. Habits of mind are hard to change, and those who stand to profit from present unequal global relations will, of course, be opposed to any restructuring that promises a piece of the pie to all. Yet, the failure to reform the international system can well have catastrophic consequences for both the powerful and the powerless.

Achieving better global governance will require effective consultation between all concerned parties. The failure of past development efforts was essentially a failure to consult with the intended beneficiaries. Past development efforts were mostly top-down projects, imposed on the hapless poor of the Third World with a disregard for their views, knowledge or input. History is a great teacher and every effort should be made to avoid the tragedy of past errors. For the potential benefits of globalization to be realized, local nongovernmental organizations, grassroots movements, national governments, and regional and international organizations must all be involved in the collaborative process. All-inclusive global consultation is now an imperative for hammering out the trajectories of the new global order. This fact was recognized over 150 years ago by one religious leader who claimed:

> The time must come when the imperative necessity for the holding of a vast, an all-embracing assemblage of men will be universally realized. The rulers and kings of the earth must needs attend it, and, participating in its deliberations, must consider such ways and means as will lay the foundations of the world's Great Peace amongst men. Such a peace demanded that the Great Powers should resolve, for the sake of the tranquillity of the peoples of the earth, to be fully reconciled among themselves. (Gleanings from the Writings of Baha'u'llah, 249)

Conclusion

Globalization is a multifaceted phenomenon that presents the world with both challenges and opportunities. It presents the challenge to post-colonial governments to recognize the interplay between international developments and national issues, and to respond with responsibility, ingenuity and creativity. It also offers a challenge to world leaders to reform the international order and its institutions according to the rules of fair play and equality, as opposed to the rules of profit maximization. Once these opportunities are utilized and attempts made at better management of the process on all levels, globalization might finally yield the fruits it can potentially bear.

Endnotes

1. East Asia was of geopolitical significance to the US in its fight against communist Russia. The US poured aid and resources into East Asia, which greatly assisted in national development. Whereas other developing countries received aid in the form of loans, East Asia received financial "gifts" which did not have to be re-paid. For more on this, see Robert Wade (1990), "Lessons from East Asia" in S. Corbridge (ed.), Development Studies: A Reader (Arnold: London) 1995.

References

Adams, WM. 1990. *Green Development: Environment and Sustainability in the Third World.* London: Routledge.

Amin, S. 2000. "The Political Economy of the Twentieth Century." *Monthly Review*, vol. 52, no. 2.

Arrighi, G. 1997. "Globalization, State Sovereignty, and the 'Endless' Accumulation of Capital." http://fbc.binghamton.edu/gairvn97.htm.

Austin, Roy, US Ambassador to Trinidad, speaking at a meeting of the Rotary Club of Princes Town. Speech entitled, "Globalization Paying off for Trinidad and Tobago" and quoted by Phoolo Dhanny-Maharaj in the *Trinidad Express Online*, July 12, 2002.

Baran, Paul. 1982. "A Morphology of Backwardness." In Alavi and Shanin (eds.), *Introduction to the Sociology of Developing Countries*. Macmillan.

Barber, B. 1995. *Jihad vs. McWorld* (NY: Times Books) quoted in A. Boyles, "World Watch" in *The Bahai World*. Haifa: Bahai World Centre, 1996.

Baha'u'llah. 1983. *Gleanings from the Writings of Baha'u'llah*. Wilmette: Baha'I Publishing Trust 1983.

Battu, H. Lecture for EC1501, "The East Asian Crisis," delivered May 1998. See Battu's website: www.abdn.ac.uk/~pec131.

Beck, S. "The way to Peace: the Great Peacemakers, Philosophers of Peace and Efforts toward World Peace." Available at http://www.san.beck.org.

Best, Lloyd. 1998. "On the Frontiers of Globalization." *Trinidad Express Newspaper*, September 26, 1998.

Birdsall, N., and Sabot, R. 1998. "Inequality as a Constraint on Growth in Latin America." In M. Seligson and J.T. Passe-Smith (eds.), *Development and Underdevelopment: The Political Economy of Global Inequality*. London: Boulder.

Bowker, M. 1997. "Nationalism and the Fall of the USSR." In A. Scott (ed.), *The Limits of Globalization: Cases and Arguments*. London: Routledge.

Bowman, K. 1997. *Should the Kuznets Curve be Relied on: Evidence from Post-1950 Development*. World Development, vol. 25, no. 1, January 1997.

Boyles, A. 1996. "World Watch." *The Bahai World 1994–1995*. Haifa: Bahai World Centre.

Brown, D.A.V. 2002. "Inbetweenity: Marginalization, Migration and Poverty among Haitians in the Turks and Caicos Islands." Unpublished paper.

Brown, M. 1993. *Fair Trade: Reform and Realities in the International Trading System*. London: Zed Books.

Bushrui et al. (eds.). 1993. *Transition to a Global Society*. Oxford: One World.

Chang, H.J. 1993. "The Political Economy of Industrial Policy in Korea." *Cambridge Journal of Economics*, Volume 17.

Chu, W. 1993. "Causes of Growth: A Study of Taiwan's Bicycle Industry." *Cambridge Journal of Economics*. Volume 21: 55–72.

Corbridge, S. 1995. *Development Studies: A Reader*. London: Arnold.

De Leong, J.B. "Lessons of History for the East Asian Financial Crisis." Available at http://www.j-bradford-deleong.net.

Durning, Charles. 1992. "How Much is Enough: The Consumer Society and the Future of the Earth" (NY: W.W. Norton and Co.) in Benjamin Barber, *Jihad vs. McWorld*. NY: Times Books, 1995.

Express. Editorial "Life After Lome." Wednesday, February 16, 2000.

Fairbank, J. 1973. *East Asia: Tradition and Transformation*. London: George Allen.

Ghai, Dharam. 1992. *Structural Adjustment, Global Integration and Social Democracy*. United Nations Research Institute for Social Development. Discussion Paper No. 37, October 1992.

Giddens, A. 2002. *Runaway World: How Globalization is Reshaping Our Lives*. London: Profile Books.

Gilpin, Robert. 1987. *The Political Economy of International Relations* (Princeton:

Princeton University Press) alluded to in Bushrui et al. (eds.), *Transition to a Global Society*. Oxford: One World, 1993.

Goldberg, Gertrude Schaffner, and Eleanor Kremen (eds.). 1990. *The Feminization of Poverty: Only in America?* New York: Praeger.

Guy, Arnold. 2000. *The End of the Third World*. Palgrave: MacMillan.

Harding, A., and Le Gales, P. 1997. "Globalization, Urban Change and Urban Policies in Britain and France." In A. Scott (ed.), *The Limits of Globalization: Cases and Arguments*. London: Routledge.

Harris, Nigel. 1987. *The End of the Third World: Newly Industrialized Countries and the Decline of an Ideology*. Viking Penguin Inc.

Haitink, A. "Small Developing States and International Organizations: The Attention for SIDS in the Work of the European Union, the United Nations and the Commonwealth." A background paper written for the seminar *Small Island Developing States: Their Vulnerability, Their Programme of Action for Sustainable Development, Their Opportunities for Post-Lome*. Brussels, 1–2 September 1998.

Hewitt de Alcántara, C. 1994. "Structural Adjustment in a Changing World." Briefing Paper No. 4, World Summit for Social Development, Submitted to United Nations Research Institute for Social Development, December 1994.

Hoogvelt, A. 1998. *Globalization and the Post-Colonial World*. MacMillan.

Isakovic, Z. 2002. "Democracy, Human Rights and Ethnic Conflicts in the Process of Globalization." Copenhagen Peace Research Institute Working Paper, no. 3.

Kassim, H. 1997. "Air Transport and Globalization: A Skeptical View." In A. Scott (ed.), *The Limits of Globalization: Cases and Arguments*. London: Routledge.

Kilminster, Richard. 1997. "Globalization as an Emergent Concept." In A. Scott (ed.), *The Limits of Globalization: Cases and Arguments*. Routledge: London.

Khoury, Inge. 1994. "The World Bank and the Feminization of Poverty." In Kevin Danaher (ed.), *50 Years Is Enough: The Case Against the World Bank and the International Monetary Fund*. Boston, MA: South End Press.

Klak, T. (ed.). 1998. *Globalization and Neoliberalism: The Caribbean Context*. Maryland: Rowman and Littlefield.

Knowles, Stephen. 2001. "Inequality and Economic Growth: The Empirical Relationship Reconsidered in the Light of Comparable Data." CREDIT Research Paper No. 01–03, March, cited in P.G. Ardeni, *Trade Liberalization and Inequality Between Households: A Review of the Recent Empirical Evidence*. Draft paper prepared for the CEPII workshop, "Methodological tools for assessing the sustainability of trade and other public policies," Brussels, 7–8 November 2002.

Lens, S. 1971. *Poverty: America's Enduring Paradox, a History of the Richest Nation's Unwon War*. New York: Crowell, 1971.

Lewis, O. 1998. "The Culture of Poverty." In M. Seligson and J.T. Passe-Smith (eds.), *Development and Underdevelopment: The Political Economy of Global Inequality*. London: Boulder.

Luard, E. 1990. "The Globalization of Politics" (Basingstoke: MacMillan) quoted in A. Scott (ed.) *The Limits of Globalization*. London: Routledge, 1997.

Maharaj, S. "Education the Key." In *Trinidad Express* Online, July 15, 2002.

Malaysia. Department of Statistics. 1996. *Overview of the Household Income Survey in Malaysia*. Income Measurement Canberra Group Papers. Canberra, 2–4 December 1996.

McDonald, Ian. 1998. "The World's New Tyranny." *Trinidad Express Newspaper,* Thursday, July 23, 1998.

McKibbin, W., and W. Martin. "The East Asian Crisis: Investigating Causes and Policy Responses." World Bank Policy Research Working Papers, Washington, August 1999.

NATUC. 1998. "Globalization and Social Policy." In The NATUC Column, *Trinidad Express Newspaper,* March 14, 1998.

Pantin, Raoul. 1999. "Caveat Emptor." *Trinidad Express Newspaper,* August 22, 1999.

_____. 1998. "No to Small Islands." *Trinidad Express Newspaper,* August 16, 1998.

Preston, P.W. 1996. *Development Theory: An Introduction.* Oxford: Blackwell Publishers.

Radelet, S., and J. Sachs. "The Onset of the East Asian Financial Crisis." A Briefing Note for Consulting Assistance on Economic Reform, Discussion Paper No. 27, Harvard Institute for International Development, March 1998.

Rampersad, C. 2002. "Knock Down Prices Breaking Locals." *Trinidad Express Online,* April 17, 2002.

Ryan, Selwyn. 1999. "Globalization and the Third World." *Trinidad Express Newspaper,* April 25, 1999.

_____. 1998. "New Rules for a Changing World." *Trinidad Express Newspaper,* August 2, 1998.

Sandrasagra, M. 2000. "Globalization Heightening Gender Inequalities." 10 Oct, 2000. Available at http://www.twnside.org.sg.

Schaeffer, R. 1997. *Understanding Globalization: The Social Consequences of Political, Economic, and Environmental Change.* Maryland: Rowman and Littlefield.

Shah, A. 2002. "Causes of Poverty: Poverty Facts and Stats." http://www.globalissues.org/TradeRelated/Facts.asp.

Sklair, L. 1994. "Capitalism and Development in Global Perspective." In L. Sklair (ed.), *Capitalism and Development.* London: Routledge.

Smith, G., and Naim, Moises. 2000. *Altered States: Globalization, Sovereignty, and Governance.* International Development Research Center.

Smith, Paul. 1992. "Industrialization and Environment." In Hewitt et al., *Industrialization and Development.* Oxford: Open University.

Stewart, P., and Garrahan, P. 1997. "Globalization, the Company and the Workplace: Some Interim Evidence from the Auto Industry in Britain." In A. Scott (ed.), *The Limits of Globalization: Cases and Arguments.* London: Routledge.

Thomas-Hope, E. 1985. "Return Migration and Its Implications for Caribbean Development." In R. Pastor (ed.), *Migration and Development in the Caribbean: The Unexplored Connection.* Boulder, CO: Westview Press.

Tsikata, Dzodzi. 1995. "Globalization: The Cause of Poor Women's Woes." A report on a UN conference entitled "Women's Empowerment, Globalization and Economic Restructuring," organized by UNIFEM, Sept. 1995.

Uimonen, P. 1997. *The Internet as a Tool for Social Development.* A paper written for the United Nations Research Institute for Social Development (Switzerland). http://www.isoc.org.

UNCTAD. 1997. Trade and Development Report. NY: UN.

UNRISD. 1995. "States of Disarray: The Social Effects of Globalization." A report for the World Summit for Social Development. In Ann Boyles, "World Watch" in *The Bahai World 1993–1994: An International Record.* Haifa: UHJ.

Wade, R. 1990. "Lessons from East Asia." In S. Corbridge (ed.), *Development Studies: A Reader*. London: Arnold, 1995.

_____. 2001. "The Rising Inequality of World Income Distribution." In *Finance and Development*. Vol. 38, no. 4, Dec. 2001.

Wallerstein, Immanuel. 1999. "Globalization or the Age of Transition? A Long-Term View of the Trajectory of the World-System." Fernand Braudel Center. http://www.rrojasdatabank.org/iwtrajws.htm.

_____. 1997. "States? Sovereignty? The Dilemmas of Capitalists in an Age of Transition." Available at: http://www.FBC.binghampton.edu/iwsovty.htm.

Watkins, Kevin. 1997. "Globalization and Liberalization: Implications for Poverty, Distribution and Inequality." In The Human Development Report, *Occasional Paper* 32.

Williams, M. "Well-travelled Trash." *Newsweek*, July 22, 2002.

"Women 2000: Gender, Equality and Peace for the 21st Century." 5–9 June 2000. Conference hosted by UN Division for the Advancement of Women.

Zakaria, F. 1996. "Paris is Burning." *The New Republic*, 22 January 1996, quoted in A. Boyles, "World Watch" in *The Bahai World*. Haifa: Bahai World Centre.

PART TWO.

The Economics of Globalization

Inequality and the Division of Gains at the Global Level: Some Reflections

Ramesh Ramsaran

Introduction

The widening gap between rich and poor nations and increasing inequality at the domestic level in many countries have led to renewed interest in the causes of poverty and the distribution of income at all levels. While a few developing states have managed to achieve significant progress in the postwar period, some others have made only moderate gains along the development path, and yet others have stagnated or retrogressed. This has happened despite a period of sustained global growth since the Second World War and some modest achievement with developmental assistance. The globalization process is benefiting some countries but a large number are being left behind, and this is raising questions about international economic policies and the role of international institutions dealing with development and governance. In response to the emerging economic and social conditions in the global economy, policies regarding trade, aid and finance are being reshaped, but there are serious questions about how well these address the concerns of poor nations who often have little influence on the decisions affecting them. Not for the first time the logic of economic theory is being overwhelmed by the interests of the powerful, and the concerns of the poor countries are seen as important only at the point where they begin to impact on the well-being of the rich.

To be sure, the division of the world into rich and poor camps is not a new phenomenon, nor is the rhetoric to reduce poverty at the national level, narrow the income gap at the international level and make the global community one rich happy family. Terms like developed and developing (or underdeveloped), industrialised and non-industrial (primary producing), center and periphery, First World as opposed to Second and Third World reflect a reality that has long plagued the international system. Setting development goals is not a new pastime. We had development decades in the 1960s and 1970s when the rich countries were expected to transfer 0.7 percent of their GNP in the form of aid to developing nations. In the early postwar decades it was widely believed that capital transfer was the catalytic factor in economic growth and development. The availability and the efficient use of technology was taken as given. All that was needed was a Marshall Plan for developing countries. Internal economic and political structures did not matter and growth could easily be translated into development benefiting the whole population. However, the experience has shown that even if total income (production) is increasing, it does not follow that average well-being is improving. "In distributing wealth economic structures both assign and respond to power. Within these structures, certain interests are privileged and resources are distributed for the benefit of some groups at the expense of others."[1]

The onset of the debt crisis in the 1980s and the resulting economic and social upheaval led to renewed interest in the problems besetting poor countries. Some gains made earlier were lost in the 1980s, and political, religious, and ethnic conflicts led to worsened conditions in a number of states with dwindling incomes and diminishing prospects. The goals adopted at the Millennium Summit in September 2000 grew out of the agreements and resolutions of world conferences organised by the United Nations in the 1990s. Among these goals is the need to reduce the number of people living in extreme poverty by half between 1990 and 2015, to reduce infant and child mortality rates by two thirds in the same period and enroll all children in primary school by 2015. While some progress was made in the 1990s, there is evidence that a number of countries are falling behind on several fronts.

There is some controversy over whether globalization is doing anything for the poor. Between 1988 and 1998, the incidence of global poverty fell by the laughable rate of 0.2 percent per year.[2] Despite this, import liberalisation is closely associated with International Monetary Fund (IMF) and World Bank loans. Poverty reduction and development involve very complex policy issues that straddle a range of concerns. With increasing interdependence at the global level, the pace of development is not only dependent on domestic conditions but on external factors as well. Political stability, appropriate social and economic policies, strong institutions and efficient management would assist in the optimal use of available resources. The state of the international economy and geopolitics affect international markets, prices and the movement of private capital. How well countries do depends critically on the interaction between domestic effort and global policies. Structural adjustment programs imposed on developing countries force changes in the domestic policy framework but provide no guarantees with respect to the liberalization of external markets or access to modern technologies and capital.

This paper looks at the nature of international economic policies and their effects on world poverty. The rest of it is organised as follows: The first section reflects on some of the premises of international trade theory. This is followed by an examination of trends in international trade and trade policy. In the third part we discuss the state of global poverty, and this is followed by a brief discussion on international economic assistance. The final section presents some concluding remarks.

Theory, Inequality and Reality

Economists tend to formulate theory based on very simplistic assumptions, both explicit and implicit, which are often far divorced from the real world, and because of this the theories are not infrequently of little use for policy. They assume efficiently functioning goods and factor markets, perfect credit markets, an impartial state, the absence of powerful interest groups and a degree of social harmony that exists neither at the local level nor the international level. Take, for example, the issue of income distribution. According to one World Bank report, "Early thinking on the effects of inequality on growth suggested that greater inequality might be good for growth, for example, by redistributing income to the rich, who save, from the poor who do not. This view implied a trade-off— more growth could be bought for the price of more inequality, with ambiguous effects on poor people."[3] This idea, however, is highly dubious. The evidence shows that in some cases the poor have a higher propensity to save than the rich. It shows that lower inequality can increase efficiency and economic growth through a variety of channels. The same World Bank report continues, "Unequal societies are more prone to difficulties in collective action, possibly reflected in dysfunctional institutions, political instability, a propensity for populist re-distributive policies, or greater volatility in policies all of which can lower growth. And to the extent that inequality in income or assets co-exists with imperfect credit markets, poor people may be unable to invest in their human and physical capital with adverse consequences for long term growth."[4]

At the international level there is no theory (fortunately) that argues for the rich countries to get richer so that earnings can be transferred back to poor countries to assist development. But by whatever means the rich get rich, the contention is that the developed nations have some kind of implied obligation to reduce international poverty and at the same time create markets for their own exports. Private capital transfers are driven by profits and take place out of self-interest arising mainly from the need for markets and national resources. In poor countries the argument is that income growth is low because savings (investment) are low, and savings are low because incomes are low. So to break out of this vicious cycle foreign capital is needed to supplement domestic savings. Interest payments on loans and profit remittances, however, often leave some countries worse off than before in the absence of an appropriate policy framework.

Trade theory is used to show how all countries can benefit from participation in international commerce. The theory of comparative advantage (or cost) in both its classical and neoclassical versions argues that if countries specialised in the production of goods in which they have a comparative advantage, world production would be maximised and all countries would be better off than they would be if they tried to meet all their needs from domestic production. The theory is founded on certain assumptions that, critics argue, make it of dubious value, since some of them do not obtain in the real world. Others contend that if some of the assumptions are relaxed the theory is still useful as an analytical tool. For example, if the idea of fixed productive resources or immobility of productive factors between nations is relaxed, this would not damage the theory. Comparative advantage can be made or achieved. The assumption that technology is fixed or similar and freely available to all nations raises more serious questions, as does perfect competition in goods markets. Other assumptions that do not accord with reality include the following: international prices are set by the forces of supply and demand, national governments play no role in international economic relations, and the gains from trade that accrue to any country benefit the nationals of that country. As M.P. Todaro explains,

> In reality the world economy is characterised by rapid change while factors of production are fixed neither in quantity nor quality. Not only do capital accumulation and human resource development take place all the time, but trade has always been and will continue to be one of the main determinants of the unequal growth of productive resources in different nations. This is especially true with respect to those resources most crucial to growth and development such as physical capital, entrepreneurial abilities, scientific capacities, the ability to carry out technological

research and development and the upgrading of technical skills in the labor force.[5]

In the context of the development debate of the 1950s, Raul Prebisch launched a blistering attack on the classical and neoclassical trade doctrine to the extent that it was used to suggest that the role of Latin America was to produce food and raw materials for industrial countries. He contended that a basic assumption was violated if the benefits of technical progress were not shared by all countries either in the form of lower prices or higher incomes. The evidence, he argued, showed that the price of primary exports tended to lag behind that of manufactured goods, or to put it differently, the secular terms of trade tended to turn against primary production in the long term. Latin America needed to industrialize if it was to benefit from international trade.[6]

Given that primary exports to the center were associated with low income and price elasticity of demand, the perception in the 1950s and 1960s was that such exports could not serve as an engine of growth. The growth of synthetics as substitutes for natural products further weakened the export position of poor countries, who saw in import substitution a way to develop a manufacturing sector and reduce their dependence on primary production. Technology was also leading to the more efficient use of materials, resulting in lower demand.

Sir Arthur Lewis approached the issue of industrialization with a different motive and from a different angle. He argued for industrialization as a means of creating employment and drawing off the excess labour from the agricultural sector where the increased productivity could lead to higher real incomes. For the small countries of the Caribbean he felt export was essential for survival. A crucial assumption was that capitalist expansion would take place through reinvestment of profits.[7] Subsequent developments would show not only that the capital intensive technologies used in the manufacturing sector resulted in little job creation but that much more was needed for increasing productivity in the agricultural sector than the simple removal of people. In fact, the higher wages paid to non-agricultural activities (including makeshift government employment programs) and the failure to increase productivity and income in agriculture have led to a flight of people from the sector resulting in its decline throughout the Caribbean.

In many developing countries, import substitution was adopted as a strategy of development and was pursued to the neglect of agriculture, which was associated with backwardness and colonialism. In most cases the industrial sector has failed to deliver either as generator of employment or as a base for export development. The protectionist framework attracted foreign investors (largely traditional suppliers) mainly interested in protecting their share of the local market, and there was little incentive to export. The poor quality product resulting from the lack of competition and the high cost of production made it difficult to penetrate foreign markets even if there was domestic pressure to do so. In few countries was the import substitution strategy converted into an export-oriented strategy producing industrial goods for foreign markets. High growth rates became closely associated with countries with vibrant export sectors.

Not surprisingly following the debt crisis of the 1980s, the international financial institutions (IFIs) became strong advocates for more open trade and investment strategies and pushed for the dismantling of the protectionist framework in developing countries, arguing that the more competitive environment would encourage export growth and a better allocation of resources. There was some doubt that the East Asian examples could be replicated several times over, and that doubt remains, given that a few countries account for most of the manufactured exports from the developing world.

Between 1970 and 1999 the merchandise exports of developing countries grew at an average annual rate of 12 percent compared to 10 percent for world trade as a whole, resulting in their share of world merchandise exports increasing from one fourth to almost one third.[8] The composition of their exports has changed particularly since the 1980s. At the end of the 1990s, manufactures accounted for 70 percent of developing countries' exports as compared to around 20 percent for much of the 1970s. The share of agricultural commodities fell from about 20 percent to 10 percent during the same period.[9] It is important to note, however, that with "the exception of a few East Asian first-tier newly industrialising economies (NIEs) with a significant industrial base, which were already closely integrated into the global trading system developing countries exports are still concentrated on products developed essentially from the exploitation of natural resources and the use of unskilled labour, which have limited prospects for productivity growth and lack dynamism in world markets."[10]

International Trade, Poverty and Developing Countries

One of the most powerful arguments for an open world trading system is that countries are not constrained by domestic markets and access to external resources allows them to produce outside the confines of domestic resource availability. Some countries, however, are better positioned than others to exploit the opportunities offered by the global system, which many agree does not offer a level playing field. A large number of developing countries are still dependent on the export of commodities that are associated with fluctuating prices and demand.[11] Even with respect to manufactures there is evidence of a decline in developing countries' terms of trade.[12] One reason is their inferior level of scientific and technological capacity. It has been estimated that although the share of developed countries in world manufactured exports fell from more than 80 percent to 70 percent over the last two decades, their share in world manufacturing income (value added) rose.[13]

Despite what was said earlier about the growth of developing countries' exports, for almost all developing countries, imports expanded at a faster rate than exports, resulting in a deterioration of their trade balance. There are several factors operating here. One of course is access to the markets of the developed countries; these are often closed to exports in which developing countries have a comparative advantage. "When developing countries export to rich country markets, they face tariff barriers that are four times higher than those encountered by rich countries. Those barriers cost them US$100 billion a year — twice as much as they receive in aid."[14] Incidentally, it is estimated that this is how much it would take in aid to cut poverty in half by 2015. A recent report has argued that while world trade could be a powerful motor to reduce poverty and support economic growth, the rules that govern it are rigged in favour of the rich.[15] "If Africa, East Asia, South Asia and Latin America were each to increase their share of world exports by one percent, the resulting gains in income could lift 128 million people out of poverty."[16] As indicated earlier, the highest tariffs (often accompanied by quotas) are on agricultural and textile products and labour intensive manufactures — the goods on which the least developed of the developing countries depend. These countries account for only 0.4 percent of total world trade.

Subsidies are another issue in contention. By subsidising their farmers the rich countries not only make it difficult for exports from other countries to compete but encourage overproduction, which is dumped on the world market. This depresses prices, thus affecting producers even in their own countries. Special interests have made it difficult to level the playing field with respect to products of particular interest to poor countries. Agricultural subsidies to farmers in the US, Europe, and Japan have risen to almost $1 billion a day.[17]

Together with the difficulties faced by developing countries in the markets of the rich nations, aid levels have been falling. The G-7 countries account for three quarters of all Official Development Assistance (ODA). The four largest donors—Japan, United States, France and Germany in that order—who account for 60 percent of ODA, made the largest cuts in the 1990s. In ODA/GNP terms, aid from the United States has fallen by half since 1990, while that of France and Germany has fallen by around 40 percent since the early part of the decade.[18] For the US the ODA/GNP ratio in 1999 was 0.10 percent as compared to 0.20 percent in the early 1980s. Over the same period the UK's ratio dropped from 0.34 percent to 0.23 percent, and France's from 0.59 percent to 0.39 percent.

While official sector flows into developing countries rose from US$30 to US$80 billion over the last 20 years, private sector investment grew even more—from US$45 billion to peak at US$300 billion during the same period.[19] These flows, however, do not go to the poorest countries. In 1998 the five largest host countries (China, Brazil, Mexico, Singapore and Indonesia) accounted for 55 percent of foreign direct investment inflows as compared to 41 percent in 1990. The concentration in fact has increased.[20]

The Social Divide

Growth in GDP is often seen as a major indicator of economic performance. It is also widely acknowledged that growth is not synonymous with development, since it says little about the distribution of income or the transformation of the economy. Trickle-down theories have proved to be highly misleading, and one simply can't assume that the poor benefit from GDP growth or exports growth.

If we look at the growth figures for developing countries as a group, these figures compare well with the world average and with those of the developed countries. In the 1990s they grew twice as fast as the developed countries. A closer look at Table 1 will show, however, that once the few high-growth countries are excluded, the performance of the rest is not so impressive.

A recent UN report has noted:

> [During] the past five decades world income increased seven fold (in real GDP) and income per person more than tripled (in per capita GDP). But this gain has been spread very unequally nationally and internationally and the inequality is increasing. Between 1960 and 1991, the share of world income for the richest 20 percent of the global population rose from 70 percent to 85 percent. Over the same period, all but the richest quintile saw their share of world income fall and the meagre share for the poorest 20 percent declined from 2.3 percent to 1.4 percent.[21]

Table 1.
Real[1] GDP Growth in the World Economy, 1981–1999
(Average Percentage Change)

Country/Region	1981–1990	1991–1999
World	2.9	2.4
Developed Economies	3.0	2.2
Economies in Transition	1.8	-3.5
Developing Countries	2.3	4.4
Of which:		
Latin America	1.1	3.0
Africa	2.0	2.1
Western Asia	-2.8	2.2
Eastern & Southern Asia	7.0	6.5
(excluding China)	6.6	5.2
East Asia	7.0	-5.3
South Asia	5.3	4.9
China	9.1	10.3

1. 1995 dollars

Source: UN, *World Economic and Social Survey,* 2000.

The gap between the developed and the developing countries has been widening. Between 1980 and 1999, real per capita GDP (1995 dollars) of the developed economies increased by 45 percent, while for the developing countries as a group it increased by 24 percent. For the economies in transition and for some developing countries it actually fell. In Africa, the decline was 12 percent while in Western Asia it was 48 percent. Table 2 shows the world distribution of income in the year 2000, and gives an indication of the concentration of wealth at the global level. In 2000, about three quarters of the world's population had a per capita income of less than US$3,000 and accounted for about 11 percent of world income. In 1993 it was estimated that the poorest 10 percent of the world's people had only 1.6 percent of the income of the richest 10 percent, while the richest 1 percent of the world people received as much income as the poorest 57 percent.[22]

In 1990 there were 1.3 billion people living on less than US$1 a day and 2.7 billion living on less than US$2 a day. In the 1990s there was a decline in the overall poverty rates, but this was largely driven by high rates of growth in countries with large numbers of poor people. In China, for example, which had one fourth of the world's poor in 1990, per capita GDP grew by 9.5 percent per year. The number of poor people in South Asia and sub-Saharan Africa actually grew in the 1990s. It might be added that the number of least-developed countries has grown in the last 30 years.

Table 2.
Gross National Income (GNP) Total and Per Capita, 2000

Income Group $US	No. of Economies	GNP US$	Pop. in Millions Bill	GNP per Capita, $US
Low ($755 or less)	63	997	2,460	410
Lower middle ($756–2,995)	54	2,324	2,048	1,130
Upper middle ($2,996–9,265)	38	3,001	647	4,640
High ($9,266 or more)	52	24,994	903	27,680
World	207	31,315	6,057	5,170

Source: World Bank, *Atlas 2002.*

Table 3
The Poor in Numbers

Region	Millions living on US$1 a day or less 1990	1998	Millions living on US$2 a day or less 1990	1998
East Asia and Pacific	452	267	1,084	885
excluding China	92	54	285	252
Europe and Central Asia	7	18	44	98
Latin America and the Caribbean	74	61	167	159
Middle East and North Africa	6	6	59	85
South Asia	495	522	976	1,095
Sub-Saharan Africa	242	302	388	489
Total	1,276	1,175	2,718	2,812
excluding China	916	961	1,919	2,179

Source: World Bank, *World Development Indicators 2001.*

The growth of the world output in the postwar period has benefited some countries more than others and has also resulted in progress in a number of areas. Life expectancy at birth has increased in most countries. "A child born today can expect to live eight years longer than one born 30 years ago. Many more people can read and write, with the adult literacy rate having increased from an estimated 47 percent in 1970 to 73 percent in 1999. The share of rural families with access to safe water has grown more than fivefold."[23] Average incomes in developing countries have also increased but not as fast as in the rich countries.

Despite some progress in the social areas, real challenges remain. Though the proportion of the world's people living in extreme poverty fell from 29 percent in 1990 to 23 percent in 1999, the richest 5 percent of the world's people have incomes 114 times those of the poorest 5 percent. One impact of poverty is malnutrition, which remains a major problem. There are 150 million underweight children in the developing world. In developing countries one child in three does not complete five years of schooling. Some 60 percent of the 110 million children not in school in developing nations are girls. In poor nations some 11 million children under five die each year, mostly of preventable causes. With respect to access to safe water, almost 20 percent of the world's people depend on unimproved water supplies to meet their daily needs.

The Aid Conundrum

Explicit (or implicit) in international relations discussions of the 1950s was the view that rising living standards worldwide would contribute to global peace. Aid grew into an industry involving a whole complex of institutions, special programs, developmental targets, consultants, high level meetings, and studies. Then the Cold War emerged and with the emphasis on security and control, aid-giving had less to do with need and poverty and was influenced more by strategic location, ideological factors and traditional ties. Economic factors such as the availability of materials and markets were not unimportant in the disbursement of aid. International institutions such as the IMF and World Bank, which were largely controlled by the United States and a few Western countries, also favoured countries taking certain ideological positions. Even after the Cold War, when it was expected that the peace dividend would lead to a more intensified fight against poverty, other types of conflicts and distractions competed for time and resources on a scale not previously envisaged. Terrorism has now replaced communism as the enemy, and the position taken by countries may well determine their qualification for assistance.

The prevailing economic and social conditions in most of the developing world have raised questions about the effectiveness of the whole postwar aid effort including the performance of the expensive international institutions, which many feel need to be restructured and reoriented, giving developing countries a greater voice in decision making. One scholar has noted that while foreign aid may have made a net addition to the stock of physical and human capital in developing countries, the indications are that "much foreign aid, once all direct and indirect effects are taken into account, has resulted in an increase in unproductive consumption, the amassing of monetary reserves and capital flight and perhaps in a decline in the productivity of investment."[24] The present reality is that one person in five lives on less than US$1 a day, and one in seven suffers from chronic hunger.[25] Health and environmental threats continue to pose major challenges to the world community. With growing populations, land and natural resources (for example, soil, forests, and freshwater) are coming under greater pressure. Already 24 million people have died from HIV/AIDS since the disease was first discovered; 40 million are living with it.[26]

While it is widely felt that aid can still play a developmental role, the real value of aid to developing countries fell by some 8 percent in the 1990s. Not all poor countries are in the same position, and there are different perspectives on solutions. Donors tend to lump all poor countries together and are placing increasing emphasis on domestic reforms while reducing their own aid effort. On the issue of trade there is pressure on developing countries to lower tariffs and other trade barriers in order to create more competitive conditions and encourage exports. Some think this is simplistic, and while they would not advocate "infant industry protection," there is need for a "more highly nuanced approach to each country's particular situation and stage of development…. Rapid trade liberalisation for all developing countries in every sector may condemn countries to low levels of industrialisation and dependence on narrow ranges of commodities for export."[27] Some rich countries seemed to have forgotten [their]

> own experience of the immense complexities of development and industrialisation policy. France, Germany, the United Kingdom and the United States all developed their domestic industries behind tariff walls and with below market rate loans. Indeed, tariffs were positively correlated with economic growth for these and six other developed countries between 1875 and 1914. More recently, Japan, Chinese Taipei and South Korea all used measures which were anything but "free trade" to industrialise, many of which are now banned under WTO rules or soon will be.[28]

Concluding Observations

It is being increasingly recognised that while the forces of globalisation have brought significant benefits to some, others have not shared in the gains. It is estimated that some 2.8 billion (nearly half the world's population) live on less than US$2 a day. Aggregate statistics on developing countries tend to hide major differences in the performance and positions of individual countries. For instance, it is often noted that since the early 1980s, the exports of the developing countries have grown faster than the world average, and much of that growth has been in manufactures; on closer examination, however, it can be seen that with "the exception of a few East Asian first tier newly industrialising economies (NIEs) with a significant industrial base ... developing country exports are still concentrated on products derived essentially from the exploitation of natural resources and the use of unskilled labour, which have limited prospects for productivity growth and lack dynamism in world markets."[29]

The level of poverty varies widely from country to country. In Bangladesh, India and most African countries, the percentage of people living below the national poverty line is over 40. In Jamaica the estimate is 34 percent (1992) as compared to 21 percent (1992) in Trinidad and Tobago. Poverty levels in rural areas are generally higher than in urban areas. It is widely recognised that poverty stems from both internal and external factors. At the domestic level, social and economic policies, educational opportunities, governance, and the quality of institutions affect the standard of living. At the external level, global trade, capital flows, official development assistance, technological advance, disease and conflicts are among the factors that affect social well-being. On the issue of poverty the rhetoric of the rich countries is not often reflected in their actions. "It is unreasonable for OECD Member country governments to continue to call for a new trade round while cutting aid budgets, delaying effective debt relief, denying exports from least developed countries and endlessly stalling and back-loading agreements on tariff reduction in such crucial areas for poor countries as agriculture, textiles and processed goods."[30]

As indicated before, the goods in which poor countries have a comparative advantage are the ones facing the highest barriers in the rich countries' markets. Official Development Assistance (ODA) not only declined in the 1990s, but as a share of total net resource flows to developing countries, the percentage dropped from 37 percent in 1992 to 21 percent in 1999. Private flows, particularly direct foreign investment, have increased significantly, but these have been confined to a small number of countries. The question of access to modern technology has always been a difficult one, given that research and development is largely undertaken by transnational corporations who seek to gain maximum benefits from their investment. A large number of countries have not been able to break the vicious circle, and therefore have not been able to participate effectively in international trade by developing products that can compete in international markets.

Endnotes

1. J. Gershman and A. Irwin, "Getting a Grip on Global Economy," in *Dying for Growth*, by J. Yong Kim et al. (Maine: Common Courage Press, Monroe House, 2000).
2. See Kevin Watkins, "Making Globalisation Work for the Poor," *Finance and Development* (March 2002).
3. World Bank, *World Development Report 2000/2001* (Washington, D.C.: World Bank, 2001), p. 56.
4. Ibid.
5. M.P. Todaro, *Economics for a Developing World* (London: Longman Group Limited, 1977), p. 305.
6. See Raul Prebisch, "The Economic Development of Latin America and Its Principal Problems," *Economic Bulletin for Latin America* (Feb. 1961).
7. See W.A. Lewis, "Economic Development with Unlimited Supplies of Labour," *The Manchester School* (May 1954).
8. See UNCTAD, *Trade and Development Report 2002* (New York: UN, 2002), p. 51.
9. Ibid.
10. Ibid.
11. Between 1998 and 2001, for example, prices of tropical beverages fell by an average rate of 18.4 percent per year. Between 1997 and 1999 the average rate of decline for sugar prices was 18.7 percent, but there was some recovery in 2000 and 2001. See UNCTAD report, *op cit.*
12. Ibid., p. 118.
13. Ibid., pp. 51–55.
14. *Rigged Rules and Double Standards*, Oxfam report, www.maketradefair.com.
15. Ibid.
16. Ibid.
17. See Wole Akande, "Agricultural Subsidies in Rich Countries: Barriers to Fair Trade for Africa," www.globalpolicy.org/globaliz/econ/2002/0406subsidies.htm.
18. See OECD, *Development Cooperation 2000* (Paris: OECD, 2001), p. 28.
119. Ibid., p. 61.
20. See UN, *World Investment Report 1999* (New York: UN, 1999), p. 18.
21. UNDP, *Human Development Report 1994* (New York: UN, 1994), p. 35.
22. Ibid, p. 23.
23. UNDP, *Human Development Report 2001* (New York: UN, 2001), p. 10.
24. K. Griffin and A.P. Khan, *Globalisation and the Developing World* (Geneva: UNRISD, 1992), p. 33.
25. See OECD, *op. cit.*, p. 44.
26. World Bank, *World Development Indicators 2002* (Washington, D.C.: World Bank, 2002), pp. 6–15.
27. OECD, *op. cit.*, p. 71.
28. Ibid.
29. UNCTAD, *op cit.*, p. 14.
30. Ibid., p. 72.

Small Regional Trade Agreements (RTAs) and Export Performance of Member Countries: Trinidad and Tobago's Experience Within CARICOM

Roger Hosein

Abstract

An increasing amount of global trade occurs within regional trade agreements. Within these trade blocs, there is generally an absence of internal trade barriers and so member country exports are offered some amount of shelter from extra-regional competitors. This paper explores the impact on Trinidad and Tobago's export patterns of membership in the regional agreement, CARICOM. Using data for the time period 1973–98 and employing specialization and regional orientation indices, this paper found that the exports of Trinidad and Tobago to CARICOM is reflective of a bias in favor of the protected regional market.

Introduction

The global economy is currently witnessing a growing wave of regionalism. In 1991, the world economy witnessed the formation of MERCO-SUR, a new regional trade agreement (RTA) in South America. In 1993, the North American Free Trade Agreement (NAFTA) between Mexico, Canada and the USA was created. In addition, in Africa several new preferential trading agreements founded on old ones have been revitalized, including the Union Economic et Monaitarie de l' Africa Occidentale, which was formerly the Communaute Economique Ouest-Africaine.

This new regionalism is such that some 55 percent to 60 percent of total international trade is transacted within the trade areas (Schiff and Winters 1998). In practice, RTAs are designed to offer reciprocal trading preferences to those within the RTA and discriminate against those countries outside it. However, this drift towards increased RTA presence in the global economy has sprouted an important concern: RTAs, while potentially acting as instruments for trade creation within the membership pact, impose an opportunity cost, especially in small economies, of diverting trade from more efficient extra-regional partners.

This paper addresses the important issue of the influence of RTA membership on the export performance of member countries, with special reference to Trinidad and Tobago (Trinidad and Tobago) within the Caribbean Community (CARICOM). The argument is developed as follows: section one provides a brief outline of Caricom and some of the main economic characteristics of its members; section two discusses the theoretical impact of an RTA on the export performance of a small developing economy; and section three provides a brief discussion of the export performance of several RTAs. In section four, the trends in total Caricom exports and Caricom exports as a proportion of total exports are discussed. This section also comments on the trends in the various single digit Standard International Trade Classifications (SITCs) in Trinidad and Tobago's total intra-Caricom exports[1] and presents evidence from specialization and regional orientation indices concerning the nature of Trinidad and Tobago's intra-Caricom export trade, to determine empirically whether any evidence exists of intra-regional bias towards the home market. The next section reviews Caricom and Trinidad and Tobago's extra-regional trade relations for the last few years and explores proposals by the Trinidad and Tobago government for the near future.

CARICOM

For Trinidad and Tobago, the issue of the influence of an RTA on export performance is especially important, as independence in this twin island republic was preceded by an attempt at integration through the West Indian Federation. Federation, which germinated in the colonial era

(1958), was terminated in 1962, when insularity prevailed and national independence was allowed ascendancy over regional integration. In the initial stages of independence, a plan for a customs union was drawn up, but more emphasis was placed on the non-economic areas of interest within the Federation. In many ways, although the Federation collapsed, it sowed the seeds of what would eventually become Caricom.

On 1 May 1968, 12 countries of the English speaking Caribbean entered into agreement to create CARIFTA (Caribbean Free Trade Area). The CARIFTA agreement, however, did not significantly boost the manufacturing export performance of Caribbean countries, especially for the larger members such as Jamaica and Trinidad and Tobago. This failure encouraged a greater call for more pronounced integration.

By 1973, the integration of the economies of the Caribbean became more of a reality with the signing of the Treaty of Chaguaramas, the objective of which was CARICOM (Caribbean Common Market). The initial signatories were Barbados, Jamaica, Guyana and Trinidad and Tobago. Other territories joined and by 4 July 1983 the Bahamas became the thirteenth member state. The British Virgin Islands and the Turks and Caicos Islands became associated members of Caricom in July 1991. Several other members of the Commonwealth Caribbean and some Latin American countries now enjoy observer status in Caricom. On 14 July 1995, Suriname became the fourteenth member of Caricom.

The basic trading rule of Caricom is that member countries allow the

Table 1.
Some macroeconomic indicators of
CARICOM member countries.

Country	GDP (US$ billions 1998)	Average annual rate of inflation (1998)	GNP per capita annual growth rate (1990-1998)	Total population (millions) 1998	Agriculture (as % of GDP) 1998	Industry (as % of GDP) 1998	Services (as % of GDP) 1998	Human Development Indicators (HDI) 1998
Antigua/Barbuda	0.6	2.8	3.5	0.1	4	18.9	77.1	0.833
Bahamas	3.7e	...	-0.9	0.3	...	...	...	0.844
Barbados	2.3	3.8	0.7	0.3	6.6	20	73.4	0.858
Belize	0.7	0.9	0.5	0.2	18.7	25.5	55.8	0.777
Dominica	0.2	-0.4	1.4	0.1	20.2	22.5	57.3	0.793
Grenada	0.3	3.6	2.2	0.1	8.4	22.2	69.4	0.785
Guyana	0.7	3.2	8.9	0.8	34.7	32.5	32.8	0.709
Jamaica	6.4	5	0.6	2.5	8	33.7	58.4	0.735
Montserrat								
St. Kitts/Nevis	0.3	3.3	4.5	...	4.6	24.3	71.1	0.798
St. Lucia	0.6	2	1.4	0.2	8.1	18.9	72.9	0.728
St. Vincent	0.3	2.3	2.6	0.1	10.9	26.9	62.2	0.738
T&T	6.4	6.7	2.1	1.3	1.8	47.5	50.7	0.793
Suriname	0.3f	...	0.5	0.4	...	...	...	0.766

Source: United Nations (2000). e: data refers to 1995, f: data refers to 1996.

unrestricted flow of goods that originate within the member countries. Tables 1 and 2 identify some basic economic characteristics of Caricom member countries.

In 1998, Trinidad and Tobago recorded a GDP of US$6.4 billion, the highest among all the member countries (Jamaica also shared a similar aggregate level of economic activity).[2] All the other Caricom territories, except the Bahamas and Barbados, have a level of economic activity lower than US$1 billion per annum, with Dominica hosting the lowest GDP of US$0.2 billion in 1998. In total the GDP of the Caricom countries is US$22.8 billion (excluding Montserrat) as compared to US$106.7 billion for a country like Portugal in 1998.[3] Only in Trinidad and Tobago and Jamaica is there an industrial base that accounts for more than 33 percent of the total level of economic activity. In particular, Jamaica's industrial sector accounted for 33.7 percent of GDP in 1998 while that of Trinidad and Tobago accounted for 47.5 percent. Only in Guyana and Trinidad and Tobago do services contribute less than 51 percent to GDP. According to the UN's *Human Development Report* (2000), Caricom member countries experience medium to high standards of living as reflected in Human Development Index (HDI) scores ranging from 0.709 in Guyana to 0.858 in Barbados.

Table 2. Openness in CARICOM countries

Country	Exports of goods and services (as % GDP) 1999, E/GDP	Imports of goods and services (as % GDP) 1999, M/GDP
Antigua/Barbuda	74.8	82.9
Bahamas	...	...
Barbados	65.4	65
Belize	48.5	53.5
Dominica	55.4	60.3
Grenada	37.9	61.4
Guyana	99	107.5
Jamaica	49.3	62.4
St. Kitts/Nevis	51.4	77.2
St. Lucia	64.9	68.2
St. Vincent	50.2	71.3
Trinidad & Tobago	41.3	56.4
Suriname	...	...

Source: United Nations, *Human Development Report 2001*.

Table 2 provides information on two standard indicators of trade openness: exports as a proportion of GDP ($^E/_{GDP}$) and imports as a proportion of GDP ($^M/_{GDP}$). Concerning $^E/_{GDP}$, the Guyanese economy is the most open among its Caricom counterparts with an $^E/_{GDP}$ ratio of 99 percent. The least open Caricom country, by this measure, is Grenada with an $^E/_{GDP}$ ratio of 37.9 percent. From the perspective of $^M/_{GDP}$, the most open Caricom economy is still Guyana with a ratio of 107.5 percent. The Caricom member country with the lowest $^M/_{GDP}$ ratio is Belize, which had an average propensity to import of 53.5 percent. Altogether these ratios reflect a high degree of trade openness among the countries which make up Caricom.

Small Regional Trade Agreements and Export Performance

For decades Caribbean thinkers have called for West Indian integration. Many of their founding arguments were based on the notion of commonalities among the islands, including language, history and culture. More importantly, integration of the countries of the Caribbean archipelago was viewed as an obvious strategy to overcome some of the vulnerability and economic weaknesses associated with small size (Demas 1965).[4]

Lewis was one of the first to call for West Indian integration, as an integral part of his industrialization proposition. In his 1950 article, "Industrialization of the British West Indies," he argued that in the small economies of the Caribbean, any serious attempts at industrialization should be preceded by a customs union. Lewis also argued that in the context of the peculiarities of the West Indian communities, an integration agreement would partly break the bottlenecks imposed by small market size, resource unavailability and uncertainty. However, although Lewis argued in favor of a customs union, he was careful to point out that it should not act as a substitute for the procurement of extra-regional markets, as the entire population of the Caribbean was insufficient to sustain an aggregate demand high enough for domestic producers to benefit from economies of scale (Lewis 1950). Thus, Lewis' idea of a customs union as a launching pad was essentially short term.

Demas (1965) argued that given the structural limitations of the small, highly open, developing countries of the Caribbean region, trade and integration could play important roles in their developmental process. Demas noted that in the context of the small markets Caribbean countries represented, manufacturing would only be successful if it pursued the extra-regional markets.

The 1960s would witness the emergence of a group of Caribbean economists popularly known as the New World Group. The New World Group was closely aligned with the University of the West Indies, and they took it upon themselves to change the very mode of thinking of Caribbean people. They also encouraged closer ties among Caribbean nations and recommended greater flirtation with elements of an import substituting strategy. These economists also recognized the potential of the Caribbean market as a starting point. Two of the main proponents, Brewster and Thomas (1967), argued that regional integration would provide the infrastructural base to bolster regional production levels. The basic proposal made by Brewster and Thomas was that since an advanced industrial economy was founded upon a few basic materials[5] and these basic but vital raw materials were available within the Caribbean region, a pooling of resources, in the context of a well laid out regional integration plan, could lead to a widening and strengthening of the production platform in the region. It should be noted that in outlining their propositions these authors, unlike Lewis and Demas, placed emphasis on the intra-regional market.

While there may be distinct economic advantages for greater trade between less developed countries in general, in the context of small regional trading blocks such as Caricom, it is likely that goods formerly produced under national Import Substituting Industrialization programs would now be produced under regional ISI programs, even though free trade existed within the trade bloc.[6] In corroboration of such an eventuality, Gonzales (1990) points out that a regional trade bloc[6] such as CARICOM can "encourage countries to postpone extra-regional plans or divert current exports to the regional market" (Gonzales 1990, 10).

In a similar mode of reasoning, Milner (1993) argued that, although possible, it is not inevitable that trade regime bias is reduced within a customs union. The precise outcome is a function of the nature and membership of the union and of the adopted external tariffs that are implemented—common or otherwise. In particular, Milner noted that

> the less competitive is regional production relative to global production and the higher are external tariffs, the greater is the degree of trade regime (i.e. anti-export) bias that will persist even with fully liberalized regional trade (367).[7]

Additionally, and from the perspective of the new growth theories, trade enhances the innovative process by facilitating economies of scale, technological spillovers, and the elimination of the need for replication of research and development in different countries. It may also be argued that by trading with developed countries, less developed countries gain greater exposure and access to the larger research and development pool of knowledge characteristic of developing countries.[8] In this sense, therefore, an RTA among less developed countries such as those of Caricom may foster the growth of export sectors which are weak in terms of technological dynamism. In addition, while the markets in developed countries are consumer oriented, demanding vibrant and responsive export capabilities, those in less developed countries are producer oriented and may allow the nurturing of X-inefficient export structures which would be unable to penetrate extra-regional markets.

In a similar vein of reasoning, Tybout (1992) notes that the absence of rigid competitive pressure (as may occur within Caricom) may allow or encourage a sheltered firm to subsist with a single, technically weak production function. In particular, Tybout notes that "new processes diffuse through an industry as managers learn about them and older vintage machines depreciate. This means that there is no single production function, and it is a mistake to think of productivity growth as an orderly shift in technology. Rather, the processes of learning, innovation, investment, entry and exit are what matter" (1992, 191).

Tybout's point implies that a vibrant and competitive export sector (as stimulated by free trade) may not be forthcoming in the context of a small RTA such as Caricom, and as a consequence export structures of member countries within small RTAs may be weak and geared towards the safer (protected) market.

Given its inception in 1973, sufficient time has since elapsed in pursuing economic integration to allow an assessment to be made of the impact of Caricom membership on Trinidad and Tobago's exports and the fertility of Caricom in terms of nurturing the growth of export sectors from Trinidad and Tobago that are competitive extra-regionally. Before such an exercise is undertaken, however, a brief discussion of the export performance of some trade blocs is in order.

Export Performance of Trade Blocs
and Member Countries

Table 3 shows the export performance for the period 1995–99 of NAFTA and the EU alongside some trade blocs in Latin America and the Caribbean. Amongst the trade blocs listed, for the period 1995–99 the European Union experienced the greatest amount of intra-regional exports amounting to US$1,259 billion in 1995 and growing to reach US$1,376 billion by 1999, an increase of 9.3 percent. The growth of NAFTA's exports

Table 3. Trade bloc exports.

year	ACS	ANDEAN GROUP	CACM	MERCOSUR	LAIA	OECS	NAFTA	EU	Caricom
1995	10448	4812	1595	14199	35299	38	394472	1259699	305
1996	10894	4692	1723	17075	37949	32	437804	1273430	906
1997	11870	5627	1973	20772	45018	35	496423	1162419	971
1998	12260	5427	1988	20352	42860	34	521649	1226988	1017
1999	12002	4012	2102	15313	35152	36	581162	1376314	1089
3(b) Exports within bloc as % of total exports									
	ACS	ANDEAN GROUP	CACM	MERCOSUR	LAIA	OECS	NAFTA	EU	Caricom
1995	8.1	12	21.7	20.3	17.1	11.7	46.2	62.4	14.6
1996	7.1	10.3	22.0	22.7	16.3	9.1	47.6	61.4	13.3
1997	7.0	11.8	18.1	24.8	17.4	9.6	49.1	55.5	14.4
1998	7.1	13.9	15.6	25	16.9	10.4	51.7	57.0	17.3
1999	5.9	9.3	11.6	20.5	13.0	7.3	54.6	62.6	15.3
3(c) Total exports by bloc as % of world exports									
	ACS	ANDEAN GROUP	CACM	MERCOSUR	LAIA	OECS	NAFTA	EU	Caricom
1995	2.6	0.8	0.1	1.4	4.1	0	16.8	39.8	0.1
1996	2.9	0.9	0.1	1.4	4.4	0	17.4	39.2	0.1
1997	3.1	0.9	0.2	1.5	4.7	0	18.4	38.0	0.1
1998	3.2	0.7	0.2	1.5	4.7	0	18.7	39.9	0.1
1999	3.6	0.8	0.3	1.3	4.8	0	18.8	38.9	0.1

*Source:*World Develomment Indicators (2001).

was much sharper, increasing 47.4 percent to move from US$394 billion in 1995 to reach US$581 billion by 1999. All of the trade blocs within the Latin American region pale in comparison to the export levels of the EU and NAFTA. Among the Latin American and Caribbean trade blocs, Caricom's exports increased from US$305 million to US$1,089 million between 1995 and 1999, at current prices. In the larger trade blocs of NAFTA and the EU, intra-regional exports as a proportion of total exports increased between 1995 and 1999. Of the other trade blocs only Caricom and Mercosur's increased.

One way to measure the international importance of a trade bloc is in terms of the amount of total exports that the intra-regional exports account for. As panel (c) of Table 3 reflects, the two largest trade blocs (by this measure) are NAFTA and the EU, which in 1999 accounted for 18.8 percent and 38.9 percent of world exports respectively. The Caricom share of world exports remained at the 0.1 percent level between 1995 and 1999.

Trinidad and Tobago's Intra-Caricom Export Performance[9]

Commodity Composition

In 1973, intra-Caricom exports of Trinidad and Tobago totaled US$76.3 million. By 1998 this increased to US$712.1 million, an increase of over 800 percent at current prices. As a proportion of total exports,

exports directed towards the Caricom market fell from 22.5 percent in 1973 to 7.7 percent in 1979. After 1979, however, the Caribbean market began to play a more prominent role in the basket of countries serviced by Trinidad and Tobago exporters, as reflected in an export share for Caricom of the total export bundle of Trinidad and Tobago of 32.5 percent in 1998 at current prices, the highest ever for the data period under review.

Table 4.
Shares (constant prices) of the various single digit sitcs in Trinidad and Tobago's intra-CARICOM trade

	xsitc0	xsitc1	xsitc2	xsitc3	xsitc4	xsitc5	xsitc6	xsitc7	xsitc8	xitc9
1973	6.04	0.85	0.08	61.62	0.07	12.36	9.55	2.23	6.85	0.35
1974	7.96	0.88	0.13	60.45	0.00	11.25	10.06	2.68	6.40	0.19
1975	9.78	2.20	0.18	54.81	0.06	8.90	11.42	3.99	8.52	0.14
1976	15.58	2.94	0.10	47.94	0.31	10.45	10.93	3.66	7.94	0.14
1977	15.59	2.18	0.05	51.14	0.17	11.54	9.64	3.11	6.34	0.23
1978	14.59	2.26	0.09	52.15	0.08	12.51	8.64	2.90	6.52	0.28
1979	12.85	3.11	0.11	56.91	0.05	11.53	8.02	2.27	4.72	0.44
1980	6.03	2.09	0.13	69.40	0.16	11.04	5.30	2.88	2.80	0.16
1981	12.10	1.82	0.06	60.30	0.07	10.97	9.25	2.44	2.80	0.19
1982	7.42	2.65	0.07	71.85	0.01	8.18	6.59	1.95	1.17	0.11
1983	10.69	2.39	0.09	66.67	0.02	7.04	7.76	2.71	2.38	0.24
1984	4.07	1.59	0.14	77.69	0.00	4.00	8.81	1.54	1.80	0.35
1985	3.25	0.99	0.23	80.79	0.00	3.31	8.23	1.20	1.46	0.54
1986	6.76	2.85	0.17	66.47	0.00	6.04	10.38	4.21	2.56	0.56
1987	7.98	3.65	0.18	58.17	0.12	7.69	12.76	5.15	3.76	0.53
1988	11.77	6.25	0.27	48.64	0.14	9.96	14.80	4.27	3.75	0.15
1989	13.48	7.80	0.27	43.03	0.28	9.35	17.32	3.83	4.34	0.29
1990	14.49	7.34	0.13	36.64	1.05	11.58	18.88	3.11	6.64	0.16
1991	14.62	5.87	0.16	37.25	0.78	11.46	20.81	3.51	5.40	0.13
1992	15.68	5.71	0.17	33.05	0.48	11.91	22.40	3.66	6.88	0.08
1993	13.72	6.46	0.11	42.37	0.39	10.93	16.88	3.18	5.90	0.05
1994	15.60	6.71	0.05	48.90	0.64	6.79	13.83	2.13	5.37	0.00
1995	16.50	7.10	0.08	50.17	0.47	5.20	12.79	2.35	5.33	0.00
1996	15.37	6.33	0.52	51.14	0.55	5.94	12.52	2.30	5.34	0.00
1997	15.86	6.42	0.09	46.17	0.50	6.85	14.64	3.77	5.69	0.01
1998	15.88	5.94	0.14	44.76	0.49	5.92	15.24	1.99	5.67	3.97
	xsitc0	xsitc1	xsitc2	xsitc3	xsitc4	xsitc5	xsitc6	xsitc7	xsitc8	xsitc9
1973-98	11.68	4.01	0.15	54.56	0.27	8.95	12.21	2.96	4.86	0.36
1973-89 (1)	9.76	2.74	0.14	60.47	0.09	9.18	9.97	3.00	4.36	0.29
1990-98 (2)	15.30	6.43	0.16	43.38	0.59	8.51	16.44	2.89	5.80	0.49
structural change (2-1)	5.54	3.70	0.02	-17.09	0.50	-0.67	6.47	-0.11	1.44	0.20

Source: computed from CSO data. sitc0: food and live animals, sitc1: beverages and tobacco, sitc2: crude materials and inedible oils except fuels, sitc3: minerals, fuels, lubricants and related materials, sitc4: animal and vegetable oils and fats, sitc5: chemicals, sitc6: manufactured goods classified by materials, sitc7: machinery and transport equipment, sitc8: miscellaneous manufactured articles, sitc9: miscellaneous transactions and commodities.

Table 4 illustrates the trends in the shares of the exports of the various single digit SITCs (Standard International Trade Classifications) from Trinidad and Tobago to other Caricom members at constant prices. The lion's share of Trinidad and Tobago's intra-regional exports have predominantly been accounted for by exports of sitc3 which, as a proportion of total intra-Caricom exports, averaged 55 percent throughout the entire data period 1973–98. The next major intra-Caricom export section for Trinidad and Tobago was sitc6, which averaged 12.2 percent and the share of which has been continually increasing (also compare the averages between the periods 1973–89 and 1990–98). If we assume that a 10 percent share constitutes an important intra-Caricom export sector, then the significant export sections by Trinidad and Tobago to its Caricom counterparts have been sitc3 and sitc6, with the marginal inclusion of sitc0. Additionally, apart from sitc3 which decreased considerably, and sitc5 and 7 which decreased marginally, all other SITCs showed signs of positive structural change between the periods 1973–89 and 1990–98, indicating that the commodity composition of Trinidad and Tobago's export portfolio to Caricom has widened into the decade of the nineties.

Trade Intensity Index

Trade intensity indices were first experimented with by Brown (1947). The index I_{ij}, is defined as follows:

$$I_{ij} = (X_{ij}/X_i) / (M_j/M_w)$$

where

X_{ij} = exports of country i to country j.
X_i = total exports of country i.
M_j = imports of country j.
M_w = imports of the world.

The theoretical range of the index is between 0 and infinity. A value tending to zero implies that countries i and j have lower bilateral trade than one would expect given the share of country j in world trade. By extension, a value greater than unity reflects that the countries i and j engage in higher levels of bilateral trade than reflected in the share of j's imports in world imports.[10] Ideally the trade intensity index should be in a time series format, as in such a format it provides the clearest picture of the evolution of the bilateral intensity of trade between the home country and foreign country or region.

Not surprisingly and in the context of the common external tariff of

Table 5. Trade intensity indices

	Guyana	Jamaica	Barbados	Caricom	Non Caricom	USA	UK
1972	188.04	36.76	114.32	50.15	0.78	2.29	1.83
1973	222.32	48.46	115.34	53.29	0.79	3.42	1.20
1974	143.56	40.93	88.81	28.83	0.87	3.74	0.56
1975	102.79	34.42	63.48	20.77	0.88	5.68	0.72
1976	123.67	22.12	63.57	18.90	0.90	4.97	0.66
1977	138.70	17.40	65.92	16.40	0.92	4.81	0.55
1978	151.12	19.41	66.71	17.79	0.93	4.75	0.48
1979	156.30	16.65	72.99	16.22	0.93	4.53	0.58
1980	162.17	27.04	79.09	15.25	0.92	4.91	0.35
1981	141.92	21.91	60.28	14.99	0.92	4.42	0.33
1982	219.34	23.60	76.13	18.02	0.91	4.02	0.33
1983	242.73	15.72	80.81	20.18	0.91	4.18	0.61
1984	300.89	16.75	71.06	23.81	0.91	3.13	1.64
1985	265.68	31.77	93.39	34.43	0.89	3.34	0.69
1986	125.47	39.06	89.06	29.84	0.91	3.39	0.81
1987	45.01	49.50	152.23	40.40	0.89	3.37	0.51
1988	88.79	46.09	160.13	52.51	0.89	3.58	0.39
1989	185.45	61.88	177.08	61.16	0.85	3.40	0.43
1990	147.86	51.01	177.80	56.44	0.88	3.73	0.45
1991	181.45	51.34	172.43	62.82	0.89	3.47	0.39
1992	199.26	38.65	256.69	94.41	0.86	3.31	0.30
1993	281.54	78.26	289.53	117.09	0.80	2.83	0.37
1994	220.96	121.02	250.86	121.11	0.81	2.73	0.35
1995	290.48	156.89	227.21	133.11	0.80	2.61	0.44
1996	292.24	155.73	221.83	159.23	0.76	3.09	0.39
1997	325.02	146.22	198.29	136.87	0.78	2.85	0.41
1998	268.43	190.74	294.62	164.48	0.71	2.61	0.39
	Guyana	Jamaica	Barbados	Caricom	Non Caricom	USA	UK
average 70s	153.31	29.52	81.39	27.79	0.88	4.27	0.82
average 80s	177.74	33.33	103.93	31.06	0.90	3.77	0.58
average 90s	245.25	109.99	232.14	116.17	0.81	3.03	0.39

Source: computed from CSO data.

the RTA, the intensity of trade of Trinidad and Tobago with its Caricom counterparts is much greater than that with its non-Caricom counterparts (Table 5). A reference to the summary statistics at the bottom of Table 4 would reflect that the intensity of trade with Caricom (and the listed member countries) has been growing while that with non-Caricom countries, including the USA and the UK, has been falling. This does not auger well, and all attempts have to be made to change this trend as exports to protected partners intra-regionally may help to nurture inefficient export sectors.

Specialization Indices

An alternative evaluation of whether or not Trinidad and Tobago's export basket to the intra-regional market has broadened over time can be gleaned through the use of a specialization index (S). Such an index may be calculated as follows:

$$S_j = \sum_{i=0}^{9} (Xsitc_{ij}/X_j)^2, i = 0, ..., 9$$

where

$Xsitc_{ij}$ = the exports of $sitc_i$ (i equals the 0 ... 9 single digit export sectors) and j = 1 or 2, (1 represents intra-Caricom exports and 2 represents extra-regional exports).

Thus, $Xsitc_{11}/X_1$: represents the export of sitc1 to Caricom, as a proportion of the total intra-Caricom exports of Trinidad and Tobago, and $Xsitc_{12}/X_2$ represents Trinidad and Tobago's extra-regional exports of sitc1, as a proportion of the total extra-regional exports of Trinidad and Tobago. This index can range anywhere between 0 and 1. A value tending towards 1 is indicative of extreme dependence on a single commodity, while a score approaching zero is reflective of a higher degree of diversification.

Figure 1 plots four specialization indices for Trinidad and Tobago: exports with and without oil, to both the intra-regional and extra-regional

---

Figure 1.
Intra- and extra-regional specialization with and without oil, 1973–1998.

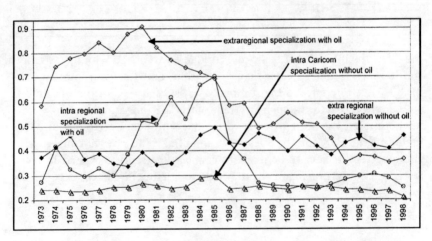

markets.[11] In particular for intra-regional exports including oil, there has been a greater element of diversification in Trinidad and Tobago's exports to its Caricom partners after 1985, as characterized by a fall in the index's value from 0.66 in 1985 to 0.21 by 1998. The non-oil version of this index also hints (although less markedly) at increasing diversification in Trinidad and Tobago as evidenced in a marginal decline in the value of this index from 0.201 in 1973 to 0.173 in 1998.

Concerning the extra-regional market, when oil is included the relevant specialization index escalates in value between 1973 and 1980 from 0.545 to 0.87. (During this period the export of oil, approximated here as the exports of sitc3, increased from US$189.2 million to US$2,293.5 million; i.e., it increased almost twelve times.) With the falloff in the exports of oil after 1980, the concentration of Trinidad and Tobago's exports in this area dampened and together with the increasing competitiveness of the non-oil areas (occasioned by devaluations in 1985 and 1988 and the dismantling of barriers to free trade in the late 1980s) led to a falloff in the value of this index to 0.31 in 1994, improving only marginally thereafter to 0.33 in 1998.[12] When oil is excluded, the extra-regional specialization index shows clear signs of increasing specialization. In particular, this version of the specialization index increased from 0.33 in 1973 to 0.42 by 1998, the increase appearing even more pronounced when it is considered that the index stood at 0.30 in 1979.

In general these specialization indices portray that the Trinidad and Tobago export basket, inclusive of oil, has broadened to both intra- and extra-regional markets. Perhaps more significantly, though, these specialization indices reflect that the extent of export commodity diversification is significantly greater in the protected regional market.

Regional Orientation Indices

In the decade of the 1990s and particularly after 1993 the Trinidad and Tobago economy experienced rapid real per capita growth motivated in part by high inflows of foreign direct investment (FDI). Rising FDI and generally high domestic investment has led to improved manufacturing (broad) exports.[13] Concerning Caricom (and as the trade intensity indices helped to reflect) Trinidad and Tobago has been doing progressively more trade and this raises important questions such as whether Trinidad and Tobago's export basket to the Caricom sphere has broadened and, if so, which export sector has expanded in a biased fashion towards the Caricom region in relation to extra-regional areas.

The first of these questions has been answered above using specialization indices. However, the analytical picture from the specialization indices as employed only provides a broad overview of the relative impact of RTA membership on the intra-Caricom export basket of Trinidad and Tobago. Certainly it would be useful to obtain a more micro-analytical picture, i.e., one that shows which component of the total export basket is targeted to the protected regional market in a greater proportion than to the extra-regional market. Such a micro-analytical perspective can be obtained by calculating regional orientation indices (ROIs). ROIs allow the determination of whether the SITCs that thrive within the regional trade bloc have passed the test of the market; that is, whether they have been able to export to non-preferential extra-regional markets. To calculate such an index for *j*th sitc, the following formula may be used:

$$ROI_j = (X_{irj}/X_{irt})/ (X_{erj} / X_{ert})$$

where

X_{irj} = exports of sitc *j* intra-regionally
X_{irt} = total value of Trinidad and Tobago's intra-regional exports
X_{erj} = exports of sitc *j* extra-regionally
X_{ert} = total value of Trinidad and Tobago's extra-regional exports.

The value of the regional orientation index ranges anywhere between 0 and infinity. A ROI value of one implies that the country's intra-regional export pattern is identical to that of its extra-regional export pattern. Yeats (1998) has noted that to be of substantive use the ROI should be calculated in a time series format, as single estimates transmit limited information. In time series format, a regional orientation index can provide useful information concerning the geographical pattern of exports.

Before attending to the interpretation of the calculated ROIs for Trinidad and Tobago, note that the exports of sitc3, sitc5 and sitc6 (principally crude oil, refined petroleum products, natural gas liquids, ammonia, methanol, urea, and iron and steel products) are targeted predominantly at the extra-regional markets and are mainly produced by branch plants of foreign multi-national corporations. If we decompose the data into the time intervals 1973–89 and 1990–98 then these SITCs have either had regional orientation values less than one for both data periods (sitc3), less than one for the 1990s (sitc3 and sitc5), or have experienced such substantive change (in terms of the target market of the SITC) that their regional orientation value has dropped considerably (sitc6). Detailed focus on these categories is therefore excluded at this point as they are especially produced for extra-regional markets.

The remaining export sectors are s0, s1, s2, s7 and s8.[14] Clearly, these

Table 6.
Regional Orientation indices for
Trinidad and Tobago 1973–98

YEAR	s0	s1	s2	s3	s5	s6	s7	s8
1973	1.20	1.41	0.27	0.55	1.17	15.70	19.69	8.51
1974	1.22	1.56	0.63	0.70	1.59	41.49	9.09	17.19
1975	1.48	5.19	1.55	0.56	2.72	86.96	9.43	23.65
1976	2.54	5.99	0.87	0.51	2.66	71.27	3.16	25.37
1977	2.85	4.85	0.89	0.54	3.01	57.62	7.53	20.88
1978	4.12	3.74	2.62	0.51	2.58	57.25	1.72	20.10
1979	3.78	5.23	0.96	0.60	3.67	72.53	2.40	18.09
1980	6.13	5.08	1.96	0.73	2.11	32.64	3.65	14.48
1981	5.58	4.71	1.00	0.75	2.14	14.06	0.45	13.87
1982	3.88	5.52	0.20	0.88	0.88	4.09	0.71	5.72
1983	6.14	6.99	0.44	0.83	0.71	3.98	0.79	6.73
1984	2.01	4.47	0.46	0.96	0.36	3.61	0.99	3.84
1985	2.17	2.55	0.67	1.02	0.25	6.04	0.38	5.25
1986	2.65	5.86	0.88	0.83	0.34	2.47	2.66	9.44
1987	2.95	9.66	0.62	0.73	0.38	2.66	4.24	15.14
1988	3.80	7.55	0.95	0.61	0.40	2.87	5.46	8.11
1989	3.52	12.87	0.76	0.57	0.39	2.52	9.75	14.27
1990	3.94	12.94	0.38	0.53	0.54	2.64	2.23	23.93
1991	3.22	7.62	2.10	0.54	0.50	2.83	9.53	12.27
1992	3.68	6.61	1.87	0.48	0.53	2.49	6.50	12.00
1993	2.71	7.11	1.16	0.62	0.50	1.90	1.63	10.83
1994	2.95	4.78	0.51	0.98	0.27	1.41	5.52	7.51
1995	3.41	8.60	0.49	0.93	0.27	1.23	1.68	5.27
1996	3.52	4.66	15.55	0.94	0.30	1.26	0.61	6.04
1997	3.07	3.14	0.52	0.96	0.26	1.31	1.15	5.96
1998	2.48	2.69	0.76	0.86	0.22	0.99	0.59	4.12
Period averages.								
	s0	s1	s2	s3	s5	s6	s7	s8
1973-98	3.27	5.82	1.50	0.72	1.10	18.99	4.29	12.25
1990-98	3.22	6.46	2.59	0.76	0.38	1.78	3.27	9.77

Source: computed from thecentral Statistical Year, Trinidad and Tobago, 1973–1998. sitc0: food and live animals, sitc1: beverages and tobacco, sitc2: crude materials and inedible oils except fuels, sitc3: minerals, fuels, lubricants and related materials, sitc4: animal and vegetable oils and fats, sitc5: chemicals, sitc6: manufactured goods classified by materials, sitc7: machinery and transport equipment, sitc8: miscellaneous manufactured articles, sitc9: miscellaneous transactions and commodities.

sitcs have ROI values that indicate a bias in favor of exporting to the intraregional protected market. It should also be noted that the concentration on the regional export market appears greatest for narrow manufacturing.[15] In part, this also reflects the superior relative size (in terms of GDP) and relative structure (in terms of industry as a proportion of GDP) of the Trinidad and Tobago economy, as compared to its Caricom counterparts.[16]

In this regard the work of Toulan and Guillen (1997) can be mentioned. These authors draw our attention to the importance of the level of sophistication that a firm faces on the demand side and the implication of this for the efficiency of the firm. In particular, when demand pressures are weak as is characteristic of less developed countries and protected markets, the incentive structure to maintain the highest levels of efficiency is compromised.[17]

One obvious way to improve the performance of the various export sectors from Trinidad and Tobago is to expose them to more robust extraregional trade. The next section outlines some of the more recent measures that the Trinidad and Tobago government has taken in this direction.

Recent Trade Developments That Widen the Preferential Market Base of Trinidad and Tobago

The decade of the 1990s was one of rapid change for Trinidad and Tobago. The government embarked upon a structural adjustment program in 1989 and this was supported by measures targeted at liberalizing foreign trade. Trinidad and Tobago's trade reform program included a sequential removal of the negative list and import duty exemptions and a general improvement in customs procedures. The removal of Trinidad and Tobago's negative import list on 1 January 1995 meant that domestic exports now had to face more intense competition from external producers.[18] In 1993, the Trinidad and Tobago dollar was floated against the US dollar.

The 1990s also witnessed the completion of the Uruguay round of trade discussions, and the World Trading Organization (WTO) was established to govern international trade on 1 January 1995. With the WTO and in the context of the agreements made at the completion of the Uruguay round of discussions, developing countries are expected to get easier access to developed country's markets.[19]

At the Caricom level, Caricom heads of government agreed in 1989 to move towards the formation of a Single Market and Economy. A West Indian Commission was established and in 1992 they submitted the "Time for Action" document. One of the major recommendations of the West Indian Commission was to widen the integration movement to include other countries from the Caribbean region.

In this regard, Caricom entered into several "spoke-to-spoke" relationships in the decade of the 1990s (see Table 7). In 1990 an Agreement on Technical Cooperation and Trade Promotion between Mexico and the Caricom was signed. Progress, however, between Caricom and Mexico has been slow, no doubt influenced by Mexico's involvement in the more beneficial NAFTA arrangement. In January 1993 an agreement between Caricom and Venezuela came into effect, with the Venezuelans granting duty free entry to a list of goods from Caricom member states. Caricom in turn has agreed not to apply quantitative restrictions to Venezuelan goods that enter the intra-regional market without first consulting the Venezuelan authorities. Caricom also entered into an agreement with Columbia and held preliminary discussions with the Dominican Republic to establish a free trade bloc. The Caricom-Columbia agreement which came into effect on 1 January 1995 includes, among other things, the phased elimination and reduction in barriers to trade between both parties.

Concerning the Dominican Republic, one author notes:

> The Dominican Republic has been a dynamic exporter in recent years and has made good use of its trade preferences under the US Caribbean Basin Initiative (CBI). It is the largest exporter in this program and accounts for over a third of total US imports from CBI countries. Its exports are highly diversified mostly as a result of the free zone provisions.... Free trade with ... the Dominican Republic would offer Caribbean producers a whole range of new business opportunities in a continuously expanding regional market. It would allow Caribbean firms to develop their competitiveness through greater economies of scale, thus preparing them for

Table 7.
List of important trade agreements between CARICOM and other states

Parties to agreement	Agreement	Preferential/ non Preferential	Year signed	Date entered into Force	Status as at dec 1999
ACP-EU	Lome IV Convention	Non reciprocal	1995	1996	Renegotiated
Caricom-Canada	Trade and investment agreement	Non reciprocal	1985	1986	Active
Caricom-Columbia	Trade, economic and Technical Cooperation	Partly reciprocal	1994	1995	Active
Caricom-Dominican Republic	Agreement on Technical cooperation	Reciprocal	1998	1999	Under discussion
Caricom-United States	(CBI), CBPTA	Non reciprocal	1983	1984	Active
Caricom-Venezuela	Agreement on technical cooperation and trade promotion	Non reciprocal	1992	1993	Active

Source: Nicholls et al. (200).

eventual hemisphere-wide free trade and continued global market integration. (Jessen et al. 1999, 20)

On a more bilateral level, Trinidad and Tobago and Cuba signed an economic and technical cooperation agreement aimed at strengthening trading ties between the two countries. Additionally, in March 1999 officials from Trinidad and Tobago visited Mexico and held discussions with the overall objective of establishing a preferential bilateral trading agreement with that country. In 2000 a fourth round of trade negotiations was completed between Mexico and Trinidad and Tobago. In 1999 a memorandum of understanding was entered into between the government of Trinidad and Tobago and Mercosur to encourage increased trade and investment (Government of Trinidad and Tobago 1999). Additionally, efforts were made to revitalize a preferential free trade arrangement between Costa Rica and Trinidad and Tobago.

In July 1994, Trinidad and Tobago also became a member of the Association of Caribbean States (ACS), which consists of the 25 countries in the Caribbean Basin, representing a market of some 200 million people (compare this with the approximately 7 million people in Caricom).[20] The ACS has emphasized the removal of tariff as well as non-tariff barriers so as to promote trade between its member countries. It has also proposed the establishment of a Caribbean Preferential Tariff (CPT) to encourage intra-bloc trade. The work program which was approved at the first ministerial council in 1996 was relatively broad in scope and covered the following priority areas: (1) tourism, (2) transportation, (3) the development of trade and external economic relations, (4) natural and environmental disasters, (5) social, cultural, scientific and technological development issues, (6) protection and preservation of the environment, and (7) natural resources and the Caribbean Sea (Nicholls 2000).

The Ministry of Planning (2000) has explicitly stated that Trinidad and Tobago will seek greater trade links with countries in Europe, Asia, the Middle East and the Pacific region. Trinidad and Tobago will also sustain its efforts towards membership in the Free Trade Areas of the Americas (FTAA).[21] These new developments, although expanding the preferential trading base of Trinidad and Tobago, mean that domestic exports would come under increased (preferential) foreign competition; this augers well for improvements in the productive efficiency of the domestic export production platform.

Conclusion

The new wave of regionalism that is currently gripping the global economy has raised several pertinent questions, one of these being the impact that RTA membership has on the export performance of member countries. This paper has demonstrated that, although initially engineered to act as a launching pad for extra-regional exports, the Caricom market was utilized as a zone of comfort for some exports from Trinidad and Tobago.

The employment of specialization indices helped to reveal that the export basket of Trinidad and Tobago to both the intra- and extra-regional markets has started to grow, although the extent of this diversification is greater within Trinidad and Tobago's intra-regional exports. The use of ROI helped to detail that there still exists an export bias in favor of the protected regional market, particularly where non-branch plant exports are concerned.

In recognition of the limitation of the intra-regional trade bloc as a catalyst for the development of vibrant export sectors, Caricom has made and is making significant attempts to broaden its preferential trading base. Commendably, the authorities in Trinidad and Tobago have also sought to broaden its preferential export base by actively pursuing several bilateral arrangements that would strengthen its individual export position.

In terms of future work in this area, a number of options are available. In the first instance it would be interesting to know whether exports from Trinidad and Tobago to the Caricom market are helping to promote the economic growth of Trinidad and Tobago. It would also be useful to explore the precise nature and extent of intra-industry trade between Trinidad and Tobago and the other members of the Caricom RTA, an issue that will be dealt with in a subsequent paper.

Endnotes

1. The single digit sitcs are: sitc0: food and live animals, sitc1: beverages and tobacco, sitc2: crude materials and inedible oils except fuels, sitc3: minerals, fuels, lubricants and related materials, sitc4: animals and vegetable oils and fats, sitc5: chemicals, sitc6: manufactured goods classified by materials, sitc7: machinery and transport equipment, sitc8: miscellaneous manufactured articles, sitc9: miscellaneous transactions and commodities.

2. When Haiti becomes fully admitted to Caricom the population of Caricom would exceed 14m (i.e. it would increase by more than 100 percent) although regional GDP would only increase by 9 percent (Jessen et. al. 1999).

3. Portugal has a population of 9.9 million people (United Nations 2000).

4. Small states face several disadvantages in terms of their relationship with the rest of the world, stemming in the main from their low bargaining capacity in the context of a

high (fixed) cost of negotiation. Integration of small states reduces their bargaining power and spreads the cost associated with negotiation.

5. See Brewster and Thomas, pp. 129–40 for a list of some of these materials.

6. Yeats (1998) in a study of MERCUSOR analyzed whether increased MERCUSOR trade took place, amongst those commodities that grew fastest, to non-MERCUSOR member countries; i.e., he examined whether intra-MERCUSOR trade passed the test of the market. Using data for the period 1988–94, Yeats found that those export areas that were dynamic within MERCUSOR were not dynamic beyond its protective walls.

7. Vamvakidis (1998) examined the economic impact of five RTAs (including the European Union) on the economic performance of its members. Apart from the EU, Vamvakidis found no significant evidence of a positive relationship between membership in the RTA and the economic growth performance of the member countries and concluded that economic integration amongst small LDCs is unlikely to have a positive impact on economic growth within these LDCs. The five regional integration agreements considered by Vamvakidis were the Central American Common Market (CACM), Union Douaniere et Economique de l' Afrique Centrale (UDEAC) and the European Union.

8. Traditional Heckscher-Ohlin theory suggests that a nation would produce and export those commodities for which it has an abundance of factors of production and import those commodities which call for factor proportions in the reverse direction. In this regard, it has become commonplace to expect that LDCs would produce and export labor and natural resource rich commodities and import human capital and research and development intensive commodities from the industrialized nations. (Nonetheless it is also recognized that a number of LDCs now export manufactured goods.)

9. Data on export and import price deflators are available for all the years included in the study, 1973–98, except the period 1991–95. To extend these deflators to cover the time period 1991–95 the following assumptions have been made: To extend the export deflator for sitc 3, the trend growth in the price of West Texas Intermediate crude oil (a blend of crude that mirrors the price that Trinidad and Tobago's crude oil attracts) for the time period 1991–95 have been used to extrapolate the values of the deflator attached to sitc 3. The trend growth of the export deflator for sitc 5 is assumed to follow that of an unweighted average growth in the prices of ammonia, urea, and methanol. Finally, the trend growth in the export deflator for sitc 6 was assumed to be equal to the unweighted average trend growth of the prices of wire rods and billets. For all the other sitcs, except sitc 9, it was assumed that the trend growth in 1990 continued in the period 1991–95. Sitc 9 is approximated by the overall export price deflator.

10. Ideally, the imports of country i should be subtracted from world imports, as a country cannot import from itself. Although the correction is made in this paper, for a small country like Trinidad and Tobago such a change would be of negligible significance.

11. Oil exports are approximated by exports of sitc3.

12. Exports of petrochemicals (approximated by the sum of exports on the sitc5 and 6 accounts) increased from TT$481.87 million in 1972 to TT$3,954.3 million in 1998 or from 12.2 percent of total exports to 88.04 percent at constant prices.

13. Caricom Secretariat (2000) has described Trinidad and Tobago as an export dynamo within Caricom.

14. Only patchy data exists for sitc4 and sitc9, forcing their exclusion.

15. Narrow manufacturing exports refer to the sum of exports of sitc7 and sitc8.

16. It also pays some amount of tribute to the Heckscher-Ohlin theory, as Trinidad and Tobago produces and exports intra-regionally those commodities in which it has a comparative advantage.

17. These authors focused on trade within Mercusor and found that Argentina's trade with its Mercusor partners runs the risk of damaging the long run competitiveness of the economy of Argentina.

18. There are also plans for the downward adjustment of the common external tariff (CET).

19. Caricom countries have supported the establishment of the WTO in the belief that such an institution would help to ensure greater fairness in the international trading system. The WTO members have agreed (in principle) to an agenda that will have important

ramifications for Caribbean countries and Caricom as a whole. Currently only Jamaica, Barbados and Trinidad and Tobago have permanent delegations to the WTO.
20. The estimated GDP of the ACS group of countries is US$500 billion.
21. The FTAA germinated in December 1994 when 34 countries from the Western Hemisphere agreed to form a Free Trade Area in the Americas by 2005.

References

Brewster, H. 1992. *The Caribbean Community in a Changing International Environment: Towards the Next Century.* Eight Adlith Brown Memorial Lecture given at the Mona Campus, The University of the West Indies, Mona, Jamaica.
_____, and C.Y. Thomas. 1967. "The Dynamics of West Indian Economic Integration." Mona, Jamaica: Institute of Social and Economic Research.
Brown, A.J. 1947. *Applied Economics.* London: George Allen Unwin.
CARICOM Secretariat. 2000. *Caribbean Trade and Investment Report 2000.* Dynamic Interface of Regionalism and Globalization. Ian Randle Publishers.
C.S.O. and Central Bank of Trinidad and Tobago. Various years. *The Balance of Payments Yearbook.* Port of Spain, Trinidad and Tobago: Government Printery.
Demas, W. 1965. *The Economics of Development in Small Countries with Special Reference to the Caribbean.* Montreal: McGill University Press.
_____. 1976. *The Political Economy of the English Speaking Caribbean: A Summary View.* Caribbean Ecumenical Consultation for Development, Study Paper #4. Barbados.
Gonzales, A. 1990. "CARICOM and Extra Regional Export Development." *Bulletin of Eastern Caribbean Affairs.* Vol. 16. Barbados: Institute of Social and Economic Research.
Jessen, A., and E. Rodriguez. 1999. "Caribbean Community: Facing the Challenges of Regional and Global Integration." Occasional paper, IDB (Intal-Ltd).
Lewis, W. A. 1950. "The Industrialization of the British West Indies." *Caribbean Economic Review* 2: 1–61.
Milner, C.R. 1994. "Identifying and Quantifying Anti-Export Bias: An Evaluation for a Small Industrializing Economy." *World Development* 22: 587–99.
_____. 1993. "'Large' and 'Small' Regional Trade Blocs and Trade Regime Bias: A Comparison of the EC and Caricom." *Weltwirtschaftliches Archiv* 129: 367–383.
Nicholls, S., et al. 2000. "The State of and Prospects for the Deepening and Widening of Caribbean Integration." *World Economy* 23 no. 9: 1161–1194.
Romer, P.M. 1992. "Two Strategies for Economic Development: Using Ideas and Producing Ideas." *Proceedings of the World Bank Annual Conference on Development Economics,* 63–92.
Schiff, M., and A. L. Winters. 1998. "Dynamics and Politics in Regional Integration Arrangements: An Introduction." *WBER* 12 no. 2: 177–95.
Toulan, O., and M. Guillen. 1997. "Beneath the Surface: The Impact of Radical Economic Reforms on the Outward Orientation of Argentine and Mendozan Firms, 1989–95." *Journal of Latin American Studies* 29 (May): 395–418.
Trinidad and Tobago. 1999. Review of the Economy. Port-of-Spain: Ministry of Finance.

Trinidad and Tobago. 1997. *Trade Policy for the Republic of Trinidad and Tobago*. Port of Spain: Ministry of Trade and Industry.

Trinidad and Tobago. Various issues. *Review of the Economy*. Port of Spain: Ministry of Finance.

Trinidad and Tobago. Various years. *Medium Term Policy Framework*. Port of Spain: Ministry of Planning.

Tybout, J. 1992. "Linking Trade and Productivity: New Research Directions." *World Bank Economic Review* May 6 (2): 189–211.

United Nations. Various years. *Human Development Report* New York: United Nations.

Vamvakidis, A. 1998. "Regional Integration and Economic Growth." *The World Bank Economic Review* 12 no. 2: 251–70.

World Bank. 2001. *World Bank Indicators*. Washington, D.C.: World Bank.

Yeats, A.J. 1998. "Does Mercosur's Trade Performance Raise Concerns about the Effects of Regional Trade Arrangements?" *The World Bank Economic Review* 12 no. 1: 1–28.

Open Regionalism: The FTAA and Implications for CARICOM Development

Bhoendranatt Tewarie and Roger Hosein[1]

Introduction

Globalization may be defined as the international integration of markets in goods and services and is an important feature of the contemporary world economy in which the Caribbean Community (Caricom) must subsist. The level of globalization is reflected in a number of features, including the fact that world merchandise trade expanded at an annual average of 6.8 percent per annum from US$3,423 billion in 1990 to reach US$6,243 billion in 2000. In a similar sense, merchandise imports expanded considerably from US$3,430 billion in 1990 to US$6,507 billion in 2000. Merchandise exports of developing countries also increased with globalization from US$969.8 million in 1990 to reach US$2,257 billion in 2000. The imports of these developing countries increased from US$1,331 billion in 1990 to US$2,187 billion in 2000.

Similarly, astonishing changes have taken place as regards global gross capital flow, which in 2000 was US$7.5 trillion as compared to US$1.4 trillion in 1990, an increase of almost 400 percent. In this environment of rapid globalization there has also been an increase in the number of regional trade agreements, albeit as steppingstones for even higher levels of multilateral trade.

Economic integration schemes in the decade of the 1960s and 1970s were mainly customs unions that reinforced the inward or import-substituting mode of industrial development. In the main these customs unions served to expand the protected market base for the manufactures

173

produced by the members of the trade agreement, and followed the line of reasoning suggested by distinguished South American economic scholars Raul Prebisch (from Argentina) and Hans Singer (from Columbia). These import substituting industrialization (ISI) models were supposed to modify the very economic structures of practicing member states by increasing the amount of economic activity that originated in the manufacturing sector and, in so doing, reducing the extent of dependence of members of the regional agreement on the industrialized nations. The main rationale for these inward oriented development strategies adopted by regional trade agreements at the time was to address the colonial division of labor, which continued the trend in which less developed countries exported primary goods and imported manufactures for their own consumption. All this occurred in the context of worsening terms of trade.

Free trade areas established by the removal of intra-regional barriers to trade are supposed to enhance the growth of trade within the trade bloc. The customs union protects domestic firms through the establishment of a common external tariff (CET). Common external tariffs are designed to allow infant industry firms within the trading agreement some margin of preference so that they can mature and then be able to compete effectively with more efficient and established producers from extra-regional areas. Import substituting industrialization models also provided supplementary support to indigenous manufacturing firms in the form of non-tariff barriers, especially quotas and licenses.

ISI models were government spearheaded and as adopted by several countries in Latin America, failed to deliver on their exant promises. In many regards, what transpired in these countries was the formation of inwardly oriented models that predominantly focused on the intra-regional market of the free trade area.

In recent times, regional integration arrangements have continued to proliferate but in a different form. The new regionalism (also called open regionalism) is in the mode of economic integration that has been adopted by most countries since the 1980s. Open regionalism is founded on the notion of liberalism, the impetus for which originated with the failure of state led attempts at ISI during the decades before. Open regionalism is strongly supported by the United States, which responded to the slow pace of liberalization in the Uruguay Trade Round for GATT (the General Agreement Tariffs and Trade) and the deepening of European economic integration by encouraging the formation of a free trade area between itself and Canada which culminated in the eventual formation of the North American Free Trade Agreement (NAFTA). This latter development provided renewed energy for Latin American economies to take another and closer look at regionalism.

Open regionalism therefore represents a sort of middle ground and has evolved to address one fundamental set of problems with contemporary trade policy. It concentrates on how trade integration can be practiced without compromising the requirements of the global trading system as specified by the World Trade Organization (WTO). The main distinction of open regionalism from free trade is that it embraces a preferential element that is reflected in integration arrangements and reinforced by the cultural and geographical closeness of the countries involved.

Perspectives: Regionalism Versus Multilateralism

There are two main schools of thought concerning the relationship between multilateral and regional trade arrangements. Proponents of multilateralism make three main arguments. In the first instance, they argue that regional trade agreements divert attention away from multilateralism and in so doing stall and threaten its development. A second concern, expressed by Bhagwati and Panagariya (1996), is that regional trade agreements may divert trade away from more efficient nonmembers towards less efficient members. These authors argue that in addition to the protection of a common external tariff, the members of a preferential trading arrangement may also benefit from terms relating to rules of origin and the amount of regional input that has to go into the production of a particular commodity.

The third concern is the geopolitical implication of growing regionalism. Bergsten (1997) has noted that in earlier periods the formation of regional agreements and trade blocs may have contributed to political and even military confrontation between the participating nations. Bergsten adds, however, that in the current mode of operation of the global economy war is an extremity that is unlikely to happen; but he notes that extensive ties among nations may exacerbate conflicts that extend beyond economics.

Economists that support regionalism have different views on all of these issues. In the first instance, they argue that these regional trade agreements promote freer trade and multilateralism in at least two important ways: a) that with regional arrangements trade creation has exceeded trade diversion; and b) that regional trade agreements also contribute to both an internal and international dynamic that enhances the likelihood of global liberalization rather than compromising it. One important attribute of the internal dynamic associated with developing countries is that regional reforms, which are much easier to negotiate than multilateral arrangements, place developing countries on a pathway that — even if governments change their perception towards free trade — would be difficult for them to reverse; i.e., open regionalism agreements provides some amount of "lock in" to developing countries to keep them on a path of liberalization (Bergsten 1996a, 1996b).

Regionalists argue, second, that many of the ideas that are experimented with concerning globalization are tried and tested at the regional level. Even further, regional liberalization will encourage other countries to join the procession and, in so doing, beef up the overall global process. Regionalism is also associated with some important demonstration effects (Bergsten 1997). In particular, government and other local officials can learn the tricks of the trade associated with multilateralism through their participation in regionalism. In this regard, regionalism increases the probability that the member states would graduate into multilateralism. The process of learning by doing applies to trade liberalization as well as to the economic development process; trade liberalization too can be more easily learned at the regional level.

Other supporters of regionalism argue, third, that the political benefits are positive rather than negative. They claim that with the formation of an economic union between two members, e.g. France and Germany in the European Union, the likelihood of a war erupting between them is much lower than otherwise (Bergsten 1997).

This paper explores some of the implications of the Free Trade Areas of the Americas (FTAA) on Caricom countries. The rest of the paper is divided as follows: in the next section, the nature of intra-Caricom trade since the formation of Caricom in 1973 is analyzed. Section three discusses the characteristics of the FTAA in terms of various macroeconomic indicators and also examines the relative size of Caricom as part of the wider FTAA. In section four a discussion of the benefits and costs of the FTAA is detailed while in the following section, two important options that Caricom countries can use to cope with the FTAA are examined.

Caricom Intra-Regional Trade Performance

The idea of West Indian integration was initiated in 1958 with the West Indian Federation but was short-lived, as the Federation was terminated in 1962 when island insularity gained ascendency over regional integration. The dismantling of the Federation, however, sowed many of the seeds necessary for some Caribbean countries to envisage the benefits of a regional integration arrangement; thus in 1973 the Caribbean Community and Common Market was formalized. The first signatories to the Caricom arrangement were Guyana, Jamaica, Barbados and Trinidad and Tobago in 1973; other Caribbean states would join shortly thereafter, and by 4 July 1983, the Bahamas would become the thirteenth member state of the Community. In July 1995 Suriname became the fourteenth member of Caricom.

Table 1 shows the trends in intra-Caricom trade for the period 1973–1998. In particular we see that the regional imports of Caricom countries increased from EC$296 million in 1973 to EC$2,099.1 million in 1998. During the same interval of time, intra-regional exports increased from

Table 1: Intra-CARICOM trade (EC$mn), 1973–1998

Year	Reg. Imports (1)	Total Imports (2)	Reg. Exports (3)	Total Exports (4)	Total intra-reg. trade (5)	Total Caricom trade (6)	1/2%	3/4%	5/6%
1973	296.5	3950	290.5	2709.8	587	6659.8	7.51	10.72	8.81
1974	508.1	7180.7	486.5	6660.9	994.6	13841.6	7.08	7.30	7.19
1975	649.2	8552.2	599.2	7020.5	1248.4	15572.7	7.59	8.54	8.02
1976	741.2	7871.7	778.7	8701.7	1519.9	16573.4	9.42	8.95	9.17
1977	723.2	9623.7	775.8	9281.9	1499	18905.6	7.51	8.36	7.93
1978	798.4	10399.4	827.4	9405.4	1625.8	19804.8	7.68	8.80	8.21
1979	1001	11063	998	10715.4	1999	21778.4	9.05	9.31	9.18
1980	1411.6	15976.2	1416.6	16002	2828.2	31978.2	8.84	8.85	8.84
1981	1615.4	16931.6	1493	15119.7	3108.4	32051.3	9.54	9.87	9.70
1982	1540.6	17646.8	1482.6	12470.7	3023.2	30117.5	8.73	11.89	10.04
1983	1349.5	14315.7	1315	10359.7	2664.5	24675.4	9.43	12.69	10.80
1984	1207.3	12461.6	1232.2	10250.6	2439.5	22712.2	9.69	12.02	10.74
1985	1154.9	11357.9	1242.7	9653	2397.6	21010.9	10.17	12.87	11.41
1986	796.7	10706.9	840.9	7660.8	1637.6	18367.7	7.44	10.98	8.92
1987	862.7	11229.6	868.9	8017.8	1731.6	19247.4	7.68	10.84	9.00
1988	986.4	11891.9	1036.7	8449	2023.1	20340.9	8.29	12.27	9.95
1989	1216.7	13856.5	1265.8	9283.6	2482.5	23140.1	8.78	13.63	10.73
1990	1350.2	14195.1	1376.1	11117.3	2726.3	25312.4	9.51	12.38	10.77
1991	1305.8	15519.3	1235.4	10205.7	2541.2	25725	8.41	12.11	9.88
1992	1363.1	14438.4	1249.1	9724.6	2612.2	24163	9.44	12.84	10.81
1993	1499.8	15591.1	1447.6	9083.6	2947.4	24674.7	9.62	15.94	11.95
1994	1722.1	19574.4	1789.2	12050.3	3511.3	31624.7	8.80	14.85	11.10
1995	1912.4	20024.1	2274.9	13775.3	4187.3	33799.4	9.55	16.51	12.39
1996	2056.7	24372.2	2363.1	13828.5	4419.8	38200.7	8.44	17.09	11.57
1997	2304.1	22122.2	2483.1	14397.1	4787.2	36519.3	10.42	17.25	13.11
1998	2099.1	22095.8	2655.5	11575.3	4754.6	33671.1	9.50	22.94	14.12

Source: El Agraa et al. and CARICOM Secretariat (2000).

EC$290.5 million to EC$2,655.5 million. What has to be noted, though, is that as a proportion of the total trade of Caricom, intra-Caricom trade averaged 10.1 percent for the period 1973–1998. Further, between 1973 and 1998 the proportionate increase in intra-Caricom trade measured a mere five percentage points.

In this context we may highlight the work of one distinguished regional commentator who has noted that "the idea of a small protected market core to facilitate the start up of economic activity is now redundant, given the increased mobility of capital, technology and expertise and the minuscule size of the market itself. The experience of Caricom itself has shown that this type of small market protection is usually excessive and in the vast majority of cases does not encourage the competitive emergence of enterprises beyond the boundaries of the region" (Gonzales 2001, 637).

Clearly then, Caricom has not fostered the expansion in intra-regional trade that one would have expected. In this regard, the pending FTAA is a valuable opportunity for Caricom member states to become part of a trading arrangement with tremendous growth potential.

During the second half of the decade of the 1990s there was a rapid increase in the number of regional trade agreements that occurred in the Western Hemisphere including Mercosur and NAFTA. These trade blocs had a very important effect on the rest of the countries in the Western Hemisphere. Importantly, many of these other countries tried to join or form trade integration arrangements of their own. These integration arrangements were principally formed with countries in close geographical proximity to each other. Important in helping the rapid increase in the number of intra-hemispheric trade arrangements were the events that unfolded after the Uruguay Round Agreement in 1995: many of the countries in the Western Hemisphere were engaged in liberalization of varying degrees, either voluntarily or with the coercion of the multilateral lending agencies.

Not wanting to be left out, Caricom countries have embarked on a set of bilateral investment or trade agreements with countries in the Western Hemisphere. These agreements are shown in Table 2.

The FTAA

The pending FTAA is in the spirit of open regionalism. The FTAA was launched in 1994 at the Summit of the Americas in Miami, the objective of which was to create a hemispheric free trade agreement by 2005. The

Table 2.
Trade investment agreements in the Western Hemisphere

Agreement in force	Date concluded	Trade agreement	Bilateral investment
Caricom-Columbia	1994	X	
Caricom–Dominica Republic	1998	X	
Caricom-Cuba	2000	X	
Caricom-Venezuela	1992	X	
Dominica Republic–CACM	1998	X	
Barbados-Venezuela	1994		X
Barbados-Canada	1996		X
Jamaica-USA	1994		X
Jamaica-Argentina	1994		X
Trinidad and Tobago-USA	1994		X
Trinidad and Tobago-Canada	1995		X

Source: UNELAC (2001b).

purpose of the FTAA is to liberalize intra-hemispheric trade. This would involve the progressive removal of both tariff and non-tariff barriers within the hemisphere. The FTAA would address the following nine areas:

- Market access
- Agriculture
- Services
- Investment
- Intellectual property rights
- Subsidies, anti-dumping and countervailing duties
- Government procurement
- Competition policy
- Dispute settlement

At the Summit the following objectives of the FTAA were expressed:

1. To enhance the prosperity of the hemisphere through economic integration and free trade;
2. To remove poverty and discrimination in the hemisphere;
3. To preserve and strengthen the democracies within the hemisphere; and
4. To guarantee sustainable development and preservation of the environment.

The interest in an FTAA was sparked in part by a similar development that had taken place on November 14 1994 (three weeks before the
announcement of the FTAA) in Bogor, Indonesia. There a group of leaders from Asia and the Pacific endorsed the attainment of free trade by 2010
for its developed country membership and by 2020 for its developing country membership. Fearing falling behind, Latin American countries pushed
at the Miami Summit for the progressive elimination of intra-hemispheric
barriers to trade by 2005.

One of the distinct features of the FTAA was the strong push made
by developing countries for its formation, despite the tremendous amount
of pressure fully liberalized trade with the most developed nation in the
world would represent. An FTAA would mean that the countries of Latin
America and the Caribbean would have to dismantle their barriers to trade
to ensure that they gain more liberalized access to the USA's market.

The FTAA, when established, would include 34 out of the 35 countries in the Western Hemisphere (the only exclusion is Cuba) and would
involve the progressive removal of substantially all barriers to trade and
investment amongst the member states. Two of the member states of the
proposed FTAA arrangement, Canada and the USA, are classified as developed nations while four others, Argentina, Mexico, Brazil and Chile, have
at various points in the recent past been classifiable as newly industrializing countries. The small member states of Caricom constitute 14 of the
34 states in the FTAA. These states are very open and depend on foreign
trade and investment for a substantial part of their economic activity.

Table 3 shows some key macroeconomic aggregates for member states
of the Western Hemisphere. In particular, the population of the countries
of the Western Hemisphere in 2000 tallied to 813.2 million out of a world
total of 6.05 billion; i.e., the population of the FTAA represents 13.4 percent of the total world population. Another indicator of the size of the
FTAA can be obtained by looking at its contribution to world GDP. In
2000, the FTAA member states accounted for 40 percent of world GDP or
US$12.47 trillion out of a world total of US$31.4 trillion. The countries of
the FTAA also accounted for 22 percent of world exports, determined by
an FTAA merchandise export value of US$1.41 trillion out of a world export
package of US$6.43 trillion in 2000. Significantly, though, this block of
countries, which represents just over one tenth of the world's population,
imports just under one third (28.4 percent) of total world imports.

Table 3.
Some macroeconomic aggregates on FTAA members, 2000

	GDP growth (annual percent)	Population, total mn	GDP (current US$m)	Merchandise exports (current US$m)	Merchandise imports (current US$m)
Nafta	5.11	410.27	11105410	1224977	1686718
Mercusor	1.56	231.49	976245	102708	107447
Andean com	2.73	113.11	279875	58027	42100
Cacm	3.25	35.83	66242	14315	24133
Caribbean	2.64	22.54	48807	13829	21830
Of which caricom1	2.64	14.17	29220	8092	12351
Antigua and Barbuda	0.41	0.07	660	10	355
Bahamas, The	4.49	0.3	4818	910	1730
Belize	11.15	0.24	773	194	450
Dominica	0.2	0.07	268	53	147
Grenada	7.97	0.1	407	50	230
Guyana	-1.38	0.76	713	570	660
Haiti	1.12	7.96	3951	164	1036
Jamaica	3.15	2.63	7709	1296	3216
St. Kitts and Nevis	5.33	0.04	328	30	160
St. Lucia	0.7	0.16	707	60	370
St. Vincent and the Grenada	2.13	0.12	337	47	163
Suriname	-14.47	0.42	846	435	526
Trinidad and Tobago	8.89	1.3	7703	4273	3308
FTAA (1)		813.24	12476579	1413856	1882228
WORLD (2)		6057.97	31498070	6425577	6626593
(1/2)		13.42	39.61	22	28.4

Source: World Bank (2002) and own derivations.

CARICOM and the FTAA

The small size of Caricom within the pending FTAA can also be gleaned from Table 3. Caricom's GDP in 2000 was US$29.2 billion, or 0.23 percent of the GDP of the pending FTAA. Caricom's merchandise exports and imports of US$8.1 billion and US$12.4 billion are a mere fraction of the total exports and imports of the FTAA nations, ranking at 0.57 percent and 0.66 percent respectively. The population of Caricom represents 1.74 percent of the FTAA total. In all regards, Caricom is a marginal player in the FTAA process, and with the reduction in the threat of a global war, the most developed nations of the pending FTAA no longer need to court Caricom member states for geopolitical reasons. For this reason, Caricom as a whole would need to ensure it meaningfully engages in the FTAA negotiations for the benefit of its people.[2]

Benefits and Costs of the FTAA for CARICOM Countries

But what are the benefits and costs to a small regional trade agreement like Caricom in a trade bloc such as the FTAA? The pending FTAA offers Caricom countries access to the markets of North America, but at the same time it also offers access to the markets of Latin America. In particular, the FTAA arrangements would provide to Caricom more stable access to Latin American countries than will be available to countries outside of the pending FTAA.[3]

Traditional trade theory suggests that trade agreements can have two predominant types of effects: these are trade diversion and trade creation. With the formation of a free trade area there is a shift from the most efficient producer towards the lowest cost intra-regional producer; this is trade diversion. The second effect is the creation of trade by allowing the high cost intra-regional producers to supply the intra-regional market. Whether or not the FTAA will be beneficial depends on the relative magnitudes of the trade diversion and trade creation effects. However, it is not unreasonable for one to expect that the benefits from the FTAA would be greater for the smaller member states of Caricom than for the larger ones, mainly because the magnitude of the trade flows that ensue from a trade integration agreement are considerably larger than the overall macroeconomic size of these small economies.

The increased competition from extra-Caricom members within the FTAA may lead to a loss in employment in inefficient industries. In the same vein of reasoning, however, the more dynamic Caricom firms would lower their operational costs and improve their efficiency in reaction to the wave of import competition that the FTAA is expected to bring.

The pending FTAA could also provide Caricom member states with a number of non-traditional benefits that are welfare enhancing but which in the absence of a regional trade agreement (RTA) would not be forthcoming. For example, Fernandez and Portes (1998) note that in becoming part of an RTA, member states have to adhere to binding rules. If extra-FTAA countries and blocs of countries perceive that the FTAA would make it difficult for Caricom countries to reverse policy action on economic reform, then their interest in Caricom may widen. In such an eventuality, Caricom countries can benefit from an increased amount of trade flows, as a foreign investor operating in the Caribbean Community would also be able to benefit from economies of scale because the other large markets in the region would become more easily accessible.[4]

How can an RTA solve problems attached to time inconsistencies? The RTA would have to be able to address two separate conditions: First, policies in the absence of an RTA must be typified by the fact that they are time inconsistent. This means that prior to the implementation of an RTA, the problem must exist but after the implementation of the RTA the problem must no longer exist. It is possible to illustrate how an RTA could fulfill these conditions with reference to trade reforms. In particular, unilateral liberalization is unlikely, even for a small country, to be a time consistent policy. Even more, it is unlikely to be politically popular with import competing infant industries. In many regards, the government in these circumstances is going to find it very difficult to maintain its political support if it practices unilateral liberalization for a variety of reasons (including traditional income redistribution, terms of trade or political economy considerations). Even though a government may extend limited protection to a few sectors for some time, the economy as a whole may become very distorted. In this context, Fernandez and Portes (1998) argue that a regional trade agreement, by making the cost of even a small deviation from the contextual arrangement very high — say by forcing the culprit member state to leave the arrangement or by some agreed punishment for deviating states— would minimize the likelihood that the RTA may engage in small distortions, which can of themselves distort the overall economy.[5] In this sense then, if the FTAA is implemented it may help to reduce time inconsistent behavior.

A further way in which membership in the FTAA can be superior to the GATT or GATT-like agencies is that the FTAA may be able to impose on the rebel member state a changing set of incentives in a way that differs from GATT. A primary example of this is domestic and foreign investment. The extent of investment is more likely to increase in a country that engages in an RTA than in a country that tries to embrace multilateral free trade. The reasoning here is that a properly implemented RTA grants a participating country preferential access to the markets of member states that are engaged in the union, whereas no such guarantee is available under the GATT.[6]

Another potential benefit of the FTAA is signaling. For an RTA to operate as a signaling mechanism it must bind the country to a set of rules that would have otherwise been time inconsistent. In this case, the motivation for the RTA is not the terms of the RTA itself but that the RTA may represent certain attributes (e.g., zero tolerance for terrorism) that the government is interested in signaling to others. The government can signal this intention to other members by joining an RTA provided that this is one of the stated intentions of the RTA.

It is possible that the FTAA can improve the welfare of at least one of its member states by providing insurance against possible future events. This type of argument may help to explain why small countries engage large countries in an RTA even though the small countries may enter on terms worse than the large countries. To explain the insurance effect of membership in an RTA, Fernandez and Portes (1998) argue as follows: Suppose that we have a country which is facing macroeconomic uncertainty as regards the level its imperfectly flexible real wages should adopt. If real wages were to increase more than a country expected, its competitiveness can be undermined; this in turn might require the country to devalue in order to prevent its output level or its level of employment from falling. However, if the country were to implement such a policy move it may realize retaliation from one or more of its trading partners. The country may still be willing to engage an RTA at terms that are in fact unfavorable to it, if it has the assurance that if it devalues, its RTA partners will not retaliate. The situation need not be in favor of only the lesser-developed or competitive member state, as any member that experiences an adverse shock may be allowed to devalue.

In a recent study, Vamvakidis (1998) found rigorous empirical evidence that small economies grow faster when they enter regional trading arrangement with larger more developed economies. To test the influence of RTAs on economic growth, Vamvakidis focused on the Association of South East Asian Nations (ASEAN), the Andean Common Market (ANCON), the Central American Common Market (CACM), the United Dounaniere et Economique de l'Afrique Centrale (UDEAC) and the European Union (EU). Of all these RTAs, Vamvakidis found that only the EU had a positive and significant effect on the growth of its member states. In this sense, therefore, the membership of the USA and Canada in the FTAA can actually work in the interest of Caricom member states.

There are a number of reasons, however, that have been cited by UNECLAC (2001b) as to why the adjustment costs of Caricom member states in an FTAA would be higher than other countries.

1. The member states of the Caricom sphere produce a narrow range of primary commodities, which are targeted at a few principal markets. These commodities are produced mainly by a group of small firms with

Table 4.
Import taxes as a percentage of fiscal revenues, 1990–99.

Country	1990	1991	1992	1993	1994	1995	1996	1997	1998	1999
Antigua & Barbuda	52.08	54.84	54.75	54.12	51.48	51.83	51.08	49.7	50.36	48.08
Anguilla	n.a.	65.97	67.84	48.33	54.92	53.23	58.25	57.04	65.57	63.18
Bahamas	65.94	62.23	55.62	54.97	53.65	52.62	52.77	52.1	49.79	52.67
Barbados	13.21	9.44	8.08	8.08	8.63	8.61	8.08	9.26	9.35	9.57
Belize	51.54	51.86	47.82	49.2	49.7	52.97	34.41	31.6	33.5	34.8
Dominica	17.8	18.2	17.4	17.6	14.7	14.3	14	15	13.5	14.6
Guyana	11.4	10.2	9.5	12.6	12.8	11.6	11.7	11.8	12.1	n.a.
Jamaica	n.a.	13.4	13.7	13.6	10.9	11.9	10.8	11.3	10.6	10.4
St. Kitts/ Nevis	53.5	50.3	48.3	26.2	49.1	45.6	45.3	44.2	42	43.5
St. Lucia	51.9	50.5	50.01	50.6	48.3	48	47.9	44.7	48.6	47.1
St. Vincent	51.1	49.6	48.7	47.6	45.9	48.9	43.6	44.9	42.7	43.3
Trinidad & Tobago	8.2	8.1	9.4	9.4	7.7	5.8	5.2	6.3	7.2	7.2

Source: Hosein (2002).

characteristically low resource endowments and small profit margins so that it would be difficult for them to make significant changes.

2. Many of the main export items from Caricom member states are sold in markets that offer them margins of preference: e.g., the USA through the Caribbean Basin Expansion Recovery Act (CBERA) and Caribbean Basin Trade Partnership Act (CBTPA);[7] Canada through the CARIBCAN arrangement; Europe through the various Lome agreements; and within Caricom, where the common external tariff exists. These margins of preference have allowed Caricom firms to subsist with inefficient production functions. The FTAA would lead to a dissipation of much of these margins of preference, with serious implications for income and employment in the affected member states.

3. Many Caricom member states, especially those of the OECS subregional blocs, depend on international trade taxes for the bulk of their revenues. The formation of an FTAA and the removal of intra-hemispheric tariffs would lead to substantial erosion of their revenues, with immediate and serious implications for their economic development. As the data in Table 4 reflect, by 1999, apart from Barbados, Dominica, Jamaica, and Trinidad and Tobago, every other Caricom member state extracted more than 34 percent (and in most cases over 40 percent) of their revenues from import taxes.[8]

Given the costs and benefits on offer from the FTAA, it should be considered as part of the global repositioning strategy of the region. Such global repositioning action is necessary to improve the position of Caricom by allowing it to adjust quickly to changes in global technology and demand. This type of strategy would include, among other things, trying to produce commodities on the upswing of the international product cycle, trying to structurally diversify the economic base so as to produce a wider range of commodities, revitalizing traditional exports, and improving the various techniques of production so as to keep abreast of world demand (Hall 2001).

Coping with the FTAA

Caricom countries would have to pay attention to the fact that trade liberalization by itself will not encourage competitiveness. In coming to terms with the FTAA, two significant options are available to Caricom countries: these are the application for special and differential status and improving the competitiveness and the efficiency of Caricom states.

Special and Differential Status

The type of argument made in favor of special and differential status by developing countries is usually premised on their inability to benefit from economies of scale and scope, but even more and especially as concerns Caricom member states, their vulnerability to the whims and fancies of natural disasters, including volcanic eruptions, hurricanes and earthquakes. The importance of devising special and differential criteria to assist the smaller economies in the pending FTAA has been recognized by the members of the FTAA. In the plan of Action and Declaration of the Summit of the Americas held in Miami in December 1995, the signatories expressed in paragraph 6, "We recognize the broad differences in the levels of development and size of the economies in our hemisphere and we will remain cognizant of those differences in our negotiations so as to ensure that these receive the treatment that they require to ensure the full participation of all countries in the construction and benefits of the FTAA" (UNECLAC 2001c).

The notion of special and differential treatment for smaller countries is not new, as it has been deployed in the past to encourage greater participation of smaller countries in the world trading system. The FTAA process has initiated a Consultative Committee that has been formed specially to deal with the proper and appropriate inclusion strategy of member states. The major role of this committee is advisorial, and it can refer matters to the Technical Negotiating Committee for further consideration.

UNECLAC (2001) has highlighted that the nature of special and differential status given to Caribbean countries is likely to take one of three forms: exemption from some of the more rigorous trade, investment and competition policy measures; the provision of a longer period for Caricom member states to implement the requirements of the arrangement; or some combination of these two. More likely, Caricom countries would encounter special and differential treatment in the form of a longer transitional time frame. In this regard, Caricom countries would eventually have to be prepared by the time the protection from any special and differential status matures. They would need to work quickly to minimize the inefficiencies in their most important comparative and dynamic comparative advantage areas. It is expected that investors in the region would capitalize on such a transitional break, if granted, and consolidate their efforts so that they can preserve or reduce the erosion of their market shares when the FTAA does eventually take effect. If small economies receive special and differential status, it is likely that those that act first will benefit most.

Improving Competitiveness and the Efficiency of CARICOM States

The Caricom economies are no longer low cost producers based on cheap wages; comparatively speaking, Caricom countries have relatively high standards of education and quality infrastructure and these can be used to foster the growth of industries (United Nations Development Program 2001).

In this regard, the strategy of development that Caricom countries can embrace would have much in common to that proposed by Lewis (1950) in his "Industrialization by Invitation" (IBI) thesis. Lewis recognized that Caricom countries were deficient in several important areas, especially the availability of physical capital, entrepreneurial capital, technology and markets.[9] One Caricom member state, Trinidad and Tobago, has adopted a particular strain of the IBI strategy as proposed by Lewis. In particular, Trinidad and Tobago embraced a resource based industrialization strategy in that they invested some of the economic rents realized during the oil boom in the formation of a series of natural gas–based plants. Trinidad and Tobago has also attracted a substantial number of foreign players to help exploit its abundant resource of natural gas. In the same vein, resource rich countries like Suriname, Guyana and Jamaica can pursue increased downstream processing of their bauxite and alumina.

Caricom member states would have to recognize that some types of investments that are cost based are very positively correlated with exports. These types of investments would flow into an economy in search of lower costs of factors of production. In this sense, therefore, the member states of Caricom should actively seek to promote their comparative advantage, which includes not only their natural resources but also the quality of their labor forces and the infrastructure of the region. For Caricom countries to encourage greater foreign direct investment, they would need to become more dynamic and try to identify sunrise industries, i.e. commodities at the early stages of the international product cycle. (Market-seeking investment will not flow into the Caricom bloc as the market size of Caricom, even with the inclusion of Haiti, is too small.) The question that arises is whether Caricom has the potential to identify and germinate such industries and, if not, what measures are being put in place to create this capacity.

One definite opportunity for Caricom states to improve their productivity rests with overall improvements in its stock of human capital and administrative infrastructure, the occurrence of which would increase the regional chance of attracting foreign direct investment in those areas where such investment is likely to experience the most rapid growth: biotechnology, information technology and microelectronics. Improvements in the labor productivity of a country through further training and education can also help to attract foreign direct investment.

Characteristically, Caricom member states are small and have undiversified export and production structures, which are very vulnerable to changes in the international conditions of trade. Consequently, these countries "cannot afford to isolate themselves from their major markets, because they are unlikely on their own to reap sufficient economies of scale and scope to compete effectively in global markets. For small economies, the issue is not whether to integrate with their hemispheric trading partners, but how" (Schott 2001, 99).

Regardless of the extent of trade liberalization practiced by Caricom member states, they would still need to administer sound macroeconomic management policies in order to take a meaningful part in the FTAA. However, one may point out that for small economies, the type of adjustment that they may be required to adopt in the context of the pending FTAA would not be significantly different from that required by multilateral liberalization. In this regard, therefore, and on the presumption that globalization is not likely to change direction, the small economies of the Western Hemisphere are on the correct pathway. Despite this—and this is where special and differential status is so very important—Caricom countries would need to be careful that the requirements of the FTAA do not force them into meeting ridiculous deadlines, as this would maximize the likeliness of error (Hall 2001). Without doubt, though, whether the FTAA will increase or decrease the amount of investment flows to the Caricom region depends on a number of factors including their comparative advantage and the degree of competition from other FTAA members.

The Challenges of the FTAA for CARICOM Member States

The FTAA process has had a checkered history. After each summit meeting there has been a serious financial crisis in the region. For example, the summit in Miami was followed by the collapse of the Mexican peso, while the Santiago summit was followed within a few months by the Brazilian financial crisis. The last summit, in 2001, mainly coincided with the Argentinean crisis.

One of the immediate challenges of the FTAA for Caricom nations is to determine whether Caricom economic growth will be sufficiently robust so as to provide the necessary financial resources for them to structurally reform their economies. One study (Itam et al. 2000) has forecast an average growth rate for Caricom countries during the period 2002–2005 of 3.6 percent. This forecast, however, was made prior to September 11, 2001, and because of important changes that have taken place in the prices of some of the key Caricom export commodities (and the falloff in tourist flows after September 11) may be overvalued.

The challenge confronting Caricom nations in the context of the FTAA is one of simultaneously determining how the regional bloc could encourage inflows of investment from other member states in the FTAA while at the same time encouraging greater trade outflows. While all this is occurring, Caricom countries need to strive towards the diversification of their production and exporting base and also try to increase their employment rates. (According to the UNECLAC [2001b]) the Caribbean Basin Initiative of May 2000 was proposed to be a gateway for greater participation of Caricom countries in the wider hemispheric context.)

For Caricom member states to achieve these goals they will need to dig even deeper and accelerate their reforms. Although some Caricom countries implemented more liberal reform oriented policies in the 1980s, it still remains optimistic to expect that a shift in the allocation of productive responsibility away from government to the private sector would lead to a change in the pace of development.[10] More specifically, a reliance on the forces of the market to instigate changes in the very nature of the resource allocation process, to affect the mobility of factors of production, and at the same time to increase efficiency has found a considerable amount of resistance from an inefficient public sector, an inefficient and small stock of physical and human capital, and a series of administrative and beaucratic procedures that weaken the investment process (Schott 2001).

In many of these small economies the political fabric in place has also not made the adjustments necessary for the economic machinery to function more efficiently. UNELAC (2001) has noted that in an open economy that is operating in a competitive environment, the existence of strong disincentives to production compounds those disadvantages that are related to resource endowments and structural factors that are historically founded.

In the first wave of reforms embarked upon by Caricom nations, there was a general element of naïve thinking premised on the idea that in all circumstances there would be a quick supply response from the market operating with minimalist state participation. However, this type of presumption ignored the limited capital endowments attributes of Caricom countries and at the same time did not pay enough attention to the influence of imperfectly operating or outright missing markets. Further, these policy directives, based as they were on the contents of the Washington Consensus, did not fully appreciate that human capital was a scarce factor in these less developed countries, and that in many instances widespread signs of surplus labor coexisted with deficient amounts of required skills. Entrepreneurial talent in Caricom member states continues to be a binding and scarce factor of production.

As a practical matter, the deficiencies outlined above must be addressed by Caricom countries if they are participate in a fuller and more meaningful way in the FTAA.[11] Consequent on the eventual context of the FTAA, developing countries would need to improve their administrative capacity or to create support units to assist them. To assist their revenue collection, the less developed countries of the Caricom sphere would need to overhaul their tax collection architecture in order to minimize the changes in their fiscal revenues, should the FTAA reduce their international trade taxes.

Conclusion

Globalization for Caricom's member states is not a choice; it is reality. Membership in this hemispheric arrangement, which accounts for 40 percent of world GDP and just under a third of world imports, does not have to require a totally open or liberalized economy; in many instances it may well be necessary for a nation to protect important parts of its economy.

Such exceptions may become necessary in order to gain the widest possible spectrum of support for FTAA participation.

In order for the people of the small highly open developing countries that typify the Caricom region to indulge freely and wholly in the FTAA, they must believe that the benefits and opportunities offered by the FTAA outweigh the costs and any associated risks. The confidence of the Caribbean people in the FTAA rests squarely on their sustained belief that the FTAA would be fully considerate of their peculiar problems and would distribute the gains from the FTAA in an equitable fashion.

As with all arrangements, membership in the FTAA would have both benefits and costs. Among the benefits are the potential creation of trade and expansion of the preferential market base of Caricom member states to the entire list of countries in the Western Hemisphere (excluding Cuba). However, attached to the FTAA are also a number of costs including the exposure of fragile infant industries to more competitive extra-regional firms. To cope with the FTAA, Caricom countries can seek an extension of the margins of preference that have carried their economies for many years in the form of special and differential status agreements. Alternatively, Caribbean countries can seek to improve their overall competitiveness and efficiency.

The FTAA is both an opportunity and a challenge for Caricom countries. It should be viewed as a vehicle for global repositioning. Moving quickly and moving in the right direction can optimise CARICOM countries' chances of coming out winners and prepare them even further for multilateral free trade.

Endnotes

1. We would like to acknowledge the assistance of Rishi Singh.
2. While Caricom may not be able to survive in the hemisphere without FTAA preferences, the non-Caricom FTAA member states may be able to do so.
3. Some authors, e.g. Krugman (1991), note that because a large RTA offers small member states the opportunity for greater productive efficiency through the opportunity of selling to a large market, one might expect them to attach more priority to joining such an RTA.
4. An RTA can encourage investment flows between Caricom states and from countries outside of the RTA in several important ways. In the first instance, by reducing the amount of distortion in production amongst member states, the RTA could lead to an expansion in the overall amount of investment that investors make. Further, and especially for lumpy investment projects, an RTA could lead to an expansion in the amount of investments made by both domestic and foreign investors because of the larger market size.
5. One may be tempted to ask why the GATT cannot implement this type of policy authority in the absence of an RTA. Fernandez and Portes argue that within the GATT, the responsibility for identifying and singling out a deviating nation rests with the GATT.
6. See Ethier (1996) for a similar type of argument.
7. In 1982, the US established a preferential trade arrangement with the countries of the

Caribbean area under the umbrella of the Caribbean Basin Initiative (CBI). With the formation of NAFTA a substantial amount of the trade preferences of the CBI countries in terms of access to the US market was eroded. It was not until May 2000 that the CBI countries were finally granted CBI enhancement through passage of the U.S.–Caribbean Basin Trade Partnership Act (CBTPA). The CBTPA is part of a broader piece of legislation, the Trade and Development Act of 2000. The CBTPA amends the CBERA and partially addressed the economic concerns of the CBI countries by reestablishing a "leveled playing field" with Mexico.

8. Increasing tax revenues to offset tariff reductions could well be the most important domestic policy challenge facing smaller economies with regard to the FTAA. The relatively high dependence of some of these countries (particularly OECS members) on tariffs as a source of income generates a reluctance on the part of policy makers to liberalize trade in general, or in relation to regional trade agreements, without alternative sources of fiscal receipts. Trade liberalization brings with it a decreased emphasis on border taxes, and the loss of what may be a considerable percentage of government revenues is a problem to the extent that alternative sources of revenues are not easily available or are yet to be developed. The range of taxable sources or even individuals is severely limited in some of the very small economies.

9. For small developing economies with limited market size, private capital flows tend to complement trade flows. More specifically, because the markets in these small countries are so small, foreign firms producing in these host economies principally target foreign markets.

10. Caricom economies have made some headway in the 1980s and 1990s in reforming their economies and by extension preparing them for more meaningful participation in the FTAA arrangement. While it may be argued that some of this economic performance was broadly satisfactory it can also be argued that even deeper reforms are necessary for Caricom states to experience the success they desire. With the pending FTAA, Caricom countries would have to be more detailed in their planning and preparation for the future, as their margins of preference in CARIBCAN and the CBI come under threat and any form of concessional assistance becomes increasingly difficult to procure.

11. It may be argued that even if the FTAA does not materialize, these type of reforms are still very necessary.

References

Bergsten, C. Fred. 1994. "APEC and World Trade: A Force for Worldwide Liberalization." *Foreign Affairs* 73, no. 3 (May/June): 20–26.

_____. 1996b. "Competitive Liberalization and Global Free Trade." In Su King, *Major Issues for the Global Trade and Financial System*. Seoul: Seoul Global Trade Forum.

_____. 1996a. "Globalizing Free Trade." *Foreign Affairs* 75, no. 3 (May/June): 105–120.

_____. 1997. "Open Regionalism." Institute for International Economics, *Working Paper* 97–3.

Bhagwati, J. 1996. "Preferential Trade Agreements: The Wrong Road." *Law and Policy in International Business* 27, no. 4 (summer): 865–871.

_____, and Arvind Panagariya. 1996. "Preferential Trading Areas and Multilateralism — Strangers, Friends or Foes?" In Jagdish Bhagwati and Arvind Panagariya, *The Economics of Preferential Trade Agreements*. Washington: American Enterprise Institute and AEI Press.

CARICOM. 2000. *Caribbean Trade and Investment Report: Dynamic Interface of Regionalism and Globalization*. Georgetown, Guyana: CARICOM.

Drysdale, Peter, and Poss Garnaut. 1993. "The Application of a General Theory of Economic Integration." In C. Fred Bergsten and Marcus Noland, *Pacific*

Dynamism and the International Economic System. Washington: Institute for International Economics.

ECLAC/CDCC. 1999. *The Fiscal Covenant: Strength, Weaknesses, Challenges — A Caribbean Perspective*. Port of Spain, Trinidad and Tobago: ECLAC.

El Agraa, A. 1997. Economic Integration Worldwide. Hampshire, England: MacMillan Press.

Ethier, W. 1996. *Regionalism in a Multilateral World. Journal of Political Economy* 106:1214–1245.

Fernandez, R., and J. Portes. 1998. "Returns to Regionalism: An Analysis of Non-traditional Gains from Regional Trade Agreements." *The World Bank Economic Review* 12, no. 2: 197–220.

Frankel, Jeffery A. 2000. "Globalization of the Economy." NBER Working Paper no. 7858, August.

Garnaut, R. 1994. "Open Regionalism: Its Analytic Basis and Relevance to International System." *Journal of Asian Economies* 5, no. 2 (summer): 273–290.

Girvan, N., M. A. Servilla, M. C. Hatton and E. Rodriguez. 1991. "The Debt Problem of Small Peripheral Economies: Case Studies from the Caribbean and Central America." *Caribbean Studies* 24, no. 1–2 (January–June): 45–115.

Girvan, Norman. 1999. "Globalization, Fragmentation and Integration: A Caribbean Perspective." International Meeting on Globalization and Development Problems, Havana, Cuba, January 18–22, 1999.

Gonzales, A. 2001. "Caribbean Integration in the Next Decade: A Strategic Vision for the New Millennium." In Kenneth Hall (ed.), The Caribbean Community: Beyond Survival. Kingston: Ian Randle Publishers.

Hall, K. (ed.). 2001. The Caribbean Community: Beyond Survival. Kingston: Ian Randle Publishers.

Hosein, R. 2002. The CARICOM Common External Tariff (CET): Development and Fiscal Implications. Forthcoming.

Itam, S. et al. 2000. *Developments and Challenges in the Caricom Region*. Washington, D.C.: International Monetary Fund.

Krugman, Paul. 1991. "Move Towards Free Trade Zones." *Federal Reserve Bank of Kansas City Economic Review* (November–December): 5–25.

Lewis W. A. 1950. "The Industrialization of the British West Indies." *Caribbean Economic Review* 2:1–61.

Schott, J. 2001. *Prospects for Free Trade in the Americas*. Washington: Institute for International Economics.

United Nations Development Program. 2001. *Human Development Report: Making new technologies work for human development*. Washington, D.C.

UNECLAC. 2001a. *Recent Development in Intra-CDCC Trade*. Washington, D.C.

_____. 1999. *Review of Caribbean Economic and Social Performance in the 1980s and 1990s*. Washington, D.C.

_____. 2001c. *Special and Differential Treatment in the FTAA*. Washington, D.C.

_____. 2001b. *Trade and Investment flows between the Caribbean and the Rest of the Hemisphere in the Context of the FTAA*. Washington, D.C.

Vamvakidis, A. 1998. "Regional Integration and Economic Growth." *The World Bank Economic Review* 12, no. 2:251–70.

World Bank. 2002. Available at http://publications.worldbank.org/WDI/.

Yusuf, S. 2001. *Globalization and the Challenge for Developing Countries*. Washington, D.C.: World Bank.

PART THREE.

Cultural and Social Integration

Cultural Policy, Globalization and the Governance of Plural Societies

John La Guerre

In this paper I set out to demonstrate that there has never been a carefully conceived cultural policy for Trinidad and Tobago; that the forces of globalization have seriously complicated the task of constructing such a policy and that such a policy is important for the governance and integration of such societies.

It has been noted that as a concept, culture has been associated with political nationalism; yet there has been a great deal of difference among anthropologists as to what actually is entailed in the concept of culture. Generally, though, there seems to be a general agreement with the conclusions reached by Kroeber and Kluckhohn that "culture is a product; is historical; includes ideas, patterns, and values; is selective; is learned; is based upon symbols; and is an abstraction from behaviour and the products of behaviour."[1] Cultural change, whether originating internally or externally, is accordingly a major factor in the relations between the institutions, ideas, values and the symbols of a particular cultural grouping. To understand the impact of change, anthropologists have employed concepts such as the "contact situation," "syncretism," "survival," "forces," "acculturation," "cultural focus," "diffusion," and "reinterpretation" to understand the impact and consequences of cultural behavior between and these among differing cultures. M.G. Smith has added to these the idea of a "contact continuum."[2] I intend to use some of these concepts in the discussion of cultural policy.

It is not surprising that anthropology and its related concerns were very much part and parcel of the imperial enterprise. Empire meant not only the subjugation of the weak by the strong, but also the contact between and among differing cultures. In the post-imperial world, contacts between the colonizer and the colonized have increased. Cultural change is very much a consequence of the forces of globalization at work throughout the world.

Over the last few years the concept of globalization has become a popular explanatory tool for almost every kind of change taking place today, as a result of what is regarded as the "end of ideology" and "system convergence." Globalization might thus be defined as "those processes by which the peoples of the world are incorporated into a single society." These processes would involve changing concepts of time and space, increasing rate of cultural interactions, common problems, growing interconnections and interdependencies, networks of powerful transnational actors and organizations, and mechanisms for the coordination of all these processes.[3] Writers and commentators contend that the world is being compressed, thus shifting visions from the village to the international arena. It has been pointed out, for instance, that whereas between 1200 and 1840 A.D. the speed of transport was 16 k.p.h., by the 1960s it had increased to 800–1120 k.p.h. Add to this the dramatic advances in telecommunications, particularly the radio, television and the Internet, and one can understand why it is now common to speak of a "global village."

It is important to note that the debates on globalization focus on three different aspects of changes and relations: economic, political and cultural. It is often pointed out that globalization has always been a force on the lives of people everywhere and that interaction between and among peoples is as old as humanity itself. While that is undoubtedly true, it is clear that over the last decade or so the pace of interaction has dramatically increased.

Writers who focus on the economic interactions point to the changes in trade and capital movements. Hirst and Thompson in their book *Globalization in Question* argue, after a review of the historical record, that levels of integration, interdependence and openness of natural borders have not changed significantly.

Ankie Hoogvelt holds that the percentage share in world trade of two continents, Africa and South America, has actually declined.[4] It has been pointed out that much of the expanded trade under globalization has been confined to the developed economies, particularly the US, the OECD and Japan.[5] Considerations such as these have led some researchers to wonder whether "globalization has not gone too far" by leading to growing inequalities between and among nations.[6]

So far as the political discussions are concerned, there are two major contending positions. One tendency is expressed by Susan Strange in *The Retreat of the State: The Diffusion of Power in the World Economy*. It is the argument of Strange that the technological innovations over the last few years, particularly the Internet, have eroded the power of the State to control the flow of capital; similarly, Held contends that increasing cultural and economic connections reduce the ability of the State to control ideas and economic transactions within its border.[7] Cerny and others, on the other hand, argue that the nation-state is still a powerful force, and that it can use the forces of globalization to position itself more effectively to compete with other states.

Clearly, these developments have serious consequences for the government of societies. In recent times, policy-makers have adopted a new term, *governance*, instead of *government*, to denote a new approach to the problem of administering societies. It will be appreciated that in the case of plural societies, the need is even greater for fresh approaches to the problems of governance. *Governance* implies less emphasis on state sanctions, power and authority; it envisages greater partnerships between the public and private sectors and a greater emphasis on market forces and the determination of policy based on the interaction of multiple actors and agencies.[8]

It has been necessary to discuss the political and economic aspects of globalization because, as we shall observe later, these are forces that have had serious consequences for the adoption of a cultural policy, particularly in a plural society as Trinidad and Tobago. Cultural policy was one of the major tasks facing the new states when they gained independence, since it was the declared aim of these states to pursue a policy of decolonization. In the case of India, the search for a cultural policy was driven by a desire to find a set of symbols that could appeal to a massive electorate. There was also a special concern to ensure that such symbols as were adopted could evoke action and commitment to a much wider community. It proclaimed a secular state but was careful to incorporate important elements and symbols from its past to ensure wide appeal. In Africa, "negritude" and "the African personality performed a similar function, something with which both the elite and masses could identify."[9]

Trinidad and Tobago was hurried into independence with little time to think out a cultural policy. The elite also believed that a small society had been successfully integrated around creole values. The forces of change, regional as well as global, would later intensify. In Trinidad it was felt that no more than a few trendy slogans and mottos were needed. If it is accepted, following Held and McGraw, that cultural globalization embraces "the specialized and professionalized discourses of the arts, the commodified output of the culture industries, the spontaneous and unorganized cultural expressions of everyday life, and of course, the complex interactions between all of these," then it is clear that decolonization should have involved cultural transformation. In such a case, the policy of the state and of the business sector would be crucial for the survival of such cultural activities, given its power to bestow or withhold resources.

The case of Trinidad and Tobago provides a clear illustration of the importance of globalization for the emergence of a cultural policy and the role of that policy in the governance of a plural society.

What is regarded as Trinidadian society was in fact, under British imperial rule, a series of labor imports from Europe, Africa, India, China and even Afghanistan. The immediate purpose of this immigration was to satisfy the labor needs of the plantation economy. Little or no attempt was made to think through a policy of integration or a corresponding cultural policy. The imperial power was convinced of the superiority of its own culture and considered it as one of the blessings of colonial rule, much as the French did with its *mission civilatric*. What the imperial power did then was to export its institutions, ideas, and practices as well as prejudices to its various colonies. In short, a global push resulted in the transplantation of cultures but with the imperial culture as the dominant ingredient. This was the process that Trinidadian sociologist Braithwaite analyzed with such insight in his pioneering study, *Social Stratification in Trinidad and Tobago*. Braithwaite, by the use of reference group theory and the concepts of superordinate and subordinate social systems, argued that people in Trinidad were all striving after metropolitan and largely British values, and that it was this aspiration after common values that held the society together. The polices by which these values were to be achieved could be summarized as one of assimilation. Such a policy emphasized a preference for European features and color and an emphasis on English language and culture. There was also a tendency to stress degrees from English universities over those obtained from Canada or the US. An English accent would also lend status to the speaker. M.G. Smith contested this view of the stratification of Trinidadian society and contended that the values claimed by Braithwaite as the bond of society were in fact shared by only a few of the elite.[10]

To some extent Smith was right, although it is clear that he and Braithwaite were analyzing differing levels of the social structure. Braithwaite was analyzing the elites of his day, while Smith was focusing his attention on the culture of the masses. What both omitted from their analyses was the impact of globalization and external forces on the local milieu. Williams also had warned that there could be no "Mother India,"

"Mother Africa" or "Mother Europe" in Trinidad and Tobago. What all failed to recognize was that the population's origins in India, Africa and Europe were all that they had that could provide a sense of identity, even though the sources were disparate. In any case, the culture of "Mother England" was quite substantial. In language, dress, diet, sporting preferences, educational systems and political institutions, the content was largely British. The policy of assimilation did in fact reach a substantial part of population. That it did not encompass a much greater part of the population was the result of the activities of a number of international organizations and individuals. African organizations such as the League of Coloured Peoples, the Negro Progress Convention, and Garvey's UNIA all challenged the basic premises of assimilationist philosophy.

The Pan African Association and George Padmore's activities in the Profintern helped to keep alive a sense of African culture and identity. In the Indian case, organizations such as the Friends of India, the Indian National Natural Congress, visiting missionaries, Indian films and confinement to or around the plantations helped to keep alive a conception of Indian identity and culture.

Different groups responded to the policies of cultural assimilation differently, and some were more assimilated than others. The rate of assimilation was understandably higher in the case of Europeans given their status in the economy. The African-descended population was more exposed to British culture than were other groups and had, after the abolition of slavery, settled mainly in the towns. There were also no African films; such films as did contain Africans usually relegated them to minor or menial roles.[11]

The Indians, on the other hand, only came in 1845 after the abolition of slavery, and it is well to remember that indentureship only ended in 1917. The vast majority of the Indians were Hindus, almost 85 percent of the Indian community, and its caste system was highly resistant to cultural assimilation. The Muslims though, given the universalist ideology of Islam, were more amendable to interaction with other cultures.

This is not to imply that any of these cultures were able to resist fully the pressures of the dominant culture. In any contact situation there is bound to be modification, acculturation, reinterpretation, syncretism and some redefinition of the key elements of the culture. To think of culture as a static system is to be guilty of reification. In this context numerous writers have pointed to change taking place in Trinidad among the various cultures. Even European culture in Trinidad, though dominant, could not escape the fact that it was distant from the center; similarly, African religion could not escape the infiltration of Christian elements. By the same token, the Hindu and Muslim cultures were heavily influenced by the prevailing cultural forms around them. Over the years the various dialects of India gave way to the lingua franca of Hindustani or Urdu which, over the years, in turn gave way to English or a French patois. In language, dress, religion, festivals, celebrations and cuisine there was much reinterpretation, syncretism and adaptation of cultural forms between and among the various cultures in the Caribbean and in Trinidad. These were the processes that were collectively described as creolization. As originally conceived, the term *Creole* referred to white settlers in the Caribbean. What it signified in fact were the cultural changes induced by residence in the Caribbean.[12] What is important though is whether the changes have taken place in the core or focal institutions, such as the family, the language, the economy or the caste system. For instance, there can be no doubt that the caste system is no longer a determinant of status position, although Hindus generally tend to marry within the Indian group. Few Indians speak Hindi except on ritual occasions, and the economy is no longer racially stratified as it once was. This does not mean that there are no identity markers. Celebrations such as Eid, Divali, Baptist Holiday and Emancipation Day serve as reminders of cultural pasts, and thereby provide their adherents with a sense of identity.

Given these disparate cultures and the differing identities to which they give rise, a cultural policy that would appeal to substantial sections of the community becomes a necessary prerequisite for effective governance. Yet political developments, national, regional and international, have over the years tended to sustain these disparate identities. In Trinidad, for example, the advent of universal adult suffrage sent aspiring political leaders scurrying for voting banks which turned out to be in fact ethnic constituencies [13] and in the run up to the 1956 elections, politics and culture became locked together as the leaders of two major blocs became identified with ethnic causes. Eric Williams, after the experience of Howard University in the USA and the Caribbean Commission, became the ideologue of the Black Man, of slavery, and of the issues surrounding slavery. Thus the People's National Movement (PNM) became identified with the urban and African community. In a similar fashion, Bhadase Sagan Maraj, as leader of the Sanatan Dharma Maha Sabha and the People's Democratic Party (PDP) became identified with Indians and Hindu culture. Thus were established the umbilical cords binding the two major political formations to African and Indian culture respectively.[14]

External developments would also be critical in sustaining these identities. Thus developments in the struggle against apartheid in South Africa and the actors involved kept alive the emotions of a separate cultural identity among the African community in Trinidad, while the various episodes in the Afro-American struggle in the US had a similar effect. Within the Caribbean, the agony of Guyanese politics struck responsive chords in Trinidad. In the case of the Indians of Trinidad, developments in Fiji and earlier the expulsion of the Indians of Uganda reverberated and ricocheted in the political controversies of the day. This explains why the Indians of Guyana and Trinidad were initially fearful of Federation and later of Caricom. To recall the silver-tongued orators of 1956 is to demonstrate that some semblance of metropolitan values still existed. Yet as Naipaul noted, even if in fiction, lurking beneath the veneer of Westminster-style debates was "the sacrament of the square."[15] Implicit in the notion was an assimilationist pecking order — white, African, then Indian. It is not that there was no cultural crossover in the two political organizations. The PNM was able to initially attract the more assimilated sections of the Indian community, namely the Presbyterians and the Muslims, while the Democratic Labour Party (DLP), successor to the PDP, was able to attract some members of the white and upscale elements of the wider community. Yet as any study of voter support would reveal, the bulk of the support of the two organizations remained the two major ethnic blocs.

It is not that the policy makers were unaware of the problems posed by cultural difference. The PNM in January 1959 sponsored a conference with the title "The Indian in West Indian Nationhood." A ministry of culture was also established, anthems devised and national mottos proclaimed. The ministry of culture, however, confined its activities largely to art in schools and later to the propagation of the steel pan, Carnival, and "Best Village" expositions, largely the cultural expression of African experience. Election manifestoes promised support for these; while tourist brochures announced Trinidad as "the land of the hummingbird, steel pan and the calypso." The national anthem sang of Trinidad as a place where every creed and race has equal place, thus inviting every creed and race to enquire whether it in truth had an equal place; and the national watchwords, "discipline, tolerance and production," led many to ask who was to tolerate whom.

It is not that the independence and post-independence policy-makers were intent on bestowing resources on some cultural expressions and withholding them from others. It was simply that they were overtaken by political developments.

Part of the problem was that the preparation for independence was inadequate. Indeed, there was no struggle for independence as there was elsewhere; anthems, mottos, flags, armies, West Indianization of the civil services and the establishment of a University College were quick-fix measures designed to allow quick entry into the world community. For these reasons the ministry of culture, then as now, was a ministry without a cultural policy for Trinidad and Tobago. In very many ways, though it seemed to be following the time-honored assimilationist policy of the British, in practice it provided far more resources for African cultural expressions than for others. Attempts to portray African cultural expressions as national were also not particularly persuasive. The adoption of a winner-takes-all model of government, the narrow majority of the PNM in 1956, and the fact that the ruling and opposition parties corresponded with ethnic blocs, ensured that patronage would follow the lines of ethnic cleavage. It is significant that only after the death of Williams in 1981 was Emancipation Day proclaimed a public holiday in 1983, whereas Eid and Divali had already been made holidays. Inspired by developments in the US and the teachings of Malcolm X, the dramatic explosion of Black Power from Kingston in Jamaica in 1965 to Port-of-Spain in 1970 forced policy makers to rethink the question of a cultural policy. Policy makers in Jamaica became concerned with the development of means to bring the country's cultural heritage into perspective, bearing in mind the imbalances of history.[16] Although the Black Power explosions were viewed by some as an expression of generational conflict, it was in fact the expression of a persistent malaise that went back to some of the racial and cultural resentments of the nineteenth century.

In Trinidad the Black Power theoreticians argued: "cultural forces have entered into the Political Being of Black People. They have created the split personalities of the Afro-Saxon and the Indo-Saxon, of contradictions. The influence has been so powerful that even when we are rebelling against the system, we often betray its values."[17] The African, they contended, could only identify with the "White Man" system. The Indian was only slightly better off in his village. Warning that "The Big System is gradually swallowing the Indian village," they called for "an understanding of our common bonds as Black, Indians and Africans." The view of the National Joint Action Committee, (NJAC) as of the Black Power movement, was that a minority of whites in alliance with foreign interests had taken control of the economic resources of the country and thereby taken control of the minds and culture of the oppressed groups. *Conventional Politics or Revolution* by NJAC was thus the most comprehensive document to date to theorize the relationship between culture and politics in Trinidad and Tobago. Yet despite the best efforts of NJAC, the movement ended up generating on the part of Indians a search for a rediscovery of their own culture. Some even became afraid of the implications of the Black Power message. Whatever the success or failure of the movement, Trinidad and Tobago was never the same again.

Policy makers concluded that the Black Power protest was essentially about economic grievances and proceeded to legislate "a people's economic sector in place." Banks were nationalized, shares in companies bought, and some of the slogans and the sartorial trends of Black Power adopted. Afro-hairdos became almost compulsory for the politically ambitious, while the slogan "Brothers and Sisters" entered the lexicon of our political vocabulary.[18] The ruling party even founded its own Black Power group. For the first time, the National Council of Indian Culture received a contribution from the government for the celebration of aspects of Indian culture. Apart from this gesture there was hardly any measure that could be regarded as a new cultural policy aimed at integrating the various segments of society. It was amazing that the government, having come so close to collapse in 1970, did not reflect on the role that a cultural policy could play in the governance of a plural society such as Trinidad.

This was the vacuum into which the National Alliance for Reconstruction (NAR) stepped with its ideology of "one nation, one love, one destiny." The NAR felt that by the political engineering of an appropriate party, cultural problems could be solved. The ever-melodramatic Basdeo Panday declared, "For the first time in our political history, we have found an effective political mechanism, the NAR, to bring our people together. Today Africans can stand in the audience and feel wanted as indeed Indians."[19]

Yet the much vaunted political mechanism barely one year later — some have claimed on the very night of the election — disintegrated in an orgy of recrimination, rancour, and racial abuse. What was lacking was an agreed policy to contain the cultural pressures seeking fulfillment within the bosom of the party and the government. Several cultural episodes illustrate the difficulties of the NAR. There was the question of ethnic imbalances in the award of citizenship to the Guyanese immigrants, the composition of state boards, the rebuke to Minister Samaroo after his speech on culture, in which he was critical of the lack of local content in the local media, and there was the issue of the Indian Cultural Centre. The offer of a cultural center was made in 1968 but was only revived in 1986. In the end the proposal was opposed by Raymond Robinson thus handing Panday, on a platter, an issue with which to fight Robinson. What was amazing was Robinson's failure to grasp the political implications of cultural issues and their capacity to unite or divide.[20] After all, in 1964, Robinson was part of the famous African safari that went to Africa and returned to write admiring articles on that land; he later actively identified with the Black Power movement in 1970 and much later wore an African headdress after acquiring the title of Chief Iqbaro.

Yet the NAR did try to work out a policy to contain the various cultural expressions within Trinidadian society. In its manifesto it promised to recognize the various cultural strains and committed itself to the establishment of a National Cultural Commission. After its assumption of power in 1986, a steering committee was assembled with the following goals:

> ... to formulate a brief regarding the National Cultural Policy with particular reference to the structure, organization, functions, scope, staffing and (overhead and operational) costs involved in the establishment of the National Commission on Culture;
> ... to propose a time-table for the establishment of the National Commission on Culture;
> ... to propose a draft Bill, in collaboration with the Ministry of Legal Affairs, for the establishment of the National Commission of Culture.[21]

The committee also recommended adequate provision of resources for the Commission; the presentation, documentation, promotion and conservation of all the cultures of the society; and the enhancement of indigenous cultural phenomena and practices. It also gave the commission the responsibility for advising the state on its cultural relations with foreign governments. It recommended an enlarged ministry of culture which was to comprise five departments, with the National Carnival Commission assigned to one of the five.

These were brave and heroic proposals. Not since 1970, when the theoreticians of NJAC had probed the importance of culture in the political process, had any group confronted the issue with such seriousness and purpose as the committee did. The authors of the NJAC report recognized that culture constituted "the sum total of ways of life, thought and action, behaviour, beliefs, customs and the values underlying them"; and most significantly the report appreciated that "cultural action by the state capitalized on the potential of the diverse cultural heritage to strengthen the fabric of society thereby facilitating of the people's creative energies and engendering a sense of well being through satisfaction with one's culture." Invoking the constitution in their support, they recommended that the commissioners be appointed by the president.

The report clearly recognized the importance of cultural divergences for the integration of the state; that cultural policy was a problem in the political management of the state; that it required a new conception of governance; and that concepts such as "unity in diversity" were mere slogans unless they could connect to the processes of interaction between and among groups. In short, cultural policy should stimulate and promote national commitment and evoke responsive chords from the major cultural segments of the society.

Yet the proposals seemed doomed from their very inception.[22] The report recommended a separate cultural Commissioner for Tobago Affairs, thus indicating a greater concern for electoral base. Indeed, the cultural policy of the NAR soon became entangled in the politics of the coalition and instead of a coherent national program, the government proceeded to the enactment of a National Carnival Commission, thus returning the policy to its former predicament. If anything this policy was reinforced by the PNM in 1991 when it decided to promulgate the steel pan as the national instrument. Indians complained that the steel pan, calypso and Carnival were integral parts of African culture and therefore the state had became committed to favor one set of institutions over another.

Similarly, CARIFESTA (the Caribbean Festival of Arts) has been the target of repeated criticisms by Indian commentators. A frequent complaint has been the underrepresentation of Indians and Indian culture at these celebrations. In some cases they complained what was being exported as Indian culture was no more than a "creolesque caricature of Indian Culture" that was Afro-nationalist in design and aesthetics. This was also the predicament of the West Indian Commission. Attempting to prescribe a cultural policy for the entire Caribbean, it called on policy makers "to formulate a regional cultural policy matched by national cultural policies."[23] But this was merely to pose the problem, not to provide solution. Although the Caribbean is predominantly African in composition, Indians are a majority in both Trinidad and Guyana. Whether national cultural policy should precede a Caribbean policy or whether they should proceed simultaneously is a valid question. There is also no Caribbean state; it is therefore neither useful nor insightful to claim that Indian culture is a mere pocket in the Anglo-Caribbean.

In 1992 the PNM introduced a Centre for Ethnic Studies, with a mandate to research the cultural issues of the day and to make recommendations. For the first time in the history of the country, researchers were allowed to examine the books, files and records of the government. A number of studies were undertaken on topics such as the media and employment practices in the public sector, from which a number of recommendations followed. However, a study of cultural policy was not undertaken since, with the coming to power of the UNC/NAR coalition in 1995, the Centre for Ethnic Studies was dismantled as one of the first acts of the new regime.[24]

Like its predecessors, the UNC (United National Congress) was without a cultural policy. Instead of a policy what transpired were a series of responses by the UNC to cultural situations as part of its politics of "inclusion and national unity." Indeed, it is more accurate to say that the UNC had a policy only for the African segment, which was to seduce voters away from the PNM; Indian critics saw this as "black appeasement."[25] The policy of the UNC seems to have been to discourage communal claims by Indians and to promote those relating to the African bloc. Thus, much of the "politics of inclusion" had led to the "politics of exclusion."

The UNC had earlier announced its cultural intentions with the abolition of the Centre for Culture Studies in 1996. Thereafter Panday, as head of the ruling UNC, became low-keyed in his address to Indian festivals and organizations, stressing parallels between Martin Luther King and Gandhi and musical forms such as chutney and calypso.[26] He threatened to rename King George V Park "Emancipation Park" and a year later suggested that Queen's Park Savannah be renamed "Emancipation Park Savannah." He also set up an Emancipation Committee within the ministry of culture. Panday even declared before the assembled audience at Indian Arrival Day celebrations in 2000 that he was not an Indian. The ministry of education and culture for its part even announced that Indian culture had received $145,000 more than African culture, leading Sat Maharaj to urge that "the Ministry of Culture be disbanded and replaced with a Ministry of Multi-Culturalism."[27] Sat Maharaj was also castigated by Panday for suggesting that if Africans were eligible for reparations, so were Indians. These episodes demonstrate that in the absence of a carefully conceived cultural policy, politicians and policy makers are reduced to symbolism and a theater of the absurd. Since coming to power, the PNM has announced the return of Best Village programs. One can understand the preoccupation with the electoral base; yet if the cultural policy of the State is to resonate among the major cultural groupings there has to be a conscious attempt to postpone political expediency and arrive at a more embracing policy. Increasingly, however, emphasis is being placed on the economic aspects of cultural policy and not only because the State is being called upon to invest heavily on cultural expression. Workers involved in cultural creation are now more concerned with the economic benefits that culture could bring. These represent forces that have begun to reshape and modify cultural expressions.

Some writers have pointed to the franchising of fried chicken outlets that has spawned what looks like a global culture. Bollywood is now an economic rather than a cultural enterprise and in Trinidad calypso, Carnival and the steel pan are now international enterprises. Chutney, once limited to Indian occasions and milieu, now joins with calypso and other African expressions to produce chutney soca. Yet the driving force is once more the dominant institutions and values. There are now Divali Queens, Chutney Soca, Chutney Kings and even "Chutney in Concert" just as there are Calypso Kings and Queens and "Pan in Concert." Clearly the forces of globalization and economic and political change have been altering the cultural landscape so that the distinctions between the basic and secondary aspects of differing cultures are now far more blurred than they ever were. Yet the current and continuing agonies over the Indian Arrival Day holiday and celebrations and the recent controversies over the Trinity Cross award illustrate the necessity for a cultural policy that would embrace the wider society. The return to power of the PNM in 2002 has not brought any fundamental change from the usual charges of racism and counter-racism. What has become clear is that the creole party is now seducing Indian voters. An Indian organization has been given permission to build a school, and chutney competitions are now receiving assistance; two schools, Vishnu Boys and Sarswattie Girls Colleges, have received funds to the tune of $7 million to assist them with their programs. The harmonium, unduly regarded as an Indian instrument, now has pride of place beside the pan in schools. Yet these are essentially responses to a changing political environment. What is needed is a clear policy. It has been argued that the politicians could not be expected to act counter to the interests of their own bases. True, but that freedom exacts a price in the politics of the country, since it becomes wired in ethnic appeal and machinations.

Conclusion

It is clear that since 1956, the issue of finding a relevant cultural policy for Trinidad and Tobago has been critical for the political processes involved in the governance of the country. The ruling party in 1956, apart from introducing a Ministry of Culture, merely followed the time-honored policy of assimilation. This was the melting-pot thesis so dear to American reformers. In practice, though, the government, for reasons of electoral advantage, was forced to allocate resources to cultural organizations along ethnic lines. The situation was further compounded by the normal operations of the Westminster model in Trinidad and Tobago. Under this model, party patronage would follow the ethnic lines on which the parties were based. The excluded groups reacted with claims of discrimination, reduced commitment to the national enterprise and recurring complaints of imbalance and alienation. From this experience emerged a tendency to interpret issues of policy, whether national or local, in terms of the advantage of one ethnic group over the other. It was clear that cultural policy — whether under the British or post-independence — was very much involved with the structures of power and therefore could not be easily altered without serious consequences.

It was the experience of 1970 and the cultural issues raised by those events that forced the government of the day to rethink its conventional wisdom. It was clear that a great deal of the impetus behind the cultural assertions of 1970 and after had its origins in the forces of globalization. Episodes in the struggle against apartheid in South Africa and the Afro-American struggle for civil and political rights and their speedy transmission to receptive audiences in Trinidad provided the oxygen for cultural nationalism. The issue was not whether African or Indian culture was authentic. Original cultures were bound to be modified in the process of transplantation into a new environment. In the process, however, institutions were given new meanings and priorities rearranged.

Yet there can be no doubt that political institutions and practices helped to keep alive the feeling and emotions of separate identities. Cultural policy was in fact neither fully assimilationist nor multicultural. Indeed what passed for cultural policy was in practice a series of ad hoc responses to gain political advantage over opponents. If policy makers were serious about such a policy they could have turned to the experience of the new states where historical and cultural experiences were ransacked to produce a set of common symbols and themes that could resonate over the entire society and with which a substantial majority could identify. Instead the politicians devised slogans and adopted the latest sartorial fashions, but shrank from the task of devising real solutions.

The traumas of politics over the last decade or so should convince policy makers that for cost-benefit reasons, the time has come for a coherent cultural policy. For too long, racial appeal and motivation have dominated the political process. At the very least, a National Cultural Commission should not only devise a policy for the country as a whole but should be assigned responsibility for the allocation of resources to cultural organizations along with responsibility for cultural activities undertaken by the state.

Endnotes

1. Quoted in M.G. Smith, *The Plural Society in the British West Indies* (Berkeley: University of California Press, 1965). See pp. 18–74 for a discussion of some of these issues.

2. Ibid., pp. 28.

3. Cohen and Kennedy, Global *Sociology* (New York: Palgrave Press, 2000), p. 24.

4. Ankie Hoogvelt, Globalization *and the Post Colonial World: The New Political Economy of Development* (Basingstoke: Macmillan, 1997), p. 115.

5. D. Held, A. McGraw, D. Goldblatt and J. Perraton, *Global Transformation* (Cambridge: Polity, 1999), pp. 171–175.

6. Dani Rodrik, *Has Globalization Gone Too Far?* (Washington: Institute for International Economics, 1997).

7. P. Held (ed.), *Political Theory Today* (Cambridge: Polity, 1991).

8. S. Strange, *The Retreat of the State* (Cambridge: Cambridge University Press, 1996); for a discussion see *International Social Sciences Journal* 155 (1998) UNESCO.

9. For a discussion of some of the problems in constructing a cultural policy see McKim Marriot, "Cultural Policy in the New States," in Clifford Geertz, Old *Societies and the New States* (London: Free Press, 1963).

10. For a summary of these early debates see Vera Robin, *Social and Cultural Pluralism in the Caribbean*, Annals of the New York Academy of Societies, vol. 82 (1960) pp. 761–916.

11. There was, though, some resistance to the policy of assimilation. See Brereton "Social Organization in Nineteenth Century Trinidad," in K. Yelvington (ed.), *Trinidad Ethnicity* (Macmillan), pp. 49–53.

12. The term Keerwal is used by Indians to refer to persons of mixed or African descent. For a discussion of creolization, see Yelvington, *Trinidad Ethnicity*.

13. For a discussion of this tendency see La Guerre, The *Politics of Communalism* (Pan Caribbean Publications, 1974).

14. See Ryan, *Race and Nationalism in Trinidad and Tobago* (ISER, 1974).

15. V.S. Naipaul, *A Way in the World* (London: Heinneman, 1994), pp. 130–131.

16. For a discussion see Rex Nettleford. *Caribbean Cultural Identity: The Case of Jamaica* (Princeton, New Jersey: Markus Weiner, 2003).

17. NJAC, Conventional *Politics or Revolution*, pp. 22–23.

18. For an assessment of this experience see Taimoon Stewart, *The Black Power Revolution 1970: A Retrospective* (ISER, 1995).

19. S. Siewah and R. Moonilal (eds.), *Basdeo Panday: An Enigma Answered* (Port of Spain: Chakra, 1991), p. 411.

20. This is not to imply that culture was the only factor in the break-up of the NAR. See the writer's *Basdeo Panday: A Political Biography* (Port of Spain: Chakra, 2002).

21. Quoted in La Guerre, *Structural Adjustment: Public Policy and Administration in the Caribbean* (St. Augustine, Trinidad: University of the West Indies, School of Continuing Studies, 1994), pp. 206–207.

22. Of the 14 members comprising the Committee, only four were Indians.

23. Report of the West India Commission, "Time for Action" (Black Rock, Barbados: West Indian Commission. 1992.

24. In its last year of office the UNC introduced the Equal Opportunity Act. It was assented to but never implemented.

25. See Kamal Persad in *Trinidad Express*, Aug. 2, 1999.

26. See *Sunday Express*, July 30, 2000; Indira Rampersand's "Cautions DM Panday" and Raffique Shah's "Jack's Chickin Lickin Lies" on page 14.

27. *Sunday Express*, Jan. 31, 1999; Kamal Persad's "UNC Turns Its Back on Hindus, Indians" on page 12 and Selwyn Cudjoe's "Militant Hinduism and the State" on page 12.

Caudillismo: A Framework of Resistance

Ann-Marie Pouchet

Abstract

Venezuela's volatile sociopolitical situation is perhaps one of the most engaging in world events of the new millennium. The election of President Hugo Chávez has been one that has been accompanied by a number of revolutions and stirrings. These uprisings have led to some turbulence internationally since Venezuela is one of the largest suppliers of oil. This article explores the tradition from which Chávez emerged, the tradition of the strongman, the *caudillo*; its origins, modifications and the new configuration that Chávez has come to personify: the *neo caudillo*. Two hypotheses are proposed: one, that this type of leader is a product of the environment, and two, that this left-leaning, nationalist strongman is generally rejected both nationally and internationally.

The world's fifth largest producer of oil and fourth largest exporter of petroleum to the United States, Venezuela finds herself in a curious position in the world today. In spite of her rich natural resources, some 80 percent of her population is still impoverished. Although she boasts of having the oldest democracy in South America, the Western world is suspicious that her present-day ruler, Hugo Chávez, may be following in the footsteps of his post-independence predecessors. Despite growing world pressure, including that from the US, which admitted to CIA involvement with the perpetrators of the short-lived coup against Chávez on April 12, 2002, President Chávez still remains closely allied to Cuba's Fidel Castro, emulating his rule and his wariness of neoliberal thinking. Even more importantly, Chávez remains popular among the poor, in spite of the many challenges he has had to face in leadership. This popularity has afforded him survival in a country that since the mid–1940s has enshrined universal suffrage in its constitution. One of the questions that arises is, how can an authoritarian, arbitrary and reactionary leader such as Chávez is alleged to be, still remain so popular with the impoverished masses? Some of the historical, religious and social factors that have helped to mold the political reality of Venezuela — namely, the heritage of *caudillismo*—are the subject of this discussion.

Caudillismo: Origins and Characteristics

Caudillismo was the dominant political system in Venezuela from her independence in 1811 until 1935 with the death of General Juan Vicente Gómez. The state of Venezuela, even after its declaration as a republic, was replete with remnants of a colonial society. After almost a quarter century of wars of independence, these remnants, still fragmented in their feudal class structure and racial diversity, a landed oligarchy and Catholicism, were preoccupied with organizing themselves.

The lack of institutional structure contributed to the rise of *caudillismo* in Venezuela. Colonial Venezuela consisted of seven provinces, each ruled by an individual governor who recognized no central authority. Regionalism and localism were rampant. Social stratification in Venezuela was a reality on caste, racial and colour lines; economic mobility was almost impossible.

The failure of national authority and social order resulted in the Federal War (1859–1864). At that time, the society was not only ripe for the rule of a strongman but he seemed to be the only real and desirable option, given the fragmented nature of the society (Vallenilla Lanz 1994, 238). The *caudillos*, referred to as military chieftains, were regional leaders whose power was largely based on military prowess displayed in the Wars of Independence and who ruled their particular region but aspired to central authority.

Gilmore defines *caudillismo* as a union of personalism and violence for the conquest of power. In the absence of a political and social structure that could cater to the functioning of representative government, these guerrilla leaders exercised local and regional political leadership as a right and allied themselves with royalist or patriot forces. The armed faction of his followers was at the call of the *caudillo*. His effectiveness was in fact related to the size of his faction.

In Venezuela, anyone could become a caudillo. He depended on three main elements in society: the landowners, the financial sector and professionals. He held power until forcibly removed by another victorious caudillo who would then enjoy public acclaim.

The Spanish American dictator is commonly termed a caudillo, as he originates from this tradition and displays certain qualities. George S. Wise highlights the lack of a fixed ideology in the Spanish American dictator (Wise 1970, 10). Pacheco (1987) points out that the dictator does not openly declare himself a dictator but rather tries to cover up this reality under the façade of being democratic, liberal, parliamentary and constitutional. Luis Britto García (1988, 208) takes up the view that in the midst of a society divided by race, class and economics, the façade of egalitarianism adopted by the caudillo was profitable to him and more palatable to his followers.

The caudillo perpetuated the myth that he was a divinely chosen leader who ruled by instinct, a man of the people, and therefore independent of any theory. People accepted his right to rule based on his personal magnetism, identifying him as a champion and deliverer. *Caudillismo* was an arbitrary regime where legitimacy was based on the personal attributes of the leader and not on the rule of law.

The power tool of this personalist regime was force. Enemies were repressed, imprisoned, tortured, exiled or killed. Media organizations that criticized or gave negative publicity to the caudillo were warned. Strict censorship was implemented and if the press did not submit and conform, it was closed down.

Critics of the Hispanic American dictator often highlight the corruption, personal embezzlement and nepotism of these regimes where the caudillo and his clan would amass a personal fortune by dishonestly misusing public funds. Yet Leo Strauss (1963, 70–71) speaks of the tyrant dating from ancient times as one who considered his fatherland his estate. Similarly, in post-independence Venezuela, the estate owner who rose to central power as political leader would implicitly believe his country to be his extended estate. The involvement of his family and relations in high places and every major transaction, receiving grants and concessions, is a natural consequence of this transference of his personal estate to his national personal estate.

Glen Dealy (1977), taking up Weber's theorizing on capitalism in *The Protestant Ethic and the Spirit of Capitalism* (1905), extrapolates that the patrimony of Catholicism left its mark on the caudillo and his society in a real way. The Catholic man, he explained, seeks to obtain public power. He needs to acquire friends, for it is through friendship that he can acquire power. Coupled with another Catholic tradition of *compadrazgo*, where godfathers are chosen for the baptized child, a network of relationships made for the particularism so commonly associated with *caudillismo*.

However, the network of mutually beneficial relationships was not based solely on family ties or friendship. Particularistic cliques took varying forms. The regional clique, in a strongly regionalist country such as Venezuela, was essential for a caudillo's ascent to power and for his survival. A caudillo would assume power, usually by an overthrow of a former caudillo; however, he would encounter the same powerful oligarchy that his predecessor had. For his survival, therefore, he had to make a pact with the economic ruling class and grant its members favors and concessions while threatening the competition.

Furthermore, the dictator could call on his *compadres*. The bonds of *compadrazgo* are so powerful that *compadres* are obliged to help each other in any circumstance. Simon Mitchell (1978) explains that *compadrazgo* or spiritual parentage establishes supernatural ties that could be used as a form of social control. In a folk system of justice and legitimacy, this *compadre* or godfather gives favors, confers high positions and grants economic concessions to his fellow *compadres*, while expecting their loyalty in return.

In *La máscara del poder*, Luis Britto García explodes the myth that the Hispanic American dictator was a ruler of humble origin (see, for example, González-Echevarría 1988; Pacheco 1987; Gilmore 1964). He proposes that this myth was propagated by the caudillo himself so as to identify himself with the people. His mobility signified the mobility of his whole ascribed class.

Hispanic American dictatorial regimes have often been termed paternalistic. The nation, like the dictator's children, is submissive and accepting of his authority. This paternalism may also be traced back to Hispanic America's Catholic heritage. The image of God as Father and Ruler of all, the Pope as holder of truth and supreme earthly legislator, the priest as parochial leader all mirror the strong, male leader in government. An almost essential counterpart of patriarchalism in a society is machismo. It was expected of the caudillo that he be virile.

Although not always attributed with formal learning and intelligence, the caudillo is always represented as a strongman. Physical strength and resistance are vital to him. From the indigenous cacique to the Spanish conquistador to the caudillo emerging from the Wars of Independence, courage and physical resistance are necessary elements for his prestige and acceptance.

Britto García points out that in many rural societies of Venezuela during the caudillesque period, speech was the only means of communication; therefore, to identify and communicate with his popular followers, the caudillo would often use popular language.

Again, Britto García (1988, 226) presents the caudillo as the emitter of the message of his political ideology and indeed as the message itself, while the people are the passive receptors. The caudillo gives; the people receive from him what they lack, even if it is he who causes the deficiency in the first place.

The caudillo is not a folkloric figure of the past. Although a specific set of historical, social, religious and economic factors gave birth to him, his essence has remained in power in many Latin American countries, including Venezuela. The deep roots of religious belief and social acculturation have caused him to transcend these factors. In Venezuela, General Juan Vicente Gómez, often hailed as the last caudillo, stamped out *caudillismo* as we knew it through his centralization of power, quelling of regional caudillos and the formation of a national army. He built industrial infrastructure and adopted a more liberal foreign policy that allowed Europe and America to invest in the petroleum sector. He ended the tradition of one caudillo's violent overthrow of the other, staying in power until death.

Yet the spirit of *caudillaje* has lived on. Even a cursory glance at the Hispanic American literary tradition shows the society's preoccupation with the figure of the *caudillo*. Often regarded as an alternative source of truth, literature has the power to reveal social and cultural realities through the heightened sensitivity of the artist.

The Literary Evolution of the Caudillo: Previous and Contemporary Manifestations

By its very violent and oppressive nature, *caudillismo* has been a framework of resistance. This resistance does not only manifest itself externally in its response to opposition but internally as well, for it engenders the very opposition it seeks to quell. The literature of and about the Spanish American dictator reflects this. Initially these works gave a voice to the oppressed, as many of the works of this genre were tools of political opposition.

The first works of this kind were written by Anti-Rosists of River Plate between 1835 and 1855, Echeverría's *El matadero* (1838), Mármol's *Amalia* (1851) and Sarmiento's *Facundo* (1845). These works were tools of political protest against the Argentine caudillo Rosas.

After the initial burgeoning of narrative works on the theme of dictatorship and dictators, this literary tradition slumped until 1925. *Tirano Banderas* by the Spaniard Valle-Inclán initiated another stage. Distance was established between the political dictator and the narrator. This novel was an expression of European and North American interest in Hispanic America at the beginning of the century, which manifested itself in the creation of a syncretistic Spanish America. By the early twentieth century, dictators who emerged out of the caudillo tradition were already being portrayed less as individual despots in particular societies than as a phenomenon of these societies, a product of their history, society, religion and culture.

El señor presidente by Miguel Ángel Asturias, a Guatemalan, was published in 1946. It is hailed as the first Hispanic American novel of the dictator of true literary quality. While not ceasing to denounce the relevant dictatorial regimes, great attention was paid to narrative structure, literary technique and the creation of an imaginary, syncretistic Spanish America.

The mid-1970s marked the turning point and arguably the peak of the novel of the dictator, particularly with the appearance of the famed trilogy *El recurso del método* (1974) by Alejo Carpentier, *Yo el supremo* (1974) by Augusto Roa Bastos, and *El otoño del patriarca* (1975) by Gabriel García Márquez. Many Latin American countries at the time of publication of these works were experiencing dictatorships or repressive military regimes.

The spirit of "El Libertador," Simón Bolívar, hailed as the first Latin American caudillo and the Father of Independence, reincarnated itself in all the caudillos of Venezuela. The fact that novelists have largely turned from depicting a specific dictator to a mythical dictator (one who transcends persons, time and space) seems to point to this figure as a recurring one. In an interview with Robert McCrum in *The Observer/Review* (April 7, 2002), Peruvian writer and former presidential candidate Mario Vargas Llosa speaks about his *La fiesta del chivo* (2000): "If you write about a dictator, you are writing about all dictators, and about totalitarianism. I was not only writing about Trujillo but about an emblematic figure and something that has been experienced in many other societies."

Venezuela seems to lend credence to the artistic imagination, allowing one to take a new look at the current Venezuelan president, his role as caudillo-style leader and his role in the pattern of resistance.

The Emergence of Hugo Chávez Frías

Hugo Chávez Frías first burst onto the political scene in Venezuela on February 4, 1992, when he led a group of rebel soldiers into an attempted coup targeting the regime of then-president Carlos Andrés

Pérez. He was arrested and imprisoned; but among the political and economic elites, he had already revived old fears of the military coups so characteristic of Venezuela's past autocratic regimes. Armed resistance and rebellion usually signaled the end of one regime and the ushering in of the next. Six years later, Hugo Chávez would win Venezuelan presidential election by a landslide victory.

Can Chávez really be considered a caudillo? Douglas Bravo, a leftist guerrilla of the 1960s and an opponent of Chávez, describes the president as having many of the characteristics of a chieftain. He explains, "Chávez is an intelligent man, he is bold, charismatic, and an excellent speaker; he has a natural ability to command ... is quite capable of making sudden changes in direction.... He can easily make agreements with one group, and then abandon them when he makes a deal with another ... it is quite dangerous now that he is the President of Venezuela" (Gott 2000, 32–33).

The Venezuela of 1998 was very different from that of 1935 and it would be erroneous to consider Chávez a caudillo in the strict, traditional sense. Venezuela in 1998 was a highly industrialized country, and had consolidated her democracy for several decades with an elected president. In spite of this, Chávez first sought legitimacy to rule by the traditional means of the caudillo: through force, instead of the ballot to which Venezuela had become accustomed since her last dictator, Pérez Jiménez in 1958.

The 1961 Constitution guaranteed civil liberties, and although the president had considerable power, he could only run for reelection after sitting out for two five-year terms. March 11, 1964, marked the first time that Venezuela passed from one constitutionally elected head of government to another. Soon a two party system emerged, where power almost alternated between the Acción Democrática (AD) and the Comité de Organización Política Electoral Independiente (COPEI), a conservative party that appealed largely to Roman Catholics.

Petroleum was the mainstay of Venezuela's economy. In fact, oil revenues had made her a wealthy nation. In 1976, Andrés Pérez nationalized all foreign and iron-mining firms. Dependency on oil revenue was extensive when in the early 1980s prices dropped, industrialized nations conserved their use and the world was hit by recession. Venezuela's income was severely affected, and through the mismanagement of President Andrés Pérez, who was given to excesses, corruption and self-enrichment, Venezuela became steeped in foreign debt with negative growth figures.

The oil boom over, COPEI president Herrera was forced to introduce austerity measures that inflicted suffering on the lower and middle classes and served to only widen the gap between them and the rich and powerful. Yet Venezuela remained peaceful largely due to the collusion of political and economic elites (Wynia, 1990). Andrés Pérez returned to power, promising prosperity, but he delivered more austerity measures as he turned to the international lending agencies for aid. In 1989, riots broke out as the poor, incensed by increased bus fares, raided businesses in Caracas. Some 300 people were killed in the rebellion known as the *Caracazo*. It was under such circumstances that Hugo Chávez attempted his first entry into politics.

Hugo Chávez had made a name for himself after the 1992 coup. Anointed as it were by supernatural decree, his failed military coup established his political career. Venezuela saw his attempt as a glimpse of hope. Many wished the coup had been successful. After the riots in 1989, it was only a matter of time before Venezuela shifted from the corrupt democratic model to an autocratic leader. Chávez had had no real idea of his effect on Venezuela when in an attempt to stop the coup, he addressed his fellow insurrectionists, saying that "por ahora" ("for the moment") their objectives could not be realized. Venezuelans saw this catch phrase of their future leader as a welcome implication that his "second coming" would bring them salvation from the throes of corrupt politicians.

By 1998, elections were due once more. Venezuelans were disenchanted with the party system of democracy, which they saw as politicians enriching themselves and the wealthy and strangling the livelihood of the poor. President Caldera, in an act of mercy, granted Chávez his freedom after serving only two years in prison. It was in this context that the nostalgia for the military strongman was felt by a large section of the population.

Yet, one cannot term Hugo Chávez a caudillo in the strict sense. The systemic change that Venezuela underwent paints a completely different scenario than Venezuela in its first hundred years after independence. Additionally, Chávez is an elected president and not a military dictator in the sense that his opponents want to evoke. He can be termed, however, a *neo-caudillo*, one who bears many of the traits of the authoritarian military man but with important differences and from a much more globalized society.

Before his win at the polls in December 1998, the upper classes of Venezuela and foreign vested interests were wary of the possible win of the neo-caudillo. His bellicose rhetoric, his military and violent past, his identification with Bolívar, his intense nationalism and hatred of the oligarchy were just some of the reasons for their concern. In an article entitled "In Latin America, the Strongman Stirs in His Grave," published in *The New York Times*, 20 December 1998, Larry Rohter reported: "With his landslide victory in Venezuela's presidential election on Dec. 6, Hugo

Chávez has revived an all-too-familiar specter that the region's ruling elite thought they had safely interred: that of the populist demagogue, the authoritarian man on horseback known as the caudillo."

Yet his landslide victory at the polls, the consequent rejection of the party system in favour of a strong, charismatic, male independent can only be read as the popular will of the people. The deep-rooted discontent coupled with the cultural acceptance of such a leader as the champion of the people must have led to the choice of Chávez.

Caudillismo is first and foremost a personalist regime. The charisma of the leader coupled with his military prowess was the source of his power and prestige. Even his enemies cannot deny Hugo Chávez his magnetism. From his early days in the military, Chávez showed signs of leadership. Starting as an unknown lieutenant, he became the most popular candidate in Venezuela.

Chávez did not need to seek legitimacy in the same way as the traditional caudillo. Instead of force, Chávez' landslide victory and continuing popularity among the poor masses gave him the legitimacy needed to rule. Although it did not stop a coup being attempted in April 2002, and a number of general strikes being called in an effort to have early elections, his popularity and his constitutional legitimacy have brought him back into the fray and continue to keep him in power. This legitimacy affords him the opportunity to do things that would have been termed arbitrary under the traditional caudillo. Chávez has extended his stay in power. The Constituent Assembly has amended the constitution to allow a six-year presidential term and the option of reelection. Although it is his political will, his popularity allows him to do this legitimately as both the Assembly and the new constitution were widely approved by referendum at the end of 1999.

Chávez, much like the mythical caudillo takes on a Messianic nature. Every Sunday, his faithful can be sure to hear their pastor speak to them of the ills of the oligarchy and his plan for their salvation on his weekly television program, Aló Presidente. He has bounced back from near death experiences: the 1992 coup attempt of which he was the protagonist and one decade later, the April 2002 coup attempt against him. His steadfastness in the midst of intense internal and external pressure over the latter part of 2002 has attested to his strength of leadership and has confirmed suspicions that he is a formidable enemy.

Chávez has claimed, as all caudillos in Venezuela have done, an affiliation with Bolívar. In this way, he assures his popularity and builds up nationalistic feelings. Simón Bolívar, "El Libertador," is a national icon. Yet Chávez' Bolivarianism goes beyond invoking the revered name; he seriously considers himself in the mold of Bolívar, renaming the Republic "La República Bolivariana de Venezuela" and seeking to unite the Latin American republics economically and militarily in another attempt at La Gran Colombia. His constitution is based on Bolivarian thinking (Rojas 2002). Flanked by a large picture of Simón Bolívar when he addresses his people, he calms fears about oppression and neo-imperialist opposition.

Chávez' choice to often appear in military garb and red beret reinforces in the minds of Venezuelans that he is one of them, but at the same time subconsciously works on the fear of all the classes of the military. The veiled threat of force is apparent lest the people's political will be different than his. On the other hand, his stay in power is completely dependent on the loyalty of the army. Given Venezuela's political tradition, it was not unusual that the major challenge to his rule in April 2002 came from dissidents among the military. However, on this occasion popular and military loyalists—coupled with the popular lack of trust in the business class, which now had a voice under democratic, constitutional rule—crippled the April coup. What one is witnessing in Venezuela, as 2002 ends, is a repeat of this pattern of resistance.

Chávez has been accused of using and abusing the press. His caudillo predecessors used the power of the word more than anything else to appeal to their often illiterate followers. Chávez has stirred the fears of and promised retribution to the wicked and corrupt oligarchy who had abused their power and enriched themselves at the expense of the poor. His divisive rhetoric strikes a chord of disapproval in the upper classes but appeals to the gut feeling of vengeance among the working class. Britto García's perception of the caudillo as the emitter of the message and the people the passive receptors is realized in Chávez. His popularity began with his unrehearsed words *"por ahora."* His gift of gab endears him to many and alienates him from others. His weekly television program guarantees him a public audience where he can popularize his propaganda and present his government's perspective on current issues in the midst of a largely hostile, privately owned media.

His mixture of machismo and paternalism also place Chávez in the mold of the culturally accepted strongman. He is a strong, virile, outspoken, military man. One of his rivals in 1998 elections, former Miss Universe Irene Sáez, made a brave attempt for the presidency, but popular opinion still showed that the socioeconomic crisis in which Venezuela found itself needed a strong male leader to save it, not the gentle touch of a female who had allied herself with corrupt political parties.

Chávez, through his paternal image, projects himself as provider and defender of the people. Not easily manipulated by his defiant children —

the trade unions, the business sector and the Church — he proceeds with his plans to redistribute the wealth and resources of Venezuela in a strongly nationalistic fashion. "Chávez plays his role as the avuncular comforter, talking, asking questions, seeking answers and spreading a sense of optimism and goodwill" (Gott 2000, 186).

Chávez and Resistance

Caudillismo by its very nature and history is a framework of resistance. It promotes, fosters and engenders internal opposition and externally from foreign opponents. The neo-caudillo, Hugo Chávez, finds himself in this very same structure of opposition.

Chávez has been vocal in his criticism of the political oligarchy, criticizing political parties, local business interests, the Church and the media who have long been the ruling elite in Venezuela. Promoting a social revolution with land reform and wealth redistribution has incurred the wrath of the elite, which he has not been able to shake off until now. In fact, the current volatility of Venezuela's current situation reveals how very strong the elite's stranglehold on power is. It has been previously noted that the caudillo's survival was in part due to his collusion with political and economic elites, even if his political discourse was one geared towards the ordinary people. But Venezuela's caudillos have traditionally been right wing. Part of the reason for considering Chávez a neo-caudillo is the fact that he tends to be leftist. This fact engenders resistance by the internal and foreign political and economic elites.

Chávez has raised eyebrows with his plan to integrate the military into the social and economic life of Venezuelan society. The caudillo is a military man and Chávez is no exception. Yet given the political history of Latin America, with the military regimes in the 1970s and 1980s renowned for political oppression and widespread violence, there is a natural distrust of the military. Chávez' plan to integrate the military into civilian society has been seen as a veiled plan to form a military dictatorship of Venezuela. His appointment of military officials to top political positions and to positions in state-owned companies has served only to confirm fears among the upper and middle classes of Venezuelan society and the international community. However, in the midst of the current strike action and demands for a consultative referendum to end his regime, Chavez' cultivation of the military is key to his survival. He depends on their loyalty to avoid a coup and on their expertise to run the oil industry and businesses shut down by his opponents.

Chávez was popularly and democratically elected on an anti-corruption, nationalist and anti-neoliberalism platform. Although constantly accused of being totalitarian, dictatorial and communist by his enemies, his major reform packages have all been popularly endorsed by referenda. The spirit of the 1999 Constitution is one of participatory democracy. Although a Datanalisis poll recently showed his popularity slipping to an overall 30 percent with up to 45 percent among the poor, he remains the most popular leader in Venezuela today even amidst calls for his resignation. In fact, in the very Constitution, the right to recall his presidency was established under him. This has been great cause for resistance as the opposition political opponents, the Confederation of Trade Unions (CTV) and the Venezuelan Federation of Chambers of Commerce and Industry (Fedecamaras), wish Chávez to step down. On the other hand, he defiantly insists that the Constitution makes provision for such a move only halfway into the six-year presidential term or in August 2003.

Why has Chávez' regime engendered so much resistance? By his very entrance onto the political scene by a violent coup, Chávez himself signaled his willingness to subvert existing orders by less than legitimate means. The use of force to oust a regime with which one was dissatisfied was the norm in nineteenth and early twentieth century Venezuela. One caudillo replaced another through their major power tool: force. In this context, it was not wholly surprising that the dissatisfied stakeholders have decided to employ means contrary to legitimacy in order to oust Chávez. Resistance engenders resistance.

But the caudillos of Venezuela were only successful in their attempts to kick out another leader if their armed faction was strong and if they had the financial means to do so. They were either self-financed or financed by the elite. Even when they had their own means, they had to rule in conjunction with the existing powers. Although he has been democratically elected, Chávez still faces the opposition of the powerful. Additionally, his criticism of neoliberalism has not endeared him to the world powers either. His Bolivarian nationalism is seen as a retrograde step and as a threat to the free market.

Chávez has faced several major challenges to his regime. There have been four general strikes up to December 10, 2002, a short-lived coup in April 2002, and speculation over other foiled and future coup attempts. The indefinite general strike that Venezuela is experiencing as of December 2002 is much like the lead-up to April's coup. The opposition — media, political opponents, trade unions and Chambers of Industry and Commerce — have accused the president of economic mismanagement, leading Venezuela to a communist style government, confrontational leadership and interventionist reforms. The economy has contracted some 6 percent in 2002 and poverty and unemployment levels remain high. The opposition have called a strike, widely publicized by an antigovernment media, and are anxious to find out the position of the military, hoping that they would move against the president in another coup d'état. Chávez, having taken the same route as a military man himself and also knowing the political history of Venezuela, would know that the key to ousting a legitimate regime is through the army. A group of some 120 army officers camped in Plaza Altamira is undoubtedly of concern to him and forces him to hold the other officers closer to his breast.

The role of the international community in the April overthrow attempt is worth noting. In the midst of accusations of US involvement, the United States admitted to certain CIA officials meeting some of the supporters of the coup but denied direct involvement. After the coup attempt, many European and Latin American governments criticized the US for tolerating the attempted overthrow of a democratically elected government and recognizing the two-day administration.

This highlights the dilemma in which the US had already found itself even before Chávez was elected. The strained relations between the US and Venezuela on economic and ideological grounds have always placed Chávez in the enemy camp. He was denied a visa before he won the election because of his involvement in the coup. But the US has supported Venezuelan military strongmen in the past. Juan Vicente Gómez (1908–1935) had excellent relations with the US, having opened up Venezuela's oil industry to foreign investment; and their last dictator, Pérez Jímenez (1948–1958) was honored by the US authorities despite his alleged corruption and atrocities. Furthermore, US intelligence has played its part in ousting democratically elected left-wing strongmen before, as was the case of Allende in Peru in 1970.

Perhaps it is Chávez' defiance, his condemnation of the acceptance of neoliberal reforms, his wariness of globalization and his desire for a multipolar world that has annoyed the world's superpower. Chávez has cultivated friendships with US enemy Fidel Castro and has expressed admiration for the Chinese communist regime as an alternative to neoliberalism. In an effort to stabilize oil prices, he has broken the UN sanctions on state visits to Saddam Hussein and Libya's Colonel Gadaffi. He has also criticized the US' use of terrorist neoliberal policies that hurt the poorer nations while claiming that they denounce terrorism (United Nations 2002). He is the self-proclaimed champion of the poor who seeks to challenge US hegemony. For economic reasons alone, the destiny of the oil rich country is of great interest to the US and other major traders. The volatility of Chávez and the Venezuelan situation must be of concern to these powers to the extent that democratic principles can be put on hold for the sake of self-interest. He has been the stubborn personification of resistance to them, accepting the need for integration but on his terms.

Chávez, in spite of his condemnation of neoliberal reforms, is still in dire need of foreign investment. Despite protectionist policies towards PDVSA, the state-owned oil company, which insist on a large market share of any joint ventures, he still quietly encourages foreign investment. Following the discovery of major natural gas reserves in the Atlantic Ocean near Trinidad and Tobago's border with Venezuela, Chávez has signaled his interest in foreign investment to assist in the exploitation of this discovery and its commercialization by the Deltana Platform while still maintaining 60 percent ownership under state-owned PDVSA Gas (Lyle 2002, 87). This shifting of ideology is consistent with the caudillo model.

Chávez's policy on the national oil company has been a major source of contention. In the midst of the current unrest, he insists that the general strike that has crippled the oil industry, drastically reducing domestic supply and threatening January exports, is motivated by business interests who would like to own private shares in the company or completely privatize it. His insistence on keeping the oil company state-owned is consistent with his nationalist outlook, so fundamentally opposed to globalization. This in turn has infuriated local and international business interests. John Ohiorhenuan (2000, 40–41) explains: "Globalization ... affects development thinking and action, relegating ethical, equity and social concerns behind market considerations and reducing the autonomy of the State. Countries of the South need to come to terms with these phenomena by adjusting their developmental strategies. Opponents present globalization as a foreign invasion that will destroy local cultures, regional cooperation and national traditions." Chávez as a nationalist strongman insists that Venezuela's wealth is for Venezuela.

Chávez's dream of a "Bolivarian republic" has both nationalist and integrationist implications, neither of which pleases the North. He attempts to fight off the effects of globalization, which "are to weaken the cultural coherence of *all* individual nation-states" (Tomlinson 2001), with his dream of a strong Venezuela and a Latin America united on economic, political and military levels. He wishes to become the second Libertador, throwing off the yoke of neo-imperialists be they political or economic. He insists that he is not against globalization but is rather for globalization with a conscience. He has formulated his own counter-globalization discourse, stating that his goal is integration, in the mold of Simón Bolívar's dream of Latin American unification at the Panama Congress in 1826.

In this light, he has proposed integration of South and Central America and the Caribbean, linking the Andean bloc with the Southern Common Market (MERCOSUR), the Association of Caribbean States (ACS) and the North American Free Trade Agreement (NAFTA). His proposal is a South American common market in response to the North American one. He also dreams of a South Atlantic Treaty Organisation made up of African and Latin American states, a united military front geared towards the security of the South instead of having the military relegated to a ceremonial role as the Western powers would like to see done.

Chávez also appears to want to play a hegemonic role. Venezuela's current administration has a troubled relationship with Colombia's President Pestaña over Chávez' support of Colombian rebels near the Venezuelan border who share his outlook on a new union between the two countries. Land disputes have also emerged with Guyana under Chavez' rule. Furthermore, plans to open the offshore Deltana Platform along Trinidad and Tobago's border, south of the island's most abundant natural gas fields, have raised concerns between the two nations on the quantity of reserves of each country and cross-border development of gas. British Petroleum already has an agreement with Venezuela on the Trinidad side of the westernmost block on the Deltana Platform, Dorado, that allows Venezuela to intervene if there is any safety or security risk on the block. This can have dangerous implications for two nations currently locked in fierce negotiations over where the liquefied natural gas from Venezuela's new discoveries will be processed.

His challenge to the US to form a multipolar world in the aftermath of the end of the Cold War has been met with its own measure of resistance. Chávez can boast of some success in the sympathies of Colombian guerrilla groups, the Revolutionary Armed Forces (FARC) and the National Liberation Army (ELN) as well as, even more significantly, the recent victory of two other left-wing populists in the Latin American continent, President Lula da Silva of Brazil and Lucio Gutierrez of Ecuador. His Bolivarian revolution has not fallen on deaf ears. Yet by and large, Latin American leaders are not willing to accept Chávez and Venezuela as leaders in a new unified Latin America. Moreover, his proposed polarization of the world and sympathy with Colombian guerrillas, when the US administration is seeking to eradicate these rebel groups and the drug trade there, also stacks US opposition against Chávez. It is therefore not surprising to hear that his government suspects US backing of the strike: Chávez sees this as another attempt to provoke a coup among the military through their financing of opposition groups, hostile media or more directly through destabilizing the economy and political order.

Perhaps one of the major obstacles to the neo-caudillo's rule is the privately-owned media in Venezuela. Except for the state-owned media which airs his *Aló Presidente*, and a few minor media houses, the privately owned press are in grave opposition to Chávez, whom they see as a budding dictator. He in turn, in true caudillo style, verbally attacks the press in a most vicious manner. The role of the media cannot be underestimated in the pattern of resistance to the caudillo. The media, which play in a major role in globalization, has made the acts of the caudillo (at least those they want to publicize) known not only to rival groups but to whole other societies where a strongman culture is unknown and not accepted. The media play their part in the subtle imposition of political and social norms of the more developed countries, which have been adopted to a large extent by the upper and middle classes of Venezuela. They undoubtedly have contributed to the instability of Hugo Chávez' rule, as they have been able to sway public opinion both locally and internationally.

The mold of the caudillo has not yet been broken in Venezuela. Although he is differently configured, Venezuela has chosen him as the present preferred type of government over the two-party system that prevailed for some 40 years. It remains to be seen how long he, Chávez and he, caudillo will last and how effective he will be in the context of a globalized world. Venezuela remains fiercely divided on class lines, the upper and middle classes largely opposing Chávez, the poor supporting him. But he is still the most popular leader at the current time in Venezuela and there is no opposition leader capable of securing the support of Venezuelans. It is indeed when a country is so divided that the caudillo flourishes. It remains to be seen if democratic principles will again be put on hold and Chávez forced out of power or if he will win some time until August 2003 when a recall is constitutionally possible. Will Chávez be challenged by one of his own military men as is the tradition? Will he consolidate his rule? Will his example continue to spread across Latin America and his eventual Bolivarian goal become a reality to challenge the hegemony of the US? Will the United States allow that to happen? If he cannot reestablish himself in a strong position, will another strongman emerge to take up the reins of power? These are some of the questions that Venezuela's neo-caudillo leaves on the minds of the national and international community.

References

Araujo, Jesus. 1990. *Juan Vicente Gómez*. Caracas.
Asturias, Miguel Ángel. 1982. *El señor presidente*. Madrid: Alianza Editorial S.A.

Bello, Walden. 2002. "Revolution and Counterrevolution in Venezuela." *Focus on Trade* 78 9 September 2002. http://focusweb.org/publications/FOT%20pdf/fot79.pdf.
Benn, Dennis, and Kenneth Hall, (eds.). 2000. "The South in an Era of Globalization." In *Globalization: A Calculus of Inequality: Perspectives from the South*. Kingston: Ian Randle Publishers.
Briceño-Iragorry, Mario. 1980. *Mensaje sin destino*. Caracas: Monte Avila.
Britto García, Luis. 1988. *La máscara del poder: 1/ Del gendarme necesario al demócrata necesario*. Venezuela: Luis Afadil Trópico.
Brossard, Emma. 2001. *Power and Petroleum: Venezuela, Cuba and Colombia, A Troika?* USA: Canaima.
Calviño Iglesias, Julio. 1985. *La novela del dictador en Hispanoamérica*. Madrid: Ediciones Cultura Hispánica.
Castellanos, Jorge and Miguel A. Mártinez. "El dictador hispanoamericano como personaje literario." *Latin American Research Review* 16, no. 2 (1981): 79–105.
Coronil, Fernando. 1997. *The Magical State*. Chicago: University of Chicago Press.
Dealy, Glen. 1977. *The Public Man: An Interpretation of Latin America and Other Catholic Countries*. Amherst: University of Massachusetts.
Dunn, Hopeton S. (ed.). 1995. *Globalization, Communications and Caribbean Identity*. Kingston: Ian Randle Publishers Ltd.
Falcoff, Mark. 1998. "Venezuela: Dancing on the Precipice." *American Enterprise Institute for Public Policy Research Latin American Outlook* (July–August).15 September 2002. http://www.aei.org/publications/pubID.9294/pub_detail.asp.
Gardels, Narthan (ed.). 2002. "Saturday's Interview with Venezuela's Hugo Chávez." *Petroleum World*. (April 27, 2002). 15 September 2002. http://www.petroleumworld.com/saturdayinterviews042702.htm.
Gilmore, Robert L. 1964. *Caudillism and Militarism in Venezuela 1810–1910*. Athens: Ohio University Press.
González-Echevarría, Roberto. 1988. *The Voices of the Masters: Writing and Authority in Modern Latin American Literature*. Austin: Institute of Latin American Studies University of Texas.
Gott, Richard. 2000. *In the Shadow of the Liberator: Hugo Chávez and the Transformation of Venezuela*. London: Verso.
Gwynne, N. Robert, and Cristobal Kay (eds.). 1999. *Latin America Transformed: Globalization and Modernity*. London: Arnold.
Kattán-Ibarra, Juan. 1995. *Perspectivas culturales de Hispanoamérica*. Illinois: NTC Publishing Group.
Lyle, Don. 2002. "Deltana Prospects Stir International Dreams." *Hart's E&P* 75, no. 9: 87.
Méndez, Rosalba. 1993. "Gómez, ¿Un Periódo Histórico?" *Juan Vicente Gómez y su época*. Elias Pino Iturrieta (compiler). Venezuela: Monte Avila Editores Latinoamericana, 27–58.
Mitchell, Simon. 1978. The Patterning of Compadrazgo Ties in Latin America. *Institute of Latin American Studies*. University of Glasgow Occasional Papers, no. 24.
Morón, Guillermo. 1970. *Historia de Venezuela*. Caracas: Italgráfica S.R.L.
Ohiorhenuan, John. 2000. "The South in an Era of Globalization." In *Globalization: A Calculus of Inequality Perspectives from the South*. Edited by Dennis Benn and Kenneth Hall. Kingston: Ian Randle Publishers.

Pacheco, Carlos. 1987. *Narrativa de la dictadura y crítica literaria.* Caracas: Eduardo Casanova.

Pizani Pardi, Antonio. 1987. *De Cipriano Castro a Rómulo Betancourt.* Caracas: Ediciones Centauro 87.

Rama, Ángel. 1976. *Los dictadores latinoamericanos.* México: Colección Testimonio del Rondo (42). Fondo de cultura económica.

Rangel, Domingo Alberto. 1964. *Los andinos en el poder: balance de una hegemonía 1899–1945.* Caracas: Talleres Gráficos Universitarios.

_____. 1975. *Gómez, el amo del poder.* Valencia: Vadell hermanos.

Reyes, Vitelio. n.d. *Juan Vicente Gómez: Epitome Biográfico: 1857–1935 a 50 años de su muerte 1935-1985.* Caracas: Editorial Logos.

Rojas, Reinaldo. 2002. *Bolívar y la constitución de 1999.* Lecture presented on 11 October 2002 at the embassy of the Bolivarian Republic of Venezuela in Trinidad and Tobago.

Rourke, Thomas. 1969. *Gómez, Tyrant of the Andes.* New York: Greenwood Press.

Strauss, Leo. 1963. *On Tyranny.* London: The Free Press of Glencoe Collier-Macmillan Ltd.

Tomlinson, John. 2001. *Cultural Imperialism.* London: Continuum.

United Nations. "Venezuelan President Hugo Chávez Urges World Leaders to Reaffirm Commitment to Address Root Cause of Terrorism." 2002. Press Release GA/10048 Fifty-seventh General Assembly Plenary 5th Meeting (PM). 13 September 2002. http://www.un.org/News/Press/docs/2002/GA10048.doc. htm.

Vallenilla Lanz, Laureano. 1994. *Cesarismo democrático: Estudios sobre las bases sociológicas de la Constitución efectiva de Venezuela.* Caracas: Monte Avila Editores.

Ward, John. 1997. *Latin American Development and Conflict.* New York: Routledge.

Wise, George S. 1970. *Caudillo: A Portrait of Antonio Guzmán Blanco.* Westport, Conn.: Greenwood Press.

Wynia, Gary W. 1990. *The Politics of Latin American Development.* Cambridge, Mass.: Cambridge University Press.

About the Contributors

Ann Marie Bissessar. Lecturer, Department of Behavioral Sciences, University of the West Indies, St. Augustine, Trinidad.

Justin Daniel. Maître de Conferences de Science Politique, and Director, Université des Antilles et de la Guyana, Faculté de Droit et d'Economie de Martinique.

Roger Hosein. Lecturer, Department of Economics, University of the West Indies, St. Augustine, Trinidad.

John La Guerre. Professor emeritus, Faculty of Social Sciences, University of the West Indies, St. Augustine, Trinidad.

Vaughan A. Lewis. Professor of international relations, Institute of International Relations, University of the West Indies, St. Augustine, Trinidad.

Ronald Marshall. Lecturer, Department of Behavioral Sciences, University of the West Indies, St. Augustine, Trinidad.

Jack Menke. Senior lecturer, University of Suriname.

Sadia Niyakan-Safy. Assistant lecturer, Department of Behavioral Sciences, University of the West Indies, St. Augustine, Trinidad.

Philip D. Osei. Research fellow, Sir Arthur Lewis Institute for Social and Economic Development, Mona Campus, Jamaica.

Ann-Marie Pouchet. Lecturer, Faculty of Humanities and Education, University of the West Indies, St. Augustine, Trinidad.

Ramesh Ramsaran. Professor of economics, Institute of International Relations, University of the West Indies, St. Augustine, Trinidad.

Gale Rigobert. Assistant lecturer, Department of Behavioral Sciences, University of the West Indies, St. Augustine.

Bhoendranatt Tewarie. Principal, University of the West Indies, St. Augustine Campus, Trinidad.

Index